THE VARIABLE SPELLINGS
OF THE HEBREW BIBLE

THE VARIABLE SPELLINGS
OF THE
HEBREW BIBLE

James Barr, FBA

Regius Professor of Hebrew
Oxford University

THE SCHWEICH LECTURES
OF THE BRITISH ACADEMY
1986

Published for THE BRITISH ACADEMY
by THE OXFORD UNIVERSITY PRESS
1989

Oxford University Press, Walton Street, Oxford OX2 6DP
Oxford New York Toronto
Delhi Bombay Calcutta Madras Karachi
Petaling Jaya Singapore Hong Kong Tokyo
Nairobi Dar es Salaam Cape Town
Melbourne Auckland

and associated companies in
Beirut Berlin Ibadan Nicosia

Oxford is a trade mark of Oxford University Press

Published in the United States
by Oxford University Press, New York

British Library Cataloguing in Publication Data

Barr, James, 1924–
The variable spellings of the Hebrew
Bible — (Schweich lectures on
biblical archaeology; 1986).
1. Bible — Criticism, Textual
I. Title II. Series
220.4'4 BS471

ISBN 0-19-726068-3

Printed in Great Britain at the Alden Press, Oxford

This book is dedicated to
Edward Ullendorff, FBA,
a great linguist
and a dear friend

CONTENTS

FIGURES

PREFACE

The material that is presented in this volume consists basically of the three Schweich Lectures which were delivered before the British Academy in May 1986. The writer's interest in the subject went back to more than ten years before that time, and something of the origin of his research upon it is outlined in the pages that follow (see pp. 13–16). By the time when the lectures were delivered, a large volume of material had been collected and analysed, and very great reductions had to be made in order to compress this into the format of three lectures of normal length. For the purpose of publication, it was necessary to expand the material somewhat, since otherwise some aspects would have had to be omitted, or treated too briefly to make a satisfactory case. Roughly speaking, the first chapter of the present volume represents the first lecture as delivered; the second chapter is the second lecture with some expansion; and the third of the original lectures has been divided and reorganized as the third and fourth chapters of the published book, since there were really two different aspects contained in it.

Various aspects and portions of the material have been presented as lectures before learned societies and organizations. Among the many such occasions I would mention my Presidential Address to the British Association for Jewish Studies in 1978, and a lecture I was invited to deliver at the meeting of the International Organization for the Study of the Old Testament in Jerusalem in 1986.

Among scholars who have assisted me with criticism, advice and information I would mention three: Dr. Emanuel Tov of the Hebrew University, Jerusalem; Dr. Michael Weitzman of University College, London; and most of all my colleague and former graduate student Dr. Jeremy Hughes of the Oriental Institute, Oxford University. I have not mentioned their names at specific points where I am indebted to their many suggestions, and think it better simply to record my indebtedness to them here in general. They are, naturally, not responsible for the way in which I have used their stimulating suggestions, nor for any mistakes I may have made in interpreting them.

The progress of research on this detailed and complicated problem was much assisted by a sabbatical year which I enjoyed in 1985. For half of that academic year I was a Member of the Institute for Advanced Study at Princeton, New Jersey, and that Institute proved to be an ideal setting in which to deepen and extend my investigations. My thanks are due to the Institute for inviting me there and providing the excellent facilities that it does. In particular, I am indebted to Professor Glen Bowersock for his support and encouragement, and for helping me with the use of the computer system for this kind of subject.

In addition I am indebted to the British Academy and the Israel Academy of Sciences and Humanities, whose joint exchange agreement enabled me to spend a month or so in Israel during 1985 for study in libraries and discussion with colleagues. And finally I am indebted to the British Academy for doing me the honour of inviting me to deliver this series of Schweich Lectures.

The work of Francis I. Andersen and A. Dean Forbes, *Spelling in the Hebrew Bible* (Biblica et orientalia, 41; Rome, Biblical Institute Press, 1986) was published at about the same time as that at which these lectures were delivered, and is devoted to more or less the same subject. It had not been seen by me at the time and the material of my lectures was not known to them. In preparing my material for publication I have added some annotations and brief remarks which refer to Andersen and Forbes's work but apart from these I have not altered my text or my arguments in order to take major account of their thinking. A full-length review of their study will, it is hoped, be published in due course in the *Journal of Semitic Studies*.

J.B
Christ Church, Oxford

ABBREVIATIONS

BDB	Brown, Driver and Briggs, *Hebrew and English Lexicon*
BJRUL	*Bulletin* of the John Rylands University Library
GK	Gesenius-Kautzsch, *Hebrew Grammar*
HTR	*Harvard Theological Review*
JBL	*Journal of Biblical Literature*
JSS	*Journal of Semitic Studies*
KBL	Koehler and Baumgartner, *Lexicon in Veteris Testamenti Libros*
VT	*Vetus Testamentum*
VTS	*Vetus Testamentum Supplements*

CHAPTER ONE

The Problem and the Approach

1. Introductory examples

It is a familiar feature of the Hebrew language, as used in the traditional Bible text, that many words can be spelt in more than one way. Thus the word known in English as 'ephod', a sacral garment, may be written אֵפוֹד with waw or אֵפֹד without it. No difference of meaning appears to be connected with the difference of spelling. Both spellings may lie within the same text and, in this case, the figures, taken over the Bible as a whole, are almost evenly balanced: 24 with waw, 25 without it. In the one book of Exodus, where this word is rather densely used, and all in one connection, namely, in the account of the tabernacle and its liturgical array, we find the short spelling 21 times and the long spelling eight times, as shown in the diagram:

A	אֵפֹד	Ex 25^7	$28^{6,12,15,25,26}$	28	$29^{5,5,5}$	
B	אֵפוֹד		28^4	27,27	28,28,31	$35^{9,27}$
A			$39^{2,7,8,18,19,20,20,21,21,21,22}$			

Fig. 1: *'epod* 'ephod', all cases in Exodus, whether with or without article

Now the conditions under which such spelling differences may occur are quite simple and, at least at a superficial level, well known: certain *o* and *u* vowels may or may not be spelt with a waw, certain *e* or *i* vowels may or may not be spelt with a yod, and certain *a* vowels may or may not be spelt with a he when in word-final position. But, since a word may contain several vowels that are eligible for the choice between short and long spelling, a very considerable degree of variation may result. Consider for instance the spellings of the one form *tol*ᵉ*dot* 'the generations of', construct but without suffix (Fig. 2).

Notice that most of these cases are within the one book of Genesis alone; and within that book four different spellings are found. The first occurrence, 2^4, uses the longest spelling, with two waws; the shortest spelling, with no waw at all, is found only once, and that in the middle of the book, at 25^{12}. The most frequent

A	תֹּלְדֹת					25[12]	
B	תּוֹלְדֹת	5[1] 6[9] 10[1] 11[10,27]				25[19]	
C	תֹּלְדוֹת						36[1,9] 37[2]
D	תּוֹלְדוֹת	Gn 2[4]					
B							Nu 3[1]
D							Ru 4[18]

Fig. 2: *tolᵉdot* 'the generations of', construct plural without suffix, all cases in the Bible

spelling, B, i.e. תּוֹלְדֹת with waw in the first syllable but not in the plural termination, is dominant in the first half of the book; in the latter part of Genesis only the spelling C, with waw of the termination but not of the first syllable, is found.

Now these first examples are only small symptoms of something that is infinitely more complicated, namely the intricate web of variable spellings that lies over and through the entire Hebrew Bible. One out of every few words is a word of potentially variable spelling, so that there are many thousands of cases in the biblical text. This in itself would not be so very complicated, if at any given point the text had a consistent preference for one mode of spelling: if, let us say, at one point where it spells the *o* of 'ephod' with waw it also spelt with waw all the other cases of this word and all the other *o* vowels in comparable conditions and in comparable words. But this is just what the text does not do: where it uses a long spelling, we find that a few words later it uses a short spelling of the same word or of a comparable word. All parts of the Bible are consistently inconsistent. No section, it seems, adopts a consistent policy of using either the longest or the shortest of the possibilities that are accepted within biblical practice, unless for a few limited cases which form a small minority within the total of words that might be liable to vary. All books and all sections of books appear to mingle shorter and longer types of spelling. The difference, therefore, is not that between a consistent short spelling and a consistent long spelling, but between different kinds of *mixtures* of the shorter with the longer.

2. Historical and distributional perspectives

In other words, the variability of biblical spelling is one of its fundamental characteristics, and for that reason the recognition of it has been placed in the title of this work and forms its starting-point.

Our first purpose, therefore, is not to overcome or obscure this variability by pressing back into a hypothetical earlier stage in which, one might suppose, some kind of uniform spelling prevailed: rather, it is to plot out and to observe the actual distribution of the sorts of spelling, as they are found in the Bible, word-type by word-type, individual word by individual word, and book by book or section by section. My main concern is not to discover an explanation of how the biblical spelling patterns arose but to describe what these patterns are: in that sense the work starts out by being descriptive rather than historical. Nevertheless it may be that in describing the patterns that are found we will also come upon clues that will suggest historical explanations. But the production of such explanations will not be our sole or primary purpose, and we will not be too disappointed if we do not make any historical discoveries at all, or if the ones which we make remain tentative and uncertain rather than definitive and clearly proved.

These remarks stand in contrast with much recent study of the subject. The study of Hebrew spelling has not been idle in the last few decades, and has been associated with the evidence of Northwest Semitic inscriptions on the one side and with the Dead Sea Scrolls on the other. Ancient inscriptions show a Hebrew in which vowel letters were used very little, certainly less than is normal even in the short-spelling parts of the Bible, and neighbouring languages like Phoenician used them practically not at all. Similarly, some portions of biblical text from Qumran show these waws and yods used much less than they are used in the Masoretic text; on the other hand many Qumran texts, and notably the major Isaiah scroll 1QIsA, use them much more extensively than the Masoretic text does. Armed with these evidences, scholars have sought to show how the system of *matres lectionis* developed; conversely, correlation of biblical spellings with this extra-biblical evidence might enable us to date the biblical spellings and thus to form hypotheses about the time and place of origin of biblical books. Could it be that the peculiar mixture of spellings in the Masoretic text results from the intermixture of usages from different past stages in this historical development?

Such a historically oriented approach, however, is not necessarily the only way, or even the primary way, in which the question may be approached. The search for a hypothesis of historical development can easily distract attention from a quite different question: what are the actual patterns of usage in the Masoretic text? How are the different options distributed there? It may be that a thorough understanding of that distribution is a necessary preliminary to any proper use of the extra-Masoretic evidence; or, stating it conversely, it may be that inadequate analysis of Masoretic text usage has had the effect that other, extra-Masoretic, evidence has led the mind into quite mistaken directions. Indeed, speaking personally, it was the deep scepticism inspired in my mind by some of the modern work on orthography and text, done with historical and comparative perspectives, that convinced me of the need to approach the subject in another way.[1] The correlation of biblical spellings with epigraphic evidences and reconstructions of orthography seems to me to be a highly speculative activity; and the premature search for diachronic, developmental and historical explanations can generate uncertain and highly unhistorical suppositions. The initial impulse of the present work, then, was directed much more in a synchronic, descriptive, direction, and the drive towards historical reconstructions, which must necessarily be speculative, was restrained. Nevertheless I must say that, having started off in this rather non-historical direction, I found in the course of my studies that the evidence gradually led me round to a more historical assessment, and that a study based on the Masoretic patterns alone led to more historical and developmental suggestions than I had originally thought likely, or wished. This is how it should be: the examination of the patterns of the basic body of evidence, the traditional biblical text, should provide a strengthening of the base for historical understanding.

In any case, then, the core of the study here presented is distributional in character. The spelling of particular Hebrew words and forms has been plotted in 'maps' such as the first two figures seen above. These maps show not only the *number* of spellings of one sort or another, but also the *way* in which the spellings alternate or are distributed. The modes of alternation, it will be argued below, are extremely important and give guidance to certain important features of spelling variability. In all cases in principle an effort is made to provide some distributional mapping of the facts before any interpretations or any historical reconstructions are attempted. For the sake of brevity and concentration in our presentation these two aspects have not always been kept as separate as might theoretically have been desirable: to keep *all* the interpretation strictly separate, and present it, let us say, as a completely separate section at the end would only entail a good deal of repetition. But the reader should be assured that the registration of the facts of spelling distri-

---

[1] See my 'Hebrew Orthography and the Book of Job', *JSS* 30 (1985) 1–33, and the work especially of D.N. Freedman there discussed.

bution within the Masoretic text has always been the primary operation of this research. Many hundreds of maps of the spelling variations of words and forms have been gathered, and only a limited selection of these have been presented in print in this volume. The intention is that the factual material should be detachable from the explanations offered and should thus be usable by those whose assessment of the patterns is quite different from my own.

3. The idea of the 'Masoretic text'

With this preamble we may turn to some of the central questions involved in our investigation: and first we should ask what we mean by the expression 'the Masoretic text', and how far that is a clearly defined unity for the purpose of our discussion. I may begin by stating simply what I have done: I have for the most part worked from the standard academic text BHS, the Stuttgart Hebrew Bible, which is based on the Leningrad manuscript B19a of 1008 AD, and also from Dothan's edition based on the same manuscript. But I have also worked a great deal from Mandelkern's well-known concordance, which is intended to be based upon the Bomberg edition of 1524, long taken as the primary standard for the printed Hebrew Bible text. In cases of uncertainty I have used facsimiles of the Leningrad manuscript itself, and of the Aleppo Codex, even older and perhaps more authoritative but unhappily not complete, and I have used the Bomberg edition itself, as well as referring at times to other editions and sources, which need not be enumerated in detail. Now these sources are, in respect of plene and defective spelling, by no means exactly agreed at every point, and this is one of the problems of research in this field.

It is commonly said, and I have said it myself, that the Masoretic text of the Hebrew Bible displays a quite uncommon degree of consistency in its readings over hundreds of manuscripts, a degree of agreement very much greater than that found in other comparable materials, such as the Greek New Testament. And this in itself is quite true. But the statement is in itself quite true only because certain qualifications are usually attached to it, such as 'except in minor details'; and these 'minor details' include differences between plene and defective spelling. And, from the point of view of the meaning of the text, and even of its exact wording, these matters of spelling may well count as minor details. But, of course, when the variable spellings are our actual subject of research, what *was*, or seemed to be, minor detail suddenly becomes central in importance. When spelling is taken into account, Masoretic manuscripts differ one from another in some fair degree, and the supposed consistency of the Masoretic text becomes somewhat reduced.

Let us take an example. What is the spelling of the plural of the familiar word דְּבוֹרָה 'bee'? In the Leningrad manuscript and in modern editions based on it, it is spelt once without waw, דְּבֹרִים Dt 1[44], and twice with waw, דְּבוֹרִים Jud 14[8] Ps 118[12]. These three are the only places where the word occurs in the plural. The Bomberg edition displays all three as spelt without waw, in other words a 66⅔% difference as against Leningrad; Letteris's long familiar edition is the same. Snaith's edition comes between, having no waw at Dt 1[44] Jud 14[8] but the waw at Ps 118[12]. And occasionally an even more extreme discrepancy may be met with. Thus the word *yoneqet* ' shoot (of a tree)' occurs in the singular only thrice, and all in the form with suffix, *yonaqto* 'its shoot'. All three are registered by Mandelkern as spelt with waw in the first syllable (they are Job 8[16] 14[7] 15[30]), and all three are without that waw in BHS, a difference of 100%. Both Snaith and Letteris have a waw in the first of the three but not in the other two.

When variable spellings are taken into account, therefore, it might seem that there is no such thing as '*the* Masoretic text' but only a collection of individual manuscripts differing at one point after another. We might have to fear that we would be in danger of producing an elaborate analysis of the spelling of one manuscript or of a handful, when the use of a different manuscript or a different group would lead in a different direction. In fact, however, things do not seem to be as difficult as this thought might suggest. The cases I have just mentioned are extreme cases and not typical. In the great majority of words that I have studied I have found a very substantial measure of agreement, in respect of plene and defective spelling, between traditional sources like Bomberg and Mandelkern on the one side, and modern critical editions based on Leningrad or Aleppo on the other. A smallish percentage of divergence must commonly be allowed for, often two or three per cent, sometimes rising to five or so; but I have not found that divergence to be of such a magnitude as to obscure the main lines of the spelling patterns in the Bible as a whole. It thus remains meaningful to continue to use the term 'the Masoretic text' even where we recognize differences between the Masoretic manuscripts in the variable spellings. In any case it seems that we hardly have a choice, not at the present stage of research. The sort of distributional analysis here attempted has not been done at all before, so far as is known to the writer; and, even when done on the basis on which it has been done, it has proved an extremely complicated piece of research occupying many years. If our maps for individual words were to be multiplied so as to present the data for (say) twenty different manuscripts or sources, the complexity of research and presentation would become intolerable. Possibly newer methods will make it possible in the future. And I should here mention with respect the work of Menahem Cohen, who has plotted the directions of movement in spelling characteristic of manuscripts of various areas, e.g. of Spain or of Germany, in the post-Masoretic period.[1] I have not myself entered into any of this kind of study. But it is generally significant, as well as in detail, for it illustrates how the spellings continued to drift in spite of the fixation of them by the work of the Masoretes.

We shall continue, then, to use the term 'the Masoretic text', not as indicating an absolute identity, but as something that in respect of variable spellings maintained a large measure of identity, sufficient to make it a workable body of material for our purpose. Moreover, by taking our basis in *early* Masoretic manuscripts like Aleppo and Leningrad we are probably seeing the Masoretic pattern at its best, close to the time when the Masora was actually fashioned and when it best fitted the realities of the writing — for, of course, the registration of unusual spellings is one of the main activities that the Masora undertook. The very numerous divergencies in spelling found in later mediaeval manuscripts can probably often in large measure be understood as a drift away from this early pattern and a harmonization of it with the general spelling tendencies of the later mediaeval period. It would be wrong, therefore, to allow the existence of differences between groups of manuscripts to obscure the fact that a central set of contours and patterns can be usefully and meaningfully perceived and described.

4. How was variation in spelling possible?

The mere existence of these spelling variations between various manuscripts of the Masoretic text does, however, point to a matter of importance. As we have said, the Masoretic text is a narrow and highly uniform tradition in general regards and displays few real variants, i.e. semantically significant variants. As is well known

---

[1] M. Cohen, *Orthographic Systems in Ancient Massorah Codices* (dissertation, Hebrew University, Jerusalem, 1973).

since the labours of Kennicott and de Rossi, the collation of numerous mediaeval manuscripts, after an enormous volume of work, brought to light few variations of substance that could be supposed to go back to ancient tradition. But so-called 'minor' variations were found in plenty, and differences between plene and defective spellings were seen to be numerous. How then, one may ask, did these numerous variations in spelling exist at all, in view of the insistence, often repeated, that manuscripts had to be letter-perfect in every detail and that even the slightest discrepancy rendered a text ritually unusable?

The explanation is obvious: because the spelling variations were non-semantic, or at least were so in the overwhelming majority of cases, they were simply not noticed. Any change of a *consonant* would be likely to make a drastic difference to meaning: for instance, the difference between אֲחַד ('*aḥad*, 'one', construct) and אַחַר '*aḥar* 'after'. The difference is of one consonant only, and the two possibilities are graphically very similar and liable to misreading; but the semantic difference thus brought about would be likely to mean that the spelling error, if there was one, would be quickly noticed. But there was no semantic difference marked by the spelling of 'ephod' with or without a waw: most readers would simply not notice. Moreover, and perhaps even more important, a difference of one consonant would be immediately *audible*, and this fact would draw attention to the difference; but no audible difference is made by one spelling of 'ephod' or the other, so that the reading of one or the other in a religious service would pass unnoticed by those present unless they looked at the actual scroll being read.

Moreover, even if they did notice, how would they know what was right? For there was not in existence any perfect, uniform, printed and generally available standard. Masoretic codices, as we have seen, themselves did not agree perfectly in this respect. Throughout the middle ages, the fact was that manuscripts showed variation in this sort of matter, and even the advent of printing did not eliminate it.

It is true that rabbinic exegesis sometimes attached interpretative significance to the spelling differences. Thus the verb *way-yiṣer* 'and he formed' is found twice in Gn 2. The first, in 2^7, is of God's 'forming' man, and here it is written וַיִּיצֶר, with two yods; the second time, at 2^{19}, it concerns his 'forming' the animals, and here it is וַיִּצֶר with one yod. The midrash points out the significance of this, the two yods in the former place marking the existence of the two *yeṣers* in man, the good and the bad formation of the soul, or else some other explanation involving the number two: the 'forming' of the animals, on the other hand, has no such double-sidedness. Repetition of such a comment in the widely-read commentary of Rashi made it very familiar.

Similarly, at Ex 13[16] 'it shall be for a sign upon your hand', this last phrase is written with the rather unusual plene spelling עַל־יָדְכָה, and it was said that this suggested יַד כֵּהָה the 'weak hand'.[1] Such an interpretation could hardly have existed unless the spelling in question was firmly entrenched in the manuscript tradition.

One would have supposed, therefore, that the existence of rabbinic comment on the precise spellings of words would on the one hand imply complete uniformity of the text, and would on the other hand tend to support and confirm the readings in conformity with what the rabbis said. Yet even at the best one must doubt whether rabbinic comments and interpretations were numerous enough to cover more than a limited number of the words in which spelling variations occurred or might occur. One may doubt whether rabbinic interpretations attached to the spelling of every one of the 49 cases of 'ephod' or to all the thirteen cases of tol'dot as mentioned above (pp. 1–2). Out of the vast number of spellings that were actually or potentially variable only a limited proportion were subject to exegetical comment on the spelling by rabbis.

Even more important, and perhaps surprising, rabbinic comments which built upon the exact spelling of the text could nevertheless fail to agree with the spelling of the texts or of the best of them or the majority among them. I will give a few instances:

Rashi, commenting on Nu 15[39] where the ṣiṣit is to remind one of the commandments, says that this is so because the gematria value of the word צִיצִית is 600 (י = 10, צ = 90, ת = 400), to which are to be added eight threads and five knots in the fringes: this gives 613, which is the number of the commandments of the Torah.

This interpretation works only if the word is spelt צִיצִית with two yods. In fact however צִצֵת with one yod is the reading of the great manuscripts and the Masora. Perhaps one may say that Rashi's interpretation can be taken to work on the basis of what would be a very common and normal spelling, even if it was not the one in the text; but even this explanation allows a very substantial gap between the interpretative comment and the actual spelling of the text.

---

[1] Cf. *Encyclopedia Judaica*, article 'Phylacteries', vol. 15 (1971), col. 901; the phylactery was laid by a right-handed man on his left hand, and vice versa. On this particular spelling see below, pp. 114–127.

Other important examples confirm the same thing. B. Men. 30a says that the length of a line in a Sepher Torah should be the space required to write לְמִשְׁפְּחוֹתֵיהֶם thrice, thus spelt; and Maimonides explicitly defines the length of the line as 30 letters. Yet in the only two places where the word occurs, namely Ex 12²¹ Nu 33⁵⁴, the expression is written without waw, and this is confirmed by the Masora; only a few manuscripts known to Kennicott spell it with waw.

The word *totapot* 'frontlets' occurs thrice and the spellings are: Ex 13¹⁶ טֹטָפֹת; Dt 6⁸ טֹטָפֹת; Dt 11¹⁸ טוֹטָפֹת. The interpretation in the Talmud, however (B. Men. 34b), connects the words with the number four which is important, because of the four paragraphs contained in the tephillin. It appears to do this by reading the word as twice singular and once plural: the plural making a minimum of two, one comes to a total of four. The passage is read as: *totepet*, *totepet*, *totapot*, implying that one of the occurrences is written with waw of the plural *-ot* termination and the others not. In fact all texts are written in the Masoretic text with defective spelling of the *-ot* ending. The interpretation, though based upon the spellings of the words, does not agree with the biblical text. An annotation in the Soncino edition, p. 215, acknowledges this to be so.

Thus, as we have shown, in post-Masoretic times the spelling of words continued to drift and change, even if only slowly, and the existence of rabbinic exegetical comments, far from constituting an obstacle to this drift, only confirms the fact of its existence. And this was in a time when, beyond doubt, the ideal was that a scribe copied with absolute exactness the text that lay before him, down to the slightest detail. Even when such exact copying was regarded as mandatory, alteration in spellings continued to go on.

But for earlier times our minds have to be open to the possibility of a situation where this requirement did not exist even as an ideal, a time when it was open to the scribe to spell his material in any way he liked, so long as it was 'the same words', a time when, for instance, if he was copying a text that had תלדת 'generations of', no one cared if he wrote תולדת or תלדות or תולדות and no one dreamt that he was doing something wrongly if he made such a change. It is totally anachronistic to read back into ancient times the ideal of slavish and letter-perfect copying. The great extent of variation as between the different Qumran texts, taken along with the Masoretic tradition, suggests that widely different spelling practices were considered acceptable. The degree of difference in the Qumran texts is not explicable in the same way as the slow drift of the text in post-Masoretic times: it is more naturally understood if we consider that scribes, while seeking to transcribe accurately the *substance* of the text before them, had no hesitation in using their own orthographic practice, if we may so call it, in the insertion or omission of waws and yods. We do not have to insist that it was so; but it is useless to approach the subject with a mind closed against the possibility that it may have been so.

5. Relation of the present study to the Masora

While we are talking about the development of the Masoretic text, something may suitably be added about the relation of our study to the Masora itself, that is, to that body of marginal annotation most of which registers peculiarities of forms in the written text. Our concern is with the distribution of shorter and longer spellings; and in fact a very high proportion of the Masoretic notes concern exactly this point. Since students of the Bible tend to neglect the Masora, and often lack understanding of the way in which to read it, some elementary guidance may be useful. In the case of words of variable spelling, the main technique of the Masora can be simply stated: it registers the minority spelling. For each class of forms, it is assumed that the majority spelling is known, and cases that have the majority spelling commonly receive no Masoretic note, while spellings that deviate from the majority spelling are commonly annotated and numbered.[1] For instance, the active qal participle in triliteral verbs is much more commonly spelt without waw, and so the Masora generally records the less common spelling, i.e. the longer, that with waw. Thus the common participle *šomer* 'keeping' occurs about fifty times in the singular masculine, and of these nine are שׁוֹמֵר plene (1S 17^{22} Ps 121^4 127^1 145^{20} Pr 10^{17} 22^5 Qo 8^5 Ne 9^{32} 2C 34^{22}); each of these is marked as such with a marginal note. This note states: 'ten cases spelt plene': there are ten because the Masora includes the personal name Shomer of 1C 7^{32} (this is one of the points requiring caution in the handling of the Masora, because it can group together as 'the same form' forms which from our point of view come from different lexemes or belong to different word-classes, the Masora being interested in many cases primarily in the fact that they have the same *written* form). The many cases without waw, e.g. שֹׁמֵר Dt 7^9, are left without annotation.

---

[1] For an account of this principle (not always correct in detail) one may have to go back to Elias Levita, *Massoreth ha-Massoreth*, ed. C.D. Ginsburg, reprint Ktav, New York, 1968, especially pp. 146ff.

Thus the modern scholar who sets out to study the distribution of spellings cannot but recognize with pleasure that he is participating in a kind of study in which the Masoretes themselves already engaged. Nevertheless the present endeavour has a number of aspects which make it quite different from their work, and this means that the Masoretic notes and lists, though sometimes useful as a heuristic device and also often welcome as confirmation, seldom solve our problems. The Masoretes wanted a system of checks and controls that would ensure that the text was written and pointed correctly by their standards; they did not want to explain *why* they were doing it in this way or what had led to the existence of these standards. They were not at all interested in the history of the text or in the discovery of an explanation of how the diversity of spellings had come about. And, more immediately important for our undertaking, their work was not really distributional in the way that the present enquiry is. The Masoretes note meticulously the places where minority spellings occur, but they show little interest in the question of *just how* these minority spellings are intermingled with the majority spellings. Thus, for instance, the difference between what I shall call 'block spellings', where a body of text uses the same spelling throughout, and what I shall call 'rapid alternation', where a text passes rapidly back and forward between two or more spellings, is seldom remarked on by them except perhaps for some limited and special cases. The Masora is to us a friend and a companion, which goes some part of the way with us, but many of the questions that interest the modern scholar lie beyond the horizon of its interests. Nevertheless we shall cite its listings from time to time, and it will be useful to use the enumeration of G.E. Weil's *Massorah Gedolah* (Rome, 1971), because, in spite of certain criticisms to which it is liable, it is fitted to the text of BHS and its figures are used in the margin thereof (e.g. for 1S 17²² שֹׁמֵר the note in the side margin refers to the lower margin and to the list Mm 3634 which specifies the ten plene spellings).

6. Practical aspects of the present study

The writer's motivation in undertaking the present work arose from a number of circumstances. One of these, dissatisfaction with what seemed to be speculative in some of the historical and reconstructive approaches of recent decades, has already been mentioned (above, p. 4). Another was the impression, left by some distinguished works, that the whole matter was a sort of chaos out of which no meaningful sense could be found — an impression which itself had doubtless been a factor in provoking the approach through supposed layers of earlier orthographies. The older grammarians seem to have been interested in tracing how the system of *matres lectionis* came into existence, rather than in giving guidance about its effect on the total graphic fabric of the Hebrew Bible. So learned a scholar as Bergsträsser (§7e; p. 45 in the German edition) gives only very slight information, telling us that the plene writing of 'naturally long' vowels was not carried out consistently, the result being 'grosse Willkür und Inkonsequenz'. Gesenius-Kautzsch before him (§8k–l; p. 44 in the English) had not said much more or much less. Bauer and Leander (§7a, pp. 91–92) likewise pay no real attention to the distribution of *matres lectionis*, apart from remarking that no *Konsequenz* or logical reason for the presence or absence of them is to be found. But they do tell us, following Rahlfs, that they were probably originally put in in order to make an outward distinction between words, written alike, that ought to be distinguished in reading (on this see again below, pp. 186–91). These slight and vague indications, coming from major scholars, seemed to invite one to discover if something more positive and detailed could not be said.

The thing that really started the writer on his research, however, was his work as editor of the *Oxford Hebrew Lexicon* (a work on which progress has now been suspended). Among the academic dictionaries of Hebrew the older Oxford dictionary, BDB, was found to be much the most precise and complete in its registration of the spellings found for the Hebrew words described in each entry. Thus, for instance, under *kabod* 'glory' (BDB, p. 458b), it is carefully registered that the long spelling occurs 71 times in the absolute כָּבוֹד and 63 times in the construct כְּבוֹד, while the short spelling, without waw, occurs only twice in the absolute, כָּבֹד Gn 31[1] Na 2[10], and twice in the construct, כְּבֹד Pr 25[2,2]. The article goes on to give similar precise figures for some of the suffixed forms. This feature of BDB seemed valuable and I wanted as editor to continue it. The major traditional German-language dictionaries, Gesenius-Buhl and Köhler-Baumgartner, tend to give less detailed registration of spellings. And even BDB's registrations are very unequal. In fact, as this book will amply show, the registration of spelling variations for many Hebrew words cannot be carried out without using a great deal of space, a commodity precious to the lexicographer.

Moreover, the dictionary posed the further problem of the *order* of entries. BDB ordered entries by the root consonants, a mode

which largely cirumvented the question of the effect of spelling of
the vowel elements in the words. But we had decided to follow the
alphabetical order for each word in itself, as the German dictionaries had always done. But this made the matter of spelling more
important. If a word had plene spelling it would be ten or twenty
pages away from the place where the same word would have been
if it had been entered under its own defective spellings. Thus šo ʿer
'doorkeeper' appears in Gesenius-Buhl on p. 815, because it is ordered under the spelling with waw, and is thus about forty pages
away from pp. 854f., where it would have been found if it had been
ordered under its own defective spelling. The same happens in
Köhler-Baumgartner: the entry is found, in the first edition (the
third edition had not yet reached this word at the time of writing),
on p. 956, while it would have been on p. 1001 if taken by the
defective spelling.

Now the obvious and objective course would be: to order the
entry according to the majority spelling of that word. But this is not
as simple as it seems. A word is entered under its 'citation form':
with nouns, the absolute singular. When we speak of a majority
spelling, do we mean the majority of cases in the absolute singular,
or do we mean the majority of all cases attaching to this word,
including constructs, plurals, and suffixed forms? For it is one of the
most elementary insights of the subject that, when words have
plural terminations or other suffixes added, this often alters the
characteristic spelling away from that found in the absolute singular (see on 'affix effect', below, pp. 25–32). In 'oyeb 'enemy' the
plene spelling אוֹיֵב is massively dominant in the unsuffixed singular
which is the citation form; but this word is very often suffixed
('your enemies', etc.), and if all cases are taken together the proportions become very different.[1]

Further details of practical lexicography need not be followed up
here. But the origins of my studies within that kind of work will
help to explain some of the characteristics of the approach followed
in succeeding pages: the way in which affix effect has been handled,
the approach through the distributional mapping of individual

---

[1] It is not clear to me that the German dictionaries followed the principle of the
majority spelling in any case. Thus with šo ʿer 'doorkeeper', though this word has an
unusually high rate of spellings with waw (see below, pp. 71f.), the defective spelling
is still the dominant one whether in the singular alone or in all cases taken together.
In the case of 'oyeb 'enemy' Köhler-Baumgartner, third edition, places the entry under
the order '–y–b (p. 37). I have not seen in any dictionary an express statement of the
principles by which they decided this sort of question.

words, the noting of lexical differences between one word and another of the same general type.

I will certainly also be asked whether I used computers in the research here presented. The answer is: a little, but not much. When I started the work, it was still difficult to obtain a computerized Hebrew Bible text, reliable in the details here involved, which also offered easy retrieval of the sort of data I wanted. It was in many ways easier to get the information from a printed concordance (essentially from Mandelkern, with verification of every case against a modern text like BHS) and from simple reading through the Hebrew Bible and making notes of spelling phenomena according to a list I had made of features that should be noted. By the time computer access became easy I had already obtained most of the data I needed and made most of the analysis I desired to make. For my sort of approach the computer seems to have two particular contributions to make. Firstly, it provides accuracy in the listing and arrangement of the material (but only in so far as no mistakes in plene and defective spelling were made when the text was fed into the computer). Secondly, it is very helpful in the retrieval of features that run across a large variety of lexemes and therefore cannot easily be traced from a printed concordance: a good example is the spelling of the *o* vowel in imperfect verb forms such as *yišmor* (on this see below, pp. 103ff.). But for much of the research, and for the linking of observation with ideas and suggestions, I found that work from printed text and concordance was just as efficient as work from the computer.

For this there is a reason, which will emerge from the study as a whole but is here stated in advance for convenience. Much of my study was done word by word, that is to say, I took individual words and made distributional diagrams for them. This means, however, that for most cases one does not have extremely long runs to deal with. The advantages of the computer are most obvious where there are very long runs of material to be processed. With Hebrew variable spellings, provided they are separated type from type, word from word, and book from book, this is seldom the case. Affix effect means that plurals have to be taken separately from singulars, forms with pronoun suffixes separately from forms that do not have them; constructs and forms with the article may require to be treated separately; as we shall see, many words show variation in one sector of the Bible (commonly in the Torah) but not in others, and the result is that for many elements of our discussion we have no longer run than a few dozen cases that have to be listed, and these are often already easily separated out and listed by a traditional concordance like Mandelkern and often confirmed by the Masora also.

To put it in another way, I am not convinced that the sort of large-scale statistical study that can be done through the computer leads to significant results. The computer can do things like count the number of *o* vowels in the Bible or compare the number of plene spellings in Exodus with that in Chronicles, but such figures appear to lump together a lot of elements which shed more light if they are considered separately. In any case, this present study does not pretend to be really a statistical one, though proportions and percentages are mentioned from time to time. Its interest is more in position and distribution than in numbers.

The accuracy of the computer, and its infallibility in producing all the information required, provided that it has been rightly charged with that information, was mentioned above; and the writer has by contrast to admit that his own work in these pages will certainly contain errors and omissions, however much effort has been made to verify everything. Some small percentage of error is simply unavoidable, and can stem from various causes: misprints in the standard texts, omissions from printed concordances, overlooking of relevant examples, and errors in typing and proof-reading; all these may be factors. I apologize in advance for such faults. However, the argument as unfolded below does not depend on *absolute* exactness. Only a small selection from the material I have gathered is here deployed, and I have made no attempt to give a full account of everything. The examples as deployed are, I think, sufficient in quantity and in accuracy to guide our understanding of biblical spelling into some creative directions.

7. Terminology and presentation

After these introductory sections, but before proceeding more deeply into our material, it will be convenient here to say something about the way in which our subject is defined and delimited and the mode in which we shall present our material.

First of all, as illustrated in our first examples, we are interested in the sort of spellings in which recurrent and persistent variation occurs. We are not interested in the collecting of occasional curiosities, such as the spelling of *dag* 'fish' as דָּאג with aleph (Ne 13[16]) or of the spelling of *halᵉku* 'they went' as הָלְכוּא (Jos 10[24]), again with aleph. Such things occur here and there and in a variety of books. But we are interested rather in the sort of spelling variation that is widespread and seems to have systemic character: it is about these, which occur in thousands and in well-marked categories, that we seek understanding. Occasional oddities may find mention here and there, but no effort will be made to collect them nor are they important for our purpose.

Secondly, our procedure begins entirely from the Masoretic text: it is the base for our operation. By 'the Masoretic text' I mean that text in both its components, i.e. the base text (commonly though not accurately called the 'consonantal text') and the vowel points and other marks such as dagesh. The question then is: in what way is a *form*, a *form* of the Masoretic text, spelt in the Masoretic text? By a *form* is meant a *pronounced form*, the word as *spoken* according to the Masoretic text and its grammar. Since the question is precisely: 'how is this form *written*?', we obviously cannot write it in Hebrew, and the form therefore is generally presented in English characters, with a gloss to indicate its meaning roughly, thus: *gadol* 'great'. The question is, then: in what way is *gadol* written in the Masoretic text, with waw or without it? This is the classic form of the question. Given the form *qoli* 'my voice', is that written with waw or not, and in what places?

The answer to that question we give by writing the spelling of the Masoretic text in written form. That written form will indicate what waws and yods and the like are there or are not there. These answers form the main data for our discussion. Commonly, as has already been illustrated, the data is presented in the form of diagrams, in which the various possibilities of the Masoretic text for the spelling of a form are set out, and the diagram gives the places where each possible spelling is found.

Some may be surprised that, when I write the form in English characters, I do not indicate vowels as long or otherwise: they may expect that I would print *gādōl* or *qōlī*. The omission of macrons, and still more of circumflexes and the like, has however a good reason and is wholly deliberate. Firstly, I do not wish to provide a phonetically exact transcription: all I want to do is to give an indication of what word it is, an indication that will be sufficient for anyone who knows Hebrew. The reader will know what sort of form *qoli* is, and he or she will know what spelling possibilities in Hebrew there may be: exactitude will come with the provision of the Masoretic text spellings as written in Hebrew.

Secondly, there is a reason that concerns the nature of the Masoretic pointing system itself. It is now widely held by scholars that the vowel points of the Masoretes do not indicate vowel length at all, but only vowel quality. This being so, it was desirable to avoid signs that suggested vowel length as a primary datum.

Thirdly, there is at present a great deal of confusion in the teaching that students receive about just this question. Is holem, for example, a long vowel? Some are told that it is a long vowel when written with waw, others that when written with waw it is a superlong vowel to be marked with a circumflex or the like. But this is just what must be avoided here. For us *qoli* is one form, with the first vowel holem, and the question is whether it is written with waw or not. Confusion is best avoided by eschewing all marks of length and the like.

Fourthly, however, there is a historical aspect to the matter. Within the period of development of the biblical text, a vowel may have been short and later became long. Here and there we shall have to take account of this sort of difference. Occasionally, therefore, we shall talk of a vowel as short or long, or mark it as long, when we are talking of the historical circumstances of some period, or when we are taking comparative philological information into account. But the spellings of the Masoretic text itself we shall not mark as short or long. Admittedly this procedure leaves the difference between sere and segol unmarked, but I think most readers will know which of these is involved, and in any case at difficult points I give them their names.

Hebrew terms, like waw and yod, occur so often that I consider them for the purposes of this book to be English words, and they are left unitalicized. Italicized are Hebrew *forms* transcribed from the Hebrew text.

The pleasing inexactness with which I handle the length of vowels is extended also to the indications of meaning that I furnish in English, such as *qol* 'voice'. Such an indication is not necessarily an exact statement of meaning, still less is it the 'correct translation' in all passages where the word occurs. It is simply a gloss, a customary or conventional expression in English that serves to give a general idea what word it is that we are talking about. Only rarely in this study are we concerned with exact semantic values.

Much of the material is presented in the form of diagrams or 'maps' which follow the incidence of a particular form throughout a book or throughout the entire Bible, as stated on each occasion. The advantage of this mode of presentation is that it enables us to follow out the way in which alternative spellings are spaced, something that I believe, in many cases, to be more important than the total numbers of one or another. These maps follow the sequence of the occurrences (order of books as in BHS) and are intended to mark each case with number of chapter and verse.

There are some kinds of spelling difference that do not fall within our discussion. For example, the name of Nebuchadnezzar is spelt both with *n* and with *r*. Though exceptions are made on some unusual occasions, this sort of difference is left untouched by the present study. For my purposes, Nebuchadnezzar with *r* is a different *form* from Nebuchadnezzar with *n*, so that we would be dealing, in this case, not with two spellings of a single pronounced form, but with two different pronounced forms, each of which might have or might not have their own variety of realizations in writing.

Where there is a KQ variation I have normally followed the Q, which is the 'pronounced form' as defined a moment ago. In a few cases I have some uncertainties. Take a case like Rt 4[5], K קניתי Q written in the margin as קניתה. The –*ta* ending which is the vocalization here appears to be written with he; but I am not sure if it should be counted as a real case of this spelling because the marginal annotation might be thought to have required a he, since it itself was unvocalized in its own position. The same applies to Ps 8[7] שתה. See below, pp. 114–27. There are thus a few doubtful cases but these will not make much difference to our discussion as a whole.

Spellings as indicated on the diagrams are generally those of BHS, following the Leningrad Codex. To build into the diagrams variant spellings from other sources is too complicated. But in the course of my work I have become increasingly struck by the importance of the Masora where it conflicts with the text of the Codex, and in many places I have made mention of the Masora's guidance even though it was not possible to give full documentation of this. Some differences in this respect will therefore appear from time to time.

8. Biblical spelling and biblical origins – a first perspective

From these preliminary considerations we may now turn to the more steady discussion of biblical spellings, and here we return to the starting point of this chapter with its diagrams of the spelling of 'ephod' and of 'the generations of'. As was there emphasized, not only does variability exist in the spelling of biblical Hebrew, but this variability exists everywhere in the Bible. It would have been easy enough, one would think, for books and passages to follow a consistent policy about spelling, but on the whole this was not done. There are indeed some few features on which one can recognize that a particular book adopted and followed a consistent policy. For example, Chronicles spelt the name David with yod,

consistently over many cases,[1] when most of the other books wrote
it without yod; certain books spell *lo'* 'not' consistently without
yod, while other books allow it to vary under certain circumstances
(see below, pp. 154–8). But consistency of this kind is not typical
of the Bible: variation is more typical. So far as I know, there is no
book, no passage, no page in the Masoretic text that does not show
the manifestations of variability in spelling. Variability in spelling,
in this sense, is a prominent feature of the traditional Hebrew Bible
text.

Take in conjunction with this another prominent fact: as has
been mentioned (above, p. 3), we have some knowledge from
inscriptions of the spelling of Hebrew within actual biblical times,
the times in which the prophets Isaiah or Jeremiah lived. A striking
feature of these inscriptions is their use of spellings for familiar
words or forms, spellings that *never* or practically never occur in the
standard Bible text. Consider such writings as these:

אש 'man'; קל 'voice';   חצבם 'diggers';
ים 'day'; נבא 'prophet'.

Spellings like these are extremely rare, or do not exist at all, in the
Masoretic text. It cannot be sufficiently strongly emphasized: there
is no part of the Hebrew Bible, as represented in the traditional text,
that spells in the way in which they spelt in the time (say) of Isaiah.
And that, after all, is not a very early time for the Bible: the same
would, no doubt, have to be said even more strongly about parts of
the Bible which originated centuries before Isaiah. This leads us to
frame as a likely possibility the following: it is likely that few parts,
or no parts, of the Hebrew Bible, as they lie before us in the Masoretic text, stand in the spelling in which they were first written, or
in which their final redaction took place. It is of course *possible* that
some parts are in that original spelling, but such a case would stand
in need of proof before it could be considered even probable, and it
would have no antecedent probability. But, if this is true, a significant consequence follows: it may well be vain to attempt to date
books, or portions of books, on the basis of the spellings that they
contain. A book, or a portion of a book, that in itself is early may
have been all the more thoroughly revised and thus appear in spelling of a 'late' type. For the same reasons it may be vain to try to
correlate the spelling of a book with a particular dialect and therefore with the locality of its origin. The whole tradition of seeking
to correlate spelling with dialect, with place, and with time of ori-

---

[1] See below, pp. 161, 165f.

gin may well be mistaken. Of course such correlations are not in principle impossible, but the evidence will show that they should not be expected, and that we should not direct our research towards the anticipation that they will be found.

To this we add another consequence, which also goes to confirm what has just been said: the difference between spellings of words cannot as a rule be correlated with documentary or source hypotheses, with the idea that a biblical book is compounded from different sources of diverse dates. This may or may not be so but matters of spelling do not necessarily affect the question one way or the other. The reason has already been hinted at in our first examples and will be confirmed by many more: the spelling differences run right across the possible source differences, the contrary spellings lie side by side within one and the same source. Thus the four spellings of *tol'dot* within Genesis (Fig. 2 above) all lie within the same source: surely no one supposes that there were four different sources all containing the exordium 'these are the generations of...' Similarly, all the spelling alternations in the word 'ephod' in Exodus (Fig. 1 above) lie within the same source. The differences of spelling do not either support or oppose the supposition that such sources existed. The reason is simple: the compounding of the sources, if such did take place, took place at a time earlier than the development of spellings that has led to our present form of text. Again, it is possible in theory that some correlation with earlier sources may be found: but it will have to be specially proved, and we should not organize our research in the expectation that it will be there. As will be shown in many cases below, the meaningful unit for the study of spellings is not the source, but the book.

9. Block spelling and rapid alternation

The terms 'block spelling' and 'rapid alternation' were briefly introduced some pages earlier (cf. above, p. 12) but these key concepts must now be explained and deployed in more detail. Let us take a simple example:

The first chapter of Numbers contains a series of very stereotyped formulae that introduce the numbers of men of military age in each tribe, and thus we have (in English):

> Nu 1[26] Of the people of Judah, their generations, by their families, by their fathers' houses, according to the number of names, from twenty years old and upward, every man able to go forth to war... (RSV)

A very similar formula is repeated again and again in the chapter. Now such a formula contains a number of words that in principle might be variable in spelling, such as תּוֹלְדֹתָם 'their generations', מִשְׁפְּחֹתָם 'their families', אֲבֹתָם 'their fathers', and יֹצֵא 'going forth'. And these words just named remain constant in their spelling throughout the repeated formulae of Nu 1, though this is not true of the same words throughout the entire book of Numbers. Within this chapter, therefore, we may perhaps speak of a 'block spelling' of these terms. Within this block of text their spelling is standardized. But there is one exception, and that is the common noun *šemot* 'names', in the absolute plural. The following diagram shows the variation of spelling in this form throughout the entire Torah; the cases in Numbers are much the most numerous:

A	שֵׁמֹת		26^{18}			$1^{26,28,30,32}$	
B	שֵׁמוֹת	Gn 2^{20} 26^{18}		Nu $1^{2,17,18,20,22,24}$			34
A		Nu $1^{36,38,40,42}$		4^{32}	32^{38}		
B			3^{43}		26^{53}		

Fig. 3: *šemot* 'names', absolute, with or without article, all cases in the Torah

In Nu 1 we can discern 'blocks' of an identical spelling: six cases from 1^2 to 1^{24}, four of the contrary spelling from 1^{26} to 1^{32} and again from 1^{36} to 1^{42}. But 'rapid alternation' can be seen, perhaps, at Gn 26^{18}, two cases in the same verse but spelt differently, and similarly at Nu 1^{34}, a sudden shift of spelling one way and back again within a very short space. And this is nothing exceptional. Our first diagram (Fig. 1, p. 1) showed rapid alternation around Ex 28^{26-28} (spelling changes three times within three verses), while chapter 39 has a block spelling, eleven cases all identical: contrast ch. 28, which has twelve occurrences of 'ephod' but shifts the spelling four times within that space.

Here is another simple example, the plural *nᵉbi'im* 'prophets' in 1 Samuel (2 Samuel has no relevant cases):

A	נְבִאָם				19^{24} $28^{6,15}$
B	נְבִאִים		$10^{10,11}$	10^{12}	
C	נְבִיאִים	1S 10^5		10^{11}	19^{20}

Fig. 4: plural absolute of *nabi'* 'prophet', all cases in Samuel

The degree of alternation in 1S 10 is obvious; and we may go on to cite a few other cases with the same word:

A נְבִאִים 22^{12} 1^5 2C 18^5 $18^{11,12}$
B נְבִיאִים 1K $22^{6,10}$ 22^{13} Zc 1^4 1^6 18^9

Fig. 5: some groups of nᵉbi'im 'prophets' in Kings, Zechariah and Chronicles

Here is another simple example: that of ṣippor 'bird'. All cases in the post-Torah books are plene and so also, even within the Torah, are all cases without the article. With the article in the Torah we find:

A הַצִּפֹּר Gn 15^{10} Lv $14^{6,6,6,7,50,51,51}$ 52,53
B הַצִּפּוֹר   Lv 14^5 52

Fig. 6: ṣippor 'bird', all cases with article in the Torah

Lv 14 has what looks like the makings of a block spelling but rapid alternation at the beginning and at vv. 51–52 makes the contrary impression.

For those who may wish to see a more extreme case of the contrast between block spellings and rapid alternation, one may put forward the case of the personal name Absalom as used in 2 Samuel. This word shows a great deal of variation, although the spelling with waw is clearly much more numerous as a whole. But there is a long block, from 2S 13^{20} to 15^{34}, in which all 46 cases are spelt with waw. Outside this block, rapid alternation occurs several times: note especially 16^{16}–16^{23}, where the name occurs nine times within eight verses, and the spelling changes seven times within that space.

A אַבְשָׁלֹם 13^4 15^{37}
B אַבְשָׁלוֹם 3^3 13^1 13^{20} to 15^{34}, block of 46 cases 16^8
A   16 18 21   23 $17^{1,4}$ 9   15,18 24,25,26
B $16^{15,16}$ 17 20 22,22   5,6,6,7 14,14 20
A   10   18,18   2
B $18^{5,5,9,9}$ 12,14,15,17 32 $19^{1,1,1}$ 5,5,7,10,11 20^6

Fig. 7: the name Absalom, all cases in 2 Samuel

The name Absalom gets off to an uncertain start, alternating briefly between two spellings, but then it settles down to a very dense and steady block, 46 cases spelt identically. But from 15^{37} it goes over to rapid alternation, and finally towards the end of 2 Samuel it begins to take up slightly longer blocks, from four to six of the longer spelling being interrupted by one or two of the shorter. I have noticed four places where Mandelkern's registration is discrepant against the BHS text: $15^{14,37}$ 16^{16b} 17^{24}. Even if 15^{14} had the defective spelling there would still be two longish blocks of identical spelling starting from 13^{20}.

Finally, the simpler case of *yošᵉbe* 'the inhabitants of', in the first chapter of Judges:

A	יֹשְׁבֵי		$1^{19,27Q}$		31	32,33,33,33,33
A	יוֹשְׁבֵי	Jud 1^{11}		27,27,30,30	31	

Fig. 8: plural construct *yošᵉbe* 'the inhabitants of', all cases in Jud 1

Notice the rapid transitions at vv. 27 and 30–32, combined with the tendency to follow one set spelling for a series of four or five cases at other points in the chapter.

Many more cases of these phenomena can be adduced; but these are enough to guide us towards one valuable conclusion. The fact of rapid alternation is extremely common and pervasive, and it is highly important that the existence of this phenomenon should be recognized. For its presence immediately makes very unlikely certain possible explanations of spelling variation that could easily occur to the mind. Very obviously, one might say, different scribes had different tendencies or different spelling conventions: one of them spelt with waw, the other spelt without it. This could well fit with examples of block spelling. But it does not fit well with rapid alternation: for it would mean that each scribe was hopping up and down, writing a few words and then leaving his bench to let a colleague write the next part. Moreover, as we have seen, we may have rapid alternation in one word when the same passage has block spelling in other variable words (cf. Nu 1, above, p. 21f.); and block spelling of one word can coexist with substantial variation of others. The rapidity of alternation, and its combination with block spelling, must support the contrary view, namely that the the differences of spelling came from the same scribe, or from the same scribal tradition. Though there may be some special cases where it is valid, it is impossible to suppose that the combination of different scribal schools or conventions is the general explanation for variation of spelling of the same word within the same text. Equally unlikely are all ideas that some sort of 'official' person or 'official' policy lay behind the distribution of spellings. Surely no 'official' or body of officials or official decision could have opted for the sort of alternation we have seen to exist, within one book or passage, with 'ephod' or with 'Absalom' or with *šemot* 'names'. Although much of the evidence has still to be assembled, we have to expect to look in a different direction than towards 'official' decisions or policies about spelling.

10. Affix effect

The matter of what I have called 'affix effect' has been briefly mentioned above (p. 14) but we now have to discuss this key concept more fully, since it is important for the entire strategy of our approach to biblical spelling.

We may begin by remarking that, while it is easy enough for beginners to learn what vowel letters (or *matres lectionis*, as we still, surely absurdly, call them) are and how they work, the actual distribution of the longer and shorter spellings is not so easily learned, and many of the grammars in common use tend to give the student a poor idea of the actual tendencies of the biblical text. Doubtless in order to simplify for the sake of the learner, they tend to standardize too much. They use plene spelling in much higher proportion than that in which the Bible itself uses it, and they give the beginner little idea of the prevalence of spellings such as אֹתֹת 'signs' with no waw at all, יְרִיעֹת without waw of the termination, or מַכְלִם written without yod for the *i* vowel of the hiphil. In particular, they tend to give little impression of the spelling patterns of the Torah, to which we shall refer below (pp. 39–43).

That the textbooks are defective in this respect is not surprising, for the more advanced works show a similar failure. One of the principles commonly inculcated is that vowel letters should not be used in successive syllables: thus, if a word is written with a vowel letter, waw or yod, and a suffix is added which contains the same vowel letter, or indeed any vowel letter, then that vowel letter is written once but not twice, by preference though not by absolute rule. 'The scriptio plena in two successive syllables was generally avoided', says GK § 8l, p. 44. The first example commonly given is that of *nabi'* 'prophet'. According to Gesenius-Kautzsch, one writes נָבִיא with yod in the singular but in the plural one writes נְבִאִים with only one yod and not two, and the one written is that of the plural termination, and not that within the body of the word. The more recent Bergsträsser says exactly the same thing (§7e, p. 45), with the same example. But no more disastrous example could be offered, for in fact the plural with two yods is massively preferred for *nᵉbi'im* in the Bible as a whole; and the same is true of the second example offered by these same authorities, who tell us that we write צַדִּיק 'righteous' with yod in the singular but plural צַדִּיקִים again with yod only of the plural termination. In fact in the Bible as a whole the double spelling צַדִּיקִים is overwhelmingly preferred; and even in the Torah, where a shorter spelling is preferred, the shorter spelling used is not צַדְקִים but צַדִּיקֵם. Clearly some of the examples offered by the learned grammarians have been traditional school examples, doubtless handed down for generations, and it had simply not been noticed that the actual biblical spelling of these words entirely transgresses the principle being inculcated. There is reason, therefore, simply as a matter of getting the facts right, for us to register afresh some of the true tendencies of biblical spelling: in particular, for instance, the student should be made aware of the number of places where the waw of the plural ending –ot or the yod of the ending –im are not written, and especially so in the Torah.

There are, then, plenty of words with two vowel letters in the Bible, and especially, one suspects, with two yods: indeed, one can have three yods, as in הַגְמִיאִינִי Gn 24[17] or הַשְׁמִיעִינִי Ct 2[14]; again, a word like p‘nimi 'interior', with its feminine p‘nimit, is always doubly plene in the singular (about thirty cases, mostly in Ezekiel indeed, but four in Kings and some in Esther). It remains, however, true that there is something in the traditional generalization that repetition of vowel letters often did not take place. Very many cases occur of forms that, when alone, are written with a waw or yod but are written without it when in some sort of combination. The observation that this is so is, however, no explanation. Why should anyone have been reluctant to write two waws or two yods in the same word, especially when, so often, they did write two, or even more? What really happened in cases of this kind?

An extensive body of evidence, some small portions of which have already been touched upon, has convinced me that this goes deeper than the mere matter of the repetition of plene spellings. A large number of words and forms seem to be written plene, either universally or in overwhelmingly high proportion, when they are 'alone', i.e. not directly connected with a prefix or suffix; but when a prefix or suffix is attached the same forms come to be written in much larger measure defectively. The case of the common word ṣippor 'bird' was mentioned above (Fig. 6, p. 23). Outside the Torah all cases are plene anyway. Within the Torah all cases of the singular without article are plene (there are four in all). But when the article is attached, as Figure 6 shows, the defective spelling becomes the *dominant* spelling within the Torah (ten cases against two).

Another prominent example is ʿolam 'eternity' or 'remotest time'. When this word is alone, it is עוֹלָם plene without exception in all parts of the Bible; there are about 205 cases. But, when preceded by l^e– (not עַד), in the familiar phrase l^e–ʿolam 'for ever', this proportion changes sharply: within the Torah we have the defective, לְעֹלָם, ten times, and the plene לְעוֹלָם only twice, as is noted by the Masora (Mm 25, 504). The position in the Torah is worth mapping precisely:

A	לְעֹלָם	Gn 3^{22} 6^3	Ex 3^{15} 15^{18}		21^6 31^{17} 32^{13}
B	לְעוֹלָם			19^9	
A		Lv 25^{46} Dt 5^{29}			32^{40}
B				23^7	

Fig. 9: l^e–ʿolam 'for ever', all cases in the Torah

Similar effects arise when ʿolam has other prefixes attached to it, such as min 'from' (Is 57^{11} וּמֵעֹלָם) and the definite article, which produces the short spelling הָעֹלָם in two cases out of about a dozen (Qo 3^{11} 1C 16^{36}).

Similarly, the common infinitive ʿašot 'to do' is always written with waw when alone, but when combined with l^e– 'to', i.e. in la–ʿašot, there is a substantial group written לַעֲשֹׂת without waw: I have noted Ex $35^{1,32}$ $36^{1,2,3,5}$ Lv 8^{34} Nu $9^{4,6}$ Ne 8^{15} 12^{27} 13^{27} — a total of twelve, which agrees with the Occidental Masora — and to these may be added Ezr 7^{10} וְלַעֲשֹׂת with the added 'and'; and in the compound with min we have the short writing מֵעֲשֹׂת Gn 18^{25} Lv 9^{22}, two cases out of a total of ten of this phrase in the entire Bible.

One important word that seems to show a different pattern of behaviour is qadoš 'holy'. With the article this adjective is always קָדוֹשׁ plene, although one cannot lay much emphasis on this because there are only four cases (Nu $16^{5,7}$ 1S 6^{20} Is 5^{16}). When the adjective is alone, on the other hand, there is considerable variation, especially in the Torah, which is mapped as below:

A	קָדֹשׁ		29^{31} Lv $6^{9,19,20}$					
B	קָדוֹשׁ	Ex 19^6		7^6 10^{13} $11^{44,45}$ 16^{24} 19^2 20^{26}				
A		Lv $21^{7,8}$	24^9 Nu $6^{5,8}$			26^{19}		
B		21^8		Dt 7^6 $14^{2,21}$ 23^{15}	28^9			

Fig. 10: qadoš 'holy', absolute without article, all cases in the Torah

Note that Leviticus favours the long spelling (ratio of 6:8), Numbers has only the short, and Deuteronomy favours the long by a ratio of 1:5. Outside the Torah the majority are long spellings; but Ezekiel has one of each, and Nehemiah has a good simple alternation: Ne 8[9] קֹדֶשׁ, 8[10] קָדוֹשׁ, 8[11] קֹדֶשׁ. The construct may be briefly mentioned: there are no cases in the Torah, and most are in the Prophets, especially Isaiah, and a few in the Psalms. The spelling is overwhelmingly plene, and short spellings seem to occur only at Is 49[7] Ps 46[5] 65[5]. It may be worth while to ask whether there may be some special explanation for the unusual pattern of the spellings of this word.

The familiar term *'aron* 'ark' has yet another pattern of distribution. In this word the absolute and the construct forms are identical, but the spellings are distributed in different ways. Outside the Torah there is uniformity: all cases, absolute or construct, with or without article, are אֲרוֹן plene, and, since books like Joshua, Samuel, Kings and Chronicles display plenty of examples, the evidence is very solid. Within the Torah there is much variation. All cases that are absolute in the Torah also have the article, and the writing is dominantly short, nineteen cases short against three long:

A הָאָרֹן   Ex 25[14,14,15,16,21,21] 31[7] 35[12] 37[1,5,5] 40[3,20,20,20,21]
B הָאָרוֹן Gn 50[26]
A   Lv 16[2] Nu 3[31] 10[35]
B   Dt 10[2,5]

Fig. 11: *'aron* 'ark', absolute with article, all cases in the Torah

This word is interesting for the distribution of the construct. As readers will have noticed, we have worked with the rather vague concept of a word being 'alone', and one might well ask whether a noun in the construct is 'alone' or not: for it is often said that it loses its own independent stress, throws its stress on to the next word, or has a low stress or medium stress, all of which might be expected to affect the spelling in a way similar to affix effect. In fact, however, at least in this word, the reverse seems to be the case: affix effect, so far as noted, seems mostly to go with a shorter spelling, while *'aron* in the construct has a very much higher proportion of plene spelling in the Torah than it has in the absolute:

A אֲרֹן   25[22]   30[6]   39[35]   Nu 4[5] 7[89]
B אֲרוֹן Ex 25[10]   26[33,34]   26   40[3,5,21]
B   Nu 10[33] 14[44] Dt 10[1,3,8] 31[9,25,26]

Fig. 12: *'aron* 'ark', construct, all cases in the Torah

In the construct, then, plene spelling is much in the majority (five defective, fifteen plene), a complete reversal of the situation in the absolute with article. Note that Deuteronomy spells *all* cases of this word plene, as do the post-Torah books. But even in Exodus the construct prefers the long spelling (three short, seven long). For further reference to this word, see below, pp. 174f., 182.

In general I have to say, perhaps surprisingly, that words in the construct, unlike the same with pronoun suffixes added, do not appear to move in the direction of more defective spelling. The contrary is the case. The absolute *'abot* 'fathers' is twice written without waw (Ex 12^3 20^5), and the same early chapters of that book have two cases of the construct *'abot* (6^{25} 10^6) but these are אֲבוֹת with waw and so are all other examples including two in Numbers. Another word of variable spelling which often occurs in the construct is *g^ebul* 'frontier', too frequent a word for us to display its writings in full here. There are said by the Masora to be nine cases spelt short גְּבֻל: Nu 21^{13} $34^{8,9,11,11}$ Dt $3^{16,17}$ Jos 13^{27} 2S 21^5. Nu 21^{13} is misprinted plene in BHS, and 34^{11b} is plene in Leningradensis against its own Masora. Anyway, of these short spellings only two are constructs, Nu 21^{13} 2S 21^5; the four in Nu 34 are all cases with definite article. The many constructs of this noun clearly do not cause it to favour a defective spelling.

The noun *qol* 'voice, sound' is an extremely common word: the absolute and construct are the same, and cases in the singular without suffix amount to two or three hundred. But there is not a single case of the defective spelling קֹל except where there is an affix conjoined with the noun; cf. on this the reference to spellings in inscriptions, above, p. 20. With affixes, however, we have a sprinkling of defective spellings: with *w^e* וְקֹל Ex 19^{16} (the only case with this prefix in the Torah), with *l^e-* לְקֹל twice, Ex $4^{8,8}$ (the Torah has לְקוֹל four times, Gn 3^{17} 16^2 Ex 15^{26} 18^{24}), with the article הַקֹּל Gn 27^{22} and וְהַקֹּל Gn 45^{16}, that is, two out of the four cases with the article in the Torah, and, finally, מִקֹּל Jr 3^9.

The importance of the presence or absence of the article is again well illustrated by the common adjective *gadol* 'great'. The absolute, without article, is almost always גָּדוֹל plene: out of over 180 cases the short spelling גָּדֹל seems to be found only at Dt 1^{17} 26^8 Ps 57^{11} (Mm 1195), a very small proportion (there are about thirty cases in the Torah alone). With the definite article, however, the pattern is quite different. Outside the Torah the spelling is always the long one, גָּדוֹל (about 70 cases); in the Torah, on the other hand, the shorter spelling is actually dominant: nineteen cases without waw as against nine with it. The following figure displays all cases with the article in the Torah ('with the article' includes prefixed prepositions if they contain the article element, e.g. Gn 44[12] בַּגָּדוֹל).

A הַגָּדֹל Gn 1[16] 15[18] 27[1,15,42] Ex 3[3] 18[22]
B הַגָּדוֹל 10[21] 44[12] Lv 21[10] Nu 34[6]
A 34[7] 35[25,28,28] Dt 1[7,17] 2[7] 4[37] 8[15] 9[29] 10[17] 11[7]
B 1[19] 4[6,32] 29[23] 34[12]

Fig. 13: *gadol* 'great', all cases with article in the Torah

It may be worth while to note, in passing, that the ratio of plene spellings is higher in Deuteronomy (see below, pp. 42, 55, 108).

Given that affixes commonly have this sort of effect, it is easy to see that the apparent 'avoidance' of successive plene spellings within the same word may be only a special case of the same thing. The presence of affixes may often reduce the proportion of plene spellings, and this is so whether the affixes themselves contain a vowel letter or not. Suffixes which contain no vowel letter often act in the same way, notably so the second-person suffix –*ka* . Thus the plural of the common word *bat* 'daughter', *banot*, is always written בָּנוֹת plene, and so also the construct בְּנוֹת; but in suffixed forms the writing without waw is common, and in some cases, as in *b*ᵉ*notaw* with the third person suffix, greatly dominant. The plural of '*ab* 'father' has only two short spellings when without suffix, and these are the first two in the Bible, Ex 12[3] 20[5], nor in this case does the presence of the article make any difference; but with possessive suffixes the spelling without waw is very common: for instance, for *ᵃbotaw* 'his fathers' the short spelling אֲבֹתָיו is overwhelmingly dominant (seventy-odd cases) and the long spelling אֲבוֹתָיו occurs only thrice (Jud 2[10] Ps 49[20] 2C 30[19]; Mm 4240).

These are sufficient evidences to establish the importance of affix effect. I do not pretend that it worked universally in the same way or that there are no exceptions; but it is clearly widespread. The fact that a word is often spelt with one vowel letter but not with two is one case within a more general phenomenon. We do not have to say that there was a principle or a rule which caused it to happen this way: rather let us say, simply, that something happened to many words when they were 'alone' that did not happen in the same proportion when they had affixes or were in certain combinations.

Now the existence of affix effect will be sufficiently obvious in much of what is to follow, and plenty of further examples will be seen. We need not discuss it further in itself. But it leads us on into some of the major questions of our entire investigation, and these can conveniently be taken up here.

Firstly, affix effect makes much difference to the strategy of our assembly and display of the evidence. For it means that affixed forms may have to be assembled, examined, and displayed and counted *separately*. Statistics based upon the global numbers of plene and defective of all forms of a word can be entirely distorting. *Nabi'* 'prophet' when 'alone' is always plene, but the plural absolute *n^ebi'im* splits into three different spellings. The (smallish) figures for some of the plurals would be dwarfed if they were placed in the same count with the singular absolute. The spellings of *qol* without waw in the singular absolute are a tiny minority: but, as soon as it is seen that they belong to a group touched by affix effect, then they become a much more substantial proportion. *'Abot* 'fathers' (absolute) has to be seen as belonging to a different group from *^abotaw* 'his fathers'. If they are simply added together on the grounds that they both have this *–ot* termination, the impression created will be false. In the case of *^olam* 'eternity', nothing is more clear than that the cases with *l^e–* affixed have to be treated as a special class and that, if they are simply enumerated as units along with the general mass of occurrences of that word, the essentials of their position will be lost and obscured.

Moreover, it seems, there is no way of knowing abstractly whether affix effect will be present in the material or in what way. No automatic test or principle can be stated or applied. Only by observation and thought can it be discerned that it is there. In some words the definite article is significant, but not in all. The effect of collocation with *l^e* in *l^e–^olam* will not be found equally clearly in many other words. In some words a difference may be made if they are in the construct state (see an example above, pp. 28f.) but in others it seems to have no effect. One has to study the distribution for each word, and each form of each word, in order to see in what ways and along what lines the material divides itself up.

This fits in with the small-scale method of research and display that has been followed here; see already above, p. 15f. Large-scale counts and statistics seem for our purpose to tend to lump together things that are distinct; and for this reason it has been possible, for many aspects, to work with fairly small units, which can fairly easily be displayed in the maps and diagrams here used.

More important, however, our discussion of affix effect introduces us to the central question of our entire investigation: do the variations in spelling go back to differences that were really there in the language at some earlier stage, or are they matters of scribal preference and convention? Though this problem will be with us constantly, this will be a good point for a first formulation.

11. The central question formulated

In the last section we have given at least a partial description and exemplification of affix effect: words which when 'alone' tend to be written with a waw or yod tend, when some particle is affixed to them or a termination added to them, to be written without such a vowel letter. But the fact that this is so is still not an explanation of how it came to be so? *Why* are these waws and yods not written? *Why* did the tendency not to write plene in two successive syllables, as so many scholars have expressed it, come about? Now there are perhaps several hypotheses that one might suggest, and two will be mentioned here, not because we have to decide between them at this point, but because the mere mention of them indicates the sort of choices that we shall have to make as we continue to explore our material farther.

Firstly, we might suppose that the affix effect had something to do with stress. The addition of a pronoun suffix, or of a definite article, or of a plural termination, might have made a difference to the total prosodic contour of the word. There may be some reason to suppose that vowel letters were most commonly used, not only on long vowels, which would be generally agreed, but on long vowels when they bear the main word stress. An added element like a definite article or a plural termination might be supposed to draw something of the stress on to itself, or otherwise to alter the balance of stress, and for that reason it might become less likely that a vowel letter would be used in a syllable other than that of the new affix. When the same word was used 'alone', i.e. without article or other affix, it might be more likely that the internal word stress would be noted, and that any relevant long vowels would be marked with a vowel letter. In principle this explanation puts the basis of the matter *within the language*: it was the language, as spoken at some past time, that provided the conditions for the spellings that we find. It was a prosodic and phonetic matter.

It should be observed that, if this were the case, the conditions for stress within words, and the pronunciation of the language in general, could well have been different at an earlier stage from the conditions implied in Masoretic Hebrew grammar, to say nothing of the conditions known in the various historical pronunciations of Hebrew by native speakers in different lands. Help might be derived from comparative philology; conversely, peculiarities of biblical spelling might confirm philological reconstructions of the shape of Hebrew as it was in a time long before the Masoretes.

The second possibility would be a matter of writing rather than of speech. The idea that scribes somehow simply did not like vowel letters, and thought that one per word was enough, is of this kind. More seriously, let us suppose that the biblical text moved very gradually from a kind of writing that used very few vowel letters towards a kind of writing that used them substantially but not universally. Vowel letters, then, were on the increase. The older manuscripts had been much more purely consonantal. As time passed by, scribes began to insert more waws and yods than had been there before. They did not do this systematically, though that would have been easy enough to do if anyone had formed a policy on the matter, but they just put them in here and there as semiconscious inclination prompted them to do. Now, when a word was 'alone', without any affix like an article or a pronoun suffix, they tended to notice that it could be more fully spelt and they tended to insert the waw or yod, now preferred. But when it had these affixes, they tended somewhat more to leave it as it was. Just why they left it alone is hard to say: perhaps they thought that the word was too long when written with both vowel letters and other affixes, perhaps they thought that the vowel letter helped to define the word more clearly when it was 'alone', perhaps it was no more than their practice and convention. These are mere hypotheses at this stage and will be discussed more seriously later. But the point is: when seen in this way, it was not so much a matter of phonetics and prosody, of relations that existed in the language as a spoken system, it was a matter of scribal technique, of the way in which scribes noticed things and put in signs according to their own habits.

The difference between these two sorts of explanation will remain with us throughout our investigation, and certainly no decision can be attempted at this point. Indeed it may be that no decision should ever be reached, and that both of the aspects here mentioned have been validly present: in that case, however, we may want to disentangle the features of spelling which derived from older states of the language from those that derived from scribal preferences.

12. The differing degrees of spelling variation

Although, as has been said, variability in spelling is pervasive and widespread in the biblical text, there are some remarkable differences between different words in the degree of variation that they undergo. Words may have vowels of the kind that normally vary in spelling, and yet these words in fact seldom vary, or not at all, while other words, apparently of the same kind, vary a lot.

Firstly, there are some words that are frequent and yet never vary in spelling although variation might have been possible. Thus נְאֻם 'prophetic saying of' occurs about 376 times and is always so spelt. It is well known that the spelling נאום (נואם) is common at Qumran, but it does not appear in MT. The constant defective spelling might theoretically be connected with the fact that this noun is practically always in the construct (exception at Jr 23³¹), but this is not very convincing, since no such effect is seen in constructs of other words of the same form. Another unvarying word is מְאֹד 'very', occurring about 300 times. *Kohen* 'priest' is כֹּהֵן over 750 times and never with waw, though 1QIsA has כוהן at Is 8² 28⁷. נָבִיא has already been mentioned. Another important case is the name מֹשֶׁה, 'Moses', never with waw. A common word of another kind is רוּחַ 'wind, spirit', and it is solidly plene in the singular, with or without suffixes, and even in the various plural forms the waw of the root is always written with the exception of Jr 49³⁶ הָרֻחוֹת, Zc 6⁵.

Secondly, there are words of exceptional variation. The defective spelling מַדֻּעַ 'why?' appears only at Ezk 18¹⁹: the word occurs 72 times in all. כֹּחַ 'strength' (about 125 cases) is always thus defective except for the one long spelling at Dn 11⁶. A much more prominent word is אֱלֹהִים 'God', which occurs in all about 2,600 times and is invariably without waw in the absolute state in which it is mainly used: in the construct, however, there is the unique Ps 18⁴⁷ אֱלֹהֵי, and with suffix the very isolated two cases of אֱלֹהַי Ps 143¹⁰ 145¹.

The singular form *'eloah*, on the other hand, varies more: dominantly plene, and universally so in Job, the book in which it is most used, it appears as אֱלָהּ in Dt 32¹⁷ (contrast 32¹⁵) and Dan 11³⁸ (where plene also a few words later); cf. also 2K 17³¹K.

Among nouns with the preformative *m*-, *maqom* 'place' (almost 300 cases singular without suffix) appears as מְקֹם only at Ex 29³¹; *mo'ed* 'agreed time, meeting', with about 185 cases without suffix, has defective spelling only once, in the construct בְּמֹעֵד Dt 31¹⁰.

Thirdly, there are words that vary more than this, but still rather little. We have already mentioned that *kabod* 'honour, glory' has only four defective spellings, out of about 135 cases without suffix (cf. above, p. 13). The well-known *šalom* has eight short spellings, four of them with affix b^e– or l^e–. 'Enemy', in the singular, without suffix, is dominantly אֹיֵב, long; the short spelling is found only at 1S 18^{29} Jr 6^{25} 15^{11}. The Torah has seven cases but all are plene.

Fourthly, at the other end of the scale there are words with a very high degree of variation: one such is *yobel* 'jubilee', which also gives us an interesting example of block spelling within the Torah, but a block that suddenly changes in the middle of a chapter:

A	יֹבֵל Ex 19^{13}		28,30,31,33,40,52,54	
B	יוֹבֵל	Lv 25^{10,11,12,13,15,28}		
A		Lv 27^{17,18,18,21,23}	Nu 36^{4}	
B			24	Jos 6^{5}

Fig. 14: *yobel* 'jubilee', all cases of singular

Note that almost all cases are affixed: the three which have the word 'alone', Lv 25^{10,11,12}, are all written with waw.

Particularly interesting in these sets of examples are the words which vary very seldom or never. It is hard to believe that this is a matter of mere chance or of failure to consider the weight of the consequences. A word like *kohen*, כֹּהֵן, belongs to a type in which spellings with waw, though seldom dominant, are usually fairly represented (cf. below, pp. 64–81), but out of over 750 cases no such spelling occurs for this word. The complete absence of variation can hardly fail to be significant. The same is true of the personal name מֹשֶׁה 'Moses'. And, though there are two or three slight and marginal exceptions, the lack of variation for אֱלֹהִים 'God' over a very large number of cases cannot be overlooked. Interesting in all these cases is the great, or indeed overwhelming, dominance of the defective spelling. Must one not consider that certain words, selected lexically, were considered to be fixed in their spelling by convention, with at the most only a very few exceptions? And, at least if this train of thought has been properly followed out, such words were more or less fixed by convention in what may have been an 'older' pattern, i.e. without waw to represent the *o* vowel.

But, if this is true, it at once makes a difference to our conception of the entire movement of Hebrew spellings. For this conception implies that certain words were picked out from the general development of Hebrew sounds and assigned a certain position, perhaps because they were ancient terms of religion and not to be changed. But this, if true, means that the spelling of certain words was fixed by scribal tradition and did not, in this tradition, change, no matter how much the phonology of the language might change historically. Even if things were done differently in other traditions of Hebrew text transmission, it would not alter these facts. But, above all, this conception would mean that the spelling of certain words was fixed by convention: it would be a matter of lexical selectivity, similar in character if not in degree to that which applies in English. It would mean that the force of lexical selectivity cut across the development of phonology; and that would mean that the laws and movements of phonology, even if perfectly known, could not be taken as a total basis from which to plot the dates and movements of texts through their spelling.

This means, however, that two quite different tracks of explanation may exist for words that have little or no variation. One might be inclined to suppose that in cases like נְאֻם or מְאֹד the basis lay in pronunciation: let us say, perhaps, these words did not, in ancient times, have the sort of vowel that qualified for plene spelling. Cases like כֹּהֵן, מֹשֶׁה and אֱלֹהִים look more plausibly like cases of lexically selective convention. The possibility of such convention will reappear in our discussion later and will remain with us to the end (see below, pp. 72, 80f., 92, 196ff.).

13. The book as the context for spelling practices

It was already stated above (p. 21) that the meaningful unit for the study of spellings is not the original source, if such there be, but the book, the biblical book within which the materials are located. Something more should now be said to amplify this.

One of the general impressions that most students will have gained from their introductory textbooks is that the Torah tends to spell defectively and the other books in increasing measure plene (so for instance GK § 8l (b), p. 44). They are also aware that, in the history of writing, the more purely consonantal writing seems to have come earlier, and the use of vowel letters to have developed later. From this it is easy to go on to the conclusion that short spellings and early sources go together. It is easy to show, however, that this is not necessarily so: generally speaking, spelling tendencies go with the tendencies of the book in which the passage stands. Thus, for instance, to take a work that will be examined more closely later (see below, pp. 168–174), the one poem that occurs both as 2S 22 and Ps 18 has a large number of striking differences of spelling between the two versions.

The Song of Deborah, Jud 5, is commonly believed to be a very ancient poem, one of the oldest in the Bible. But, if this is so, and I do not doubt it, it is not reflected in the spelling tendencies of the text. Even a brief glance will show that this poem has many long spellings in words in which a shorter spelling would be possible and even normal. A few examples follow:

5⁶   נְתִיבוֹת This is written with both yod and waw; words of this pattern are often spelt shorter: cf. for instance zᵉmirot, which is never written with both yod and waw and which at Is 24¹⁶ has the doubly short spelling זְמִרֹת. Jud 5 is scarcely a later text than Is 24.

5⁹   חוֹקְקֵי The writing of the qal participle plural with waw is a distinctively long spelling; it is not uncommon with verbs of this kind (double ʿayin), e.g. in the Psalms. This particular word is found in the participle twice in Isaiah, often a markedly long-spelling book, and both times without waw: Is 10¹ הַחֹקְקִים, 22¹⁶ חֹקְקִי.

5¹³,²⁵   אַדִּירִים This doubly long spelling is actually the common one for this word in the plural and is found also in the (old?) poem Ex 15¹⁰. The short spelling אַדִּרִים is found at Zc 11² and the ultra-short אַדִּרִם at Ezk 32¹⁸, both undeniably late books.

5¹⁷   יִשְׁכּוֹן The long spelling of a qal imperfect of this sort is found primarily in Ezekiel, the Minor Prophets and Job. In this particular verb, שׁכן, taking together the various persons of the singular, plene spellings are found at Is 57¹⁵ Jb 29²⁵ (1st person); Ps 104¹² (3rd person masculine), as well as here in Judges; Jr 50³⁹ Jb 18¹⁵ (3rd person feminine).

5¹³,²³   בַּגִּבּוֹרִים An obvious example of repetition of a long spelling, one which in this word in the plural is favoured in sources like Jeremiah, Ezekiel, the Minor Prophets, while the writing without waw is dominant in Samuel, Chronicles, and even Song of Songs, Ezra and Nehemiah.

Even a quick look at the Song of Deborah, then, is enough to explode the supposed correlation between ancient origins of a text and defective spelling of it — unless, of course, we are seriously to think that Jud 5 is a late poem after all. But — and this is our point — it is not a matter of proving a date for the Song of Deborah, for the whole book of Judges is involved in the same question. Much of Judges must be of ancient origin; but its spelling styles throughout include many long spellings and, like those of Joshua, present a marked contrast with the spelling tendencies of the Torah which in the Bible just precedes them. One other note about the Song of Deborah should be added: it often has a mixture of short and long spellings in close juxtaposition, e.g. גְּדֹלִים 5[15] defective, but גְּדוֹלִים plene in the very next verse, 5[16]; in 5[11] we have both the long צְדָקוֹת and the short צִדְקֹת in the same verse; so again אֹרוּ, אוֹרוּ 5[23]. Even Deborah's own name is spelt defectively only once (5[15]) as against plene spellings in all other cases. Among other long spellings we may note 5[21] קְדוּמִים and 5[31] אוֹיְבֶיךָ.

The principle that 'the more archaic the spelling, the earlier the completion and publication of the work'[1] is thus entirely wrong, and no enormous amount of observation and penetration is necessary in order for this to become obvious.

In particular, care should be taken to avoid taking the presence of defective spellings as an argument for the early origin of particular texts or passages. Defective spellings, sometimes quite surprising ones, continue to appear down to the very latest books. Daniel, as we just saw, has the rare spelling אֱלֹהַּ (Dn 11[38]), Esther has the only case of שֵׁשׁן defective (Esth 8[16]), Nehemiah has נֶגֶד 11[11], a surprising spelling since this i vowel is overwhelmingly written plene (cf. the case of בְּרִית 'covenant', with about 280 cases and all of them written with yod, even when affixed, except for the one case of Jr 34[18] בְּרִתִי).

Some years ago I heard a paper read in which it was argued that the latter part of Ex 3[15] was an extremely ancient text. The phrase is:

זֶה־שְּׁמִי לְעֹלָם וְזֶה זִכְרִי לְדֹר דֹּר

and it was argued that the two expressions לְעֹלָם and לְדֹר דֹּר were both striking for their defective spelling and that this was an indication of early date. Now the passage may well be very early, indeed I have no doubt that it is so, but the spelling of these words is no argument of any kind, as can easily be shown.

First of all, לְעֹלָם: we have already shown above (p. 27) that this is a classic case of affix effect. The spelling here used is the dominant spelling throughout the Torah. Moreover, there are eight or nine cases of לְעֹלָם, so spelt, outside the Torah: 1K 1[31] 2[33] 9[5] 10[9] Ps 45[18] 75[10] 92[9] (136[3]) Jb 7[16].[2] The Psalm cases are a small

---

[1] Anderson and Forbes, p. 317.

[2] Ps 136[3] is interesting, since it is (in BHS) a solitary short spelling within a series of 26. It seems, however, to be a mistaken writing. It is indeed defective in the Leningrad Codex but its Masora does not note it. In the Aleppo Codex the word is plene.

minority since the phrase is common in these poems, but the pattern in Kings is striking: the four cases in 1 Kings are all the four cases of *l^e–^{c}olam* in the book, while the two cases in 2 Kings are both spelt with waw. 1 Kings appears to have a steady preference for the short spelling. Some short spellings of ^{c}*olam* in other combinations occur in late books, cf. the unusual הָעֹלָם in Qo 3[11] and the striking מִן הָעוֹלָם וְעַד הָעֹלָם with both spellings in the same phrase, at 1C 16[36].

The short spelling of לְעֹלָם, then, is no indication of date. But neither is the short spelling of לְדֹר דֹר. Although the singular *dor* is always plene when alone, when the word is repeated twice in succession, which is a common idiom, it is very common that both words should be spelt defectively. That this is so is no new idea: Elias Levita stated it as a principle of Masoretic spelling centuries ago.[1] I should say, however, that I have found an unusually high degree of variation between manuscripts and editions in precisely this phrase: for example, Dt 32[7] דּוֹר וָדוֹר is printed as doubly defective in many editions, e.g. Snaith's. But, whatever the exact proportion of spellings in this phrase, there seem to be a substantial number of double defective spellings, especially in the Psalms (sixteen cases in all), and thus enough to show that the short spelling is the common practice for this phrase in many sources, whatever their date, and thus provides no evidence for the date of any particular passage that contains it.

We reiterate, then, that biblical spellings should not be attached by us to the origin, date or provenance of the sources, but considered in the first place in relation to, and as a part of, the spelling tendencies of the book in which they are found. This is not to say that books are uniform within themselves: they are not. All books are mixtures of spellings, and sometimes the strength or weakness of the mixture alters as we go through the book. In order to go farther into the character of books as spelling units, we may first of all consider what is in many ways the most important group, the spellings of the Torah.

14. Particular aspects of Torah spellings

The vague impression that the Torah tends to spell shorter than 'other books' or 'later books' is a very rough distinction and not

---

[1] Levita, ed. Ginsburg, pp. 163f.

sufficient for serious work. If we say 'later books', we should understand that this is meant in a spatial rather than a temporal sense: the books that come nearer the 'end' of the Bible come 'after', the Torah comes 'before'. The Psalms form a 'late' book in the sense that they come near the 'end' and far from the 'beginning', although some of the poems in the Psalter may well be earlier than parts of the Torah.

Experience quickly shows that the facts are much more complicated than would be suggested by the simple idea that the Torah is the prime locus for the shorter spellings. In order to take account of the facts, we shall have to notice differences between various books within the Torah; and, outside the Torah, distinctions have equally to be made. It is not the case that spellings simply become longer as we move away from the Torah and into the other books: many 'late' books contain many short spellings, and perhaps the prime example is Jeremiah. Conversely, in spite of the many literary similarities between Chronicles and Nehemiah, there are many differences in spelling between them, and many interesting similarities between Nehemiah and the Torah. Here and there we can find in the Torah a plene spelling which is quite unusual in the other books: for example, the name 'Jacob'. This is said to occur 349 times in all, and of these only five are יַעֲקוֹב plene: four cases in Jeremiah, and one in the Torah, Lv 26[42].

A more exact statement of the difference between the Torah and the other books might begin with this observation: there are certain words and forms which are universally plene outside the Torah, so that variation exists only within the Torah. We saw, for example, on pp. 29–30 that the adjective *gadol* 'great', when with the definite article, is always spelt long outside the Torah, הַגָּדוֹל, while within the Torah it varies. Similarly, on p. 23, with Fig. 6, we saw that all cases of *ṣippor* 'bird' in the singular are plene outside the Torah, while within the Torah, when with the article, there is variation, and the shorter spelling is actually dominant. Figure 3, p. 22, showed that *šemot* 'names', plural absolute, has many cases defective in the Torah, but in the non-Torah books it is always plene, as it is in the construct also (fourteen cases absolute, nine construct). *Ḥᵃmor* 'ass' appears to be with waw in all cases outside the Torah in the singular; but in the plural it varies freely in the non-Torah books, while in the Torah it is uniformly without waw. It is all these many cases (for I have cited only a few) that combine together to support the impression of the Torah as the locus *par excellence* of defective spelling: all these are cases where spelling outside the Torah is uniformly plene. To these can be added, as additional support, those words in which, outside the Torah, defective spelling is very rare. For instance, the personal name of Sihon, king of the Amorites, outside the Torah is defective only once, Jos 2^{10} (the first case after the end of the Torah), while within the Torah the defective spelling סיחן is dominant, and the plene סיחון occurs only four times.

In such cases, then, plene spelling is universal or dominant in the non-Torah books; but this carries with it, in most cases, a corollary that is not so often noticed or expressed. In words such as those mentioned, the Torah itself *is divided*. It is not the case that the other books use plene spelling but the Torah uses defective. The Torah is the area of greater variation, of greater diversity: words of this kind, spelt uniformly in the rest of the Bible, are divided in their spelling within the Torah. Thus it is rather less usual for the Torah to use a shorter spelling *uniformly*.

Thus many of our diagrams have already shown how divided the Torah can be. Fig. 1 showed its deep division in the spelling of 'ephod'; Fig. 2 showed how it used four different spellings for *tol^{e}dot*, and the shortest of these spellings only once. Fig. 6 shows its strong preference for the shorter spelling of *sippor*, but only when with the article; Fig. 9 showed its strong preference for the shorter spelling of *^{c}olam*, but only when collocated with *l^e-*. With *šemot* 'names', however (Fig. 3, p. 22), the two spellings are practically equal in numbers, and if we add the figures for the plural construct *š^{e}mot* the preference will go to the plene spelling, since in the construct we have שְׁמֹת defective only thrice, Ex 28^{11,21} 39^{14}, but plene four times in Genesis, six in Exodus and nine in Numbers.

And with some expressions the short spellings, though found only in the Torah, are *actually a small minority* within the Torah. This is a key point for our understanding. The plural absolute *'abot* 'fathers' occurs as אֲבֹת defective only in the Torah, indeed only in Exodus, but even there it occurs only twice, Ex 12^3 20^5, the first two cases in the Bible, and all other cases in the Torah are with waw, six without article, two with article; and the construct forms also are all אֲבוֹת with waw, four cases in the Torah, including Ex 6^{25} 10^6 which come before the two defective cases of the absolute. We have seen (p. 29) that *qol* 'voice' occurs without waw almost only in the Torah, but even if all cases are taken together they are a small minority as against the spelling קוֹל. *Bor* 'pit' occurs only once as בֹר without waw, in Ex 21^{33}, immediately after the full spelling בּוֹר in the same verse; but the short spelling is in a small minority within the Torah, which has about eleven cases of the plene writing (though, as in other books, defectives occur when with affixes, e.g. הַבְּדָה Gn 37²⁴, וּבֹדֹת Dt 6¹¹. With *'ot* 'sign' in the singular Exodus has, as so often, the only short spellings: with *lᵉ* it has לְאֹת Ex 12¹³, but this is the only short spelling in the Torah, as against nine of לְאוֹת; and it has, with the article, three times הָאֹת defective (Ex 4⁸⋅⁸ 8¹⁹ — and note that 4⁸ also has the short לְקֹל twice) but the Torah also has the same twice plene (Ex 3¹² Dt 13³), and *'ot*, when 'alone', is of course universally plene. With בְּכוֹר 'firstborn', singular, without article, all cases outside the Torah are plene; within the Torah six or so are בְּכֹר defective but these are swamped by a much larger number of plene spellings. With the article the proportion of the short spelling הַבְּכֹר is higher (four to six in the BHS text) but the long spelling is still the dominant one even within the Torah. Collocated with *min* 'from', there are two of each.

These examples are sufficient to give a clearer idea of the way in which the short spellings of the Torah are distributed.

Another aspect of the spellings of the Torah must now be added. The Torah's content of defective spelling is by no means evenly distributed. Even the casual reader of these pages can hardly have failed to notice how often the rather exceptional short spellings come within Exodus, and especially the earlier chapters of that book. This observation seems correct: for many phenomena, the major concentration of short spellings lies within Exodus. The Torah is not a flat continuum in these respects, but its spelling tendencies appear to be shaped like a curve. Genesis, the first book, appears to try out a variety of spellings: consider the four writings of *tolᵉdot* (Fig. 2, p. 2). In Gn 10⁸⁻⁹, introducing Nimrod, and using the word *gibbor* for the first time in the Bible, it writes it twice defectively and once plene in the space of a few words.

In its very first chapter Genesis spells *mᵉˀorot* 'luminaries' in two different ways, defective מְאֹרֹת Gn 1¹⁴⋅¹⁶ but מְאוֹרֹת with waw 1¹⁵; and it uses the participle with waw, רוֹמֵשׂ Gn 1³⁰ (and again 8¹⁹), though that is a rather unusual style for the Torah (and this same form is without waw at Gn 7⁸ Dt 4¹⁸ and in all cases with the article).

With *ha-gadol*, as we saw above (Fig. 13, p. 30), Genesis prefers the shorter spelling by a ratio of 5:2, while Exodus uses only the shorter; Deuteronomy has a higher proportion of the longer spelling (five long v. eight short). In its latter chapters Deuteronomy at times seems to move towards the longer spellings more characteristic of the non-Torah books. These are only a few and slight examples, but as we progress through the material similar tendencies will be seen again.

One other characteristic should be mentioned here: although it is not found only in Torah spellings it is particularly evident in them. It has already been touched upon above (see pp. 22f., 25f. on the plural of *n ᵉbi'im*). I refer to the plurals of words which in the singular have a vowel letter within the body of the word, and where the plural retains that vowel letter but uses no vowel letter in the plural terminations *–im* or *–ot*. Here is an example which has also been briefly mentioned on p. 26: the plural of *ṣaddiq* 'righteous':

A	צַדִּיקִם Gn $18^{24,24,26,28}$		Dt 4^8 16^{19}
B	צַדִּקִים		1K 2^{32} 2K 10^9
C	צַדִּיקִים	Ex 23^8	
B			Ho 14^{10}
C		Is 5^{23} 60^{21} Ezk 23^{45}	

Fig. 15: *ṣaddiqim*, plural absolute masculine, all cases in the Torah and Prophets

It is not necessary to extend the diagram to include the Writings, for there all cases are the same, that is, they spell with two yods, spelling C: 19 cases in the Psalms, 23 in Proverbs, one in Job, one in Lamentations, and three in Qohelet. Thus over the Bible as a whole the longest spelling, צַדִּיקִים, is massively dominant; but in the Torah it is an exceptional spelling, found only once out of seven times — and, strikingly, in Exodus, so often the primary locus of the shortest spellings. The dominant spelling in the Torah is צַדִּיקִם. This style of spelling plurals is interesting, and poorly known, perhaps because it may have been little used after biblical times: in the Bible it is quite common, and especially so in the Torah, but few textbooks pay attention to it. Thus בְּרִיחִם 'bars' is always so spelt in the absolute plural except for one case at 2C 14^6; תַּנִּינִם 'sea monsters' has three cases in the Torah, and all so spelt (Gn 1^{21} Ex 7^{12} Dt 32^{33}; with two yods only at Ps 74^{13} 148^7); יְרִיעֹת 'curtains' is very frequent in the description of the tabernacle, and every case in the Torah is thus written. Similarly the pattern תְּמִימִם 'perfect' is practically standard over many cases of this common term in the Torah (Lv 14^{10} has תְּמִימִים in the Leningrad Codex but many texts have תְּמִימִם, e.g. Snaith); and note in this the agreement with Ezekiel (five cases in his concluding chapters, and only one of them תְּמִימִים plene, Ezk 43^{25}). Something more will be said in discussion of this type of spelling at a later point (see below, pp. 45f.).

We have now said enough to unfold the basic ramifications of our study and to introduce the approach that will be taken. The next stage will be to discuss in order various types of words in which variable spellings occur. This task will occupy the next chapter.

CHAPTER TWO
The Central Groups of Evidence

In this chapter studies are made of various types of words in which variable spellings occur. It was not possible to aspire to completeness, and I have selected types which are prominent in the language and, especially, those which seem to yield important clues for the understanding of biblical spelling in general. Other types have also been studied by me and have influenced my judgement on the question as a whole, but it would be an extremely complicated task to cover all types in which spelling variation is to be found.

There is no particularly logical order in the following sections. I begin with the plural terminations –*im* and –*ot*, because these may be a special case of affix effect, as discussed above, and their influence extends over thousands of the noun forms that have to be discussed, so that it seemed to be good to take first the effect of these ubiquitous terminations. Thereafter we pass to some major nouns and adjectives of the pattern *qatol* and to the highly interesting class of monosyllabic nouns. The qal participle of the normal triliteral verb is a very important case and comes next. Thereafter treatments, sometimes brief, of various other types within verbs are provided. A very important case is the second person masculine singular suffix, –*ta* or –*ka*, and it is given a more extended treatment, followed by a shorter study of the similar case of the feminine plural verb suffix –*na*. There follow some problems concerning yod (or its absence) with *e* vowels and finally, the numerals, the short word לֹא 'not', the particle '*ot*– with suffixes, and some personal names and place names.

1. The plural terminations –*im* and –*ot*

The importance of the plural terminations for any study of spellings has already been touched upon (e.g. pp. 25f., 43 above). It will be convenient to say something more about these endings at this point, before we go into the various classes of words, since the plural elements have something pervasive about them and they recur very frequently. The average reader of Hebrew is accustomed to think of these terminations as written plene, i.e. with yod in –im and with waw in –ot, and grammars tend to present them in this way. In fact, as has already been amply shown, the plural endings are often spelt without these vowel letters. In this, however, there is a very large difference between the two endings: the –ot without waw is a very common spelling, notably in the Torah but also in other sections of the Bible; the –im without yod, by contrast, is much less common. We shall therefore look at these two endings separately.

A. THE TERMINATION –IM

The first thing to notice is that, in nouns of the common pattern $q^e talim$, or in nouns, to put it in another way, where the vowel before the termination is a, it is extremely rare for the yod of the termination not to be written. Thus, out of many hundreds of cases, we simply never get spellings like:

*אֲנָשׁם 'men';   *דְּבָרם 'words, matters';   *שָׁנם 'years';

*מְלָכְם 'kings';   *בָּנם 'sons'

Such spellings are extremely rare. It is not the case, however, that they never exist: there is, for instance, one case of וַעֲבָדָם Gn 24³⁵. There are sporadic other cases, such as the peculiar writing הַיֵּמָם Gn 36²⁴ ('mules', KJV and NEB; 'water', New American Bible; 'hot water', Vulgate and Mandelkern). Most striking of all, beyond doubt, among the numerous occurrences of yamim 'days', is the writing הַיֵּמָם at Nu 6⁵, which is coupled by the Masora with Gn 36²⁴ just mentioned. Cf. also Ex 8¹⁰ חֲמָרם twice in immediate succession.

The place where we do find –im written without yod in substantial measure is in words that have an i vowel in the previous syllable, giving a pattern like $q^e tilim, qattilim$, etc. We have already shown (p. 43) that this is the dominant spelling of saddiqim, צְדִיקָם, in the Torah, and includes also the one case in Ezekiel; similarly with בְּרִיחָם 'bars', תַּנִּינָם 'sea monsters', and תְּמִימָם 'perfect (masc. plur.)'. $N^e bi'im$ 'prophets' might well have more cases but for the fact that this word seldom occurs in the Torah and never in the plural. On p. 22 above we display the distribution in Samuel, showing three cases of this spelling, the last three in the book. The one other case of נְבִיאָם is in Jeremiah, at 23³¹. Since this term is important, and is richly used by Jeremiah, and since his distribution is interesting, we display it here:

A   נְבִיאָם 23^{31}

B   נְבִאִים $14^{13,14,15,15}$ $23^{9,15,16,21,25,26,30}$

C   נְבִיאִים   Jr 2^8 4^9 $5^{13,31}$ 7^{25} 8^1 13^{13}

B 25^4 $26^{5,7,8,11}$ $27^{14,15,18}$ ^{15,19} 35^{15}

C ^{16} 28^8 29^1 44^4

Fig. 16: plural absolute of *nabi'* 'prophet', all cases in Jeremiah

In this word the Jeremiah text begins with seven cases of the long spelling C and then, in two blocks in chs. 14 and 23, uses only נְבִאִים; but after 23^{30} he moves in the very next verse to the unusual spelling used only once by him (and thrice in Samuel); thereafter he alternates, using the long spelling נְבִיאִים less frequently. 26^8 has spelling C in a number of texts.

A few other cases can be added: 2S 1^{23} has וְעִימָם, Ex 20^{18} has לַפִּדֹם, of which word all other cases are in non-Torah books and have the yod of the termination. Even in the Torah, it should be added, there are words in which this type of spelling is not found: for example, the word 'cups' is גְּבִעִים, so spelt, in all seven cases, Ex $25^{33,33,34}37^{19,19,20}$ Jr 35^5. On the other hand שְׂעִירֻם 'goats' is so spelt in all three cases in the Torah (Lv $16^{7,8}$ 17^7) and the homonym meaning 'showers' is the same at Dt 32^2.

These are sufficient examples. They lead us on, however, to a further and perhaps more striking point, seldom noticed: namely, that in words of this type we sometimes have the yod of the termination –*im* and the yod of the *i* within the body of the word omitted, producing a doubly defective writing with no vowel letter at all.

Thus, to confound all those who think that short spelling goes with early date of origin, in *'addir* 'glorious' the dominant plural spelling is the doubly plene אַדִּירִים, found in the ancient sources Ex 15^{10} Jud $5^{13,25}$. But the shorter אַדִּרִים is found once, at Zc 11^2, and the ultra-short אַדִּרֹם at Ezk 32^{18}.

An important example is the plural of *naśi'* 'prince':

A   נְשִׂאָם 35^{27}

B   נְשִׂיאָם   Gn 17^{20} 25^{16} ^{10} 27^2

C   נְשִׂאִים   Ex 34^{31} Nu $7^{3,10}$ 36^1

D   נְשִׂיאִים 10^4

C continued 22^{14}

D continued   Jos $9^{18,19,21,21}$ 17^4 22^{32} 1C 4^{38} 7^{40}

Fig. 17: plural absolute of *naśi'* 'prince', with or without definite article

The ultra-short spelling נְשִׂאָם is used only by Exodus, and by it only once. The Torah uses all four spellings but with a preference for the two intermediate ones, B and C. In this case there is a complication, in that we should perhaps include also the four cases of the homonymic *nᵉśi'im* that means 'clouds' or the like; but if we do it does not make much difference: the spellings are נְשִׂאִים at Jr 10¹³ 51¹⁶ Ps 135⁷ and נְשִׂיאִים at Pr 25¹⁴.

The ultra-short spellings, though few in number, are very suggestive. They confirm that the avoidance of plene spelling is not something caused by the antecedent presence of another vowel letter in the same word (pp.26–30 above): for here there is no other vowel letter in the word, and the point is rather the quite different one, namely that there is in the word one of the vowels that *might* have had such a vowel letter. The importance of this will be much confirmed when we consider the cases with termination –*ot*. These ultra-short spellings suggest a different series of suppositions: there may, at an earlier stage, have been a much larger number of such spellings in the text, and the few that remain may in many cases be remnants from that earlier stage: that is, that the *yods* were added to a text which lacked them, but were added haphazardly and sporadically. Hence, in a case like *nᵉśi'im* above, when yods came to be added, they were sometimes added in the –*im* termination, sometimes in the body of the word, sometimes not at all, and occasionally both, but this last possibility was less often taken up in the Torah.

Much more common than the writings that have no vowel letter at all are those that have it within the body of the word but not in the termination –*im*, and this sort of writing, like תְּמִימִם, is, as we have seen, particularly prominent in the Torah but noticeable elsewhere, as in Samuel, Jeremiah and Ezekiel. Yet, taken over the Bible as a whole, there is no doubt that a spelling with the yod on the termination, like נְשִׂאִים, is very much more frequent in a wide variety of words. This brings us back to affix effect and the question raised above, p. 38f.: might there be a shift of accent involved in this? If the Torah, and some other sources, liked a spelling like תְּמִימִם, might it go back to a stage when the word was stressed in that way, *tᵉmímim*, with the stress on the final syllable of the stem and not on the termination as it is in Masoretic grammar? Or might it be that the vowel of the –*im* ending was at one time a shorter vowel, or a different vowel in some other way, so that it was not always felt to be a candidate for plene spelling? I am not sure that we have means to answer the question but it should at least be borne in mind.

It remains to add that the spelling with –*im* without yod is also found in some other cases, like hiphil participles in the plural: so Lv 21⁶ מַקְרִיבִם, 2S 20¹⁵ מַשְׁחִיתִם.

B. THE TERMINATION -OT

As was said above, the termination –ot is quite commonly written without waw, and in proportion very much more commonly than the writing of –im without its yod. In some words, indeed, as mentioned above, (p. 43), the defective spelling of the termination is universal in the Torah, as with יְרִיעֹת 'curtains', 23 cases in all, while the four in non-Torah books are all יְרִיעוֹת. The same is true of the term עֲבֹתֹת 'interwoven work', five times in the Torah, Ex 28[14,24,25] 39[17,18], but with waw in the one non-Torah case, עֲבוֹתֹ Hos 11[4]. Here and there in the Torah one may find a whole string of words so written, e.g. Ex 28[14] שַׁרְשֹׁרֹת הָעֲבֹתֹת עַל־הַמִּשְׁבְּצֹת. In the first chapter of Genesis every one of the four words with ending –ot is written without waw: 1[14] מְאֹרֹת, 1[15] לְמָאֹרֹת, 1[16] הַמְּאֹרֹת. Ex 15 has five such words, and all are without waw. At this stage, it should be added, we are dealing with the termination –ot, whether in the absolute or the construct, but not with the –ot– of the plural when further pronoun suffixes are added to it, for that forms a separate case.

We can illustrate the situation from a few familiar words. שִׁפְחָה 'maidservant' begins in Genesis with three cases of the plural (Gn 12[16] 20[14] 24[35]), all written without waw as שְׁפָחֹת, followed by one of שְׁפָחוֹת with waw, 30[43]; all these are preceded by w[e] 'and'. After this come three more, spelt with waw, and having the article, הַשְּׁפָחוֹת Gn 33[1,2,6]. Dt 28[68] also has this long spelling. The spelling with waw is shared also by all the nine or so cases in non-Torah books. Cf. also below, p. 184.

Take similarly the plural of אֶרֶץ 'land'. With article we have the defective writing הָאֲרָצֹת Gn 26[3,4] Ne 9[30], and in the construct אַרְצֹת with prefix b[e] at Lv 26[36,39]. The four in Genesis and Leviticus form a majority of the total usage of this word in plural without suffix in the Torah: the only exception is Gn 41[54] הָאֲרָצוֹת. Note the agreement of the case in Nehemiah, which has however its counterpart in the spelling with waw at Ne 10[29].

The familiar נֶפֶשׁ has the absolute plural נְפָשֹׁת at Ex 12[4] Lv 27[2]; these are without article, and the other Torah cases, Lv 18[29] Nu 19[18], are spelt נְפָשׁוֹת and have the article. The plural construct is similarly נַפְשֹׁת at Lv 21[11] but נַפְשׁוֹת at Gn 36[6]. Those in other books are written with waw.

Mišpaha 'family' has the plural מִשְׁפָּחֹת at Zc 12[14], twice in juxtaposition, contrast the spelling with waw at 12[12,14a]. In the construct, which is a common form, though the first case in the Bible is מִשְׁפְּחוֹת plene (Gn 10[18]), the short spelling מִשְׁפְּחֹת is massively dominant through a long run of cases in the Torah (I think 40 cases without suffix; by Mm 3361 there are six plene in the Torah).

The examples are enough to show us two things: firstly, that the spelling of –ot without waw is substantially more common than the spelling of –im without yod; secondly, that the short spelling of –ot is more independent of the presence of an o vowel in the body of the word, since in fact the cases so far cited have no such o vowel. This is not to say that words containing o are excluded: a good evidence that they are just the same is provided by אָתוֹן 'she-ass', which has the doubly defective plural אֲתֹנֹת in Gn 12[16] 32[16] 45[23] 1S 9[3b]: these are all the Torah examples, and 1S 9[3b] is sandwiched between two spellings with waw. Other cases in non-Torah books are אֲתֹנוֹת with waw, including Jud 5[10] within the Song of Deborah, and Job 1[3] 42[12] have the writing with two waws, אֲתוֹנוֹת.

On the other hand, as we saw with words that take the plural ending –im, there are some words that take the ending –ot but never have it without the vowel letter except when suffixes are appended. Banot 'daughters', a very frequent form, is always written with waw, both absolute and construct, though not the forms with suffixes. 'Fathers', already mentioned above, p. 29, has only two cases without waw in the absolute, and all in the construct have waw. Šemot 'names', as was shown on Fig. 3, p. 22, varies a great deal in the absolute; its construct is more preponderantly plene, the short writing שְׁמֹת being found only thrice, at Ex 28[11,21] 39[14], as against four of שְׁמוֹת in Genesis, six in Exodus and nine in Numbers. It is interesting to compare also another kind of –ot termination, namely that of 'ahot 'sister', אָחוֹת, which is not a plural ending at all but has the same form: it is plene in all cases, absolute or construct, except with suffixes, and this includes a good number of cases within the Torah. The very frequent צִבְאוֹת 'armies', with close to 300 occurrences, seems to be always with waw, including the construct; but this may be connected with the fact that there are practically no cases in the Torah (only Dt 20[9] and, in the construct, Ex 12[41]). The uniformity of the many cases in the Prophets is striking.

Another word that seems to have uniformity is בָּמוֹת 'high places' (but again only Nu 21[28] within the Torah). Does it seem that words that have the vowel a (qamets) in the syllable before the ending –ot have a stronger tendency to write the ending with waw, as we have seen with banot 'daughters' above, and with banim 'sons' correspondingly in the words with –im? Contrast, for example, mizbᵉhot 'altars', which has a fairly substantial group of writings without waw (all cases in the Torah, five in number, plus 2K 21[3,4]), with mamlakot 'kingdoms', apparently always plene in the termination, including the two cases in the Torah (Dt 3^{21} 28^{25}), and including the construct, with the solitary exception of Is 10^{10} לְמַמְלְכֹת.

Before leaving this subject we have to add some mention of some other word-types: participles with the feminine plural ending, adjectives with the same, and, most important, monosyllabic nouns like *qol* 'voice' which take the plural termination –*ot*.

Qal participles with the ending –*ot* are not very numerous but a few examples will show some tendencies: יֹצֵאת 'going out', thus defective only at Gn 24^{13}, the only case in the Torah, while four in other books are written with waw; יֹשֶׁבֹת 'living', thus short at 1K 3^{17} but long in the termination at 1S 27^8 Ezk 8^{14} Ct 5^{12}; צֹבְאֹת 'working' (?), thus short at Ex 38^8 but long at 1S 2^{22}; נֹשְׂאֹת 'carrying', thus short at Gn 45^{23} but long at 2C 9^{21}; הֹלְכֹת 'going', thus short at Ex 2^5 but long at 1S 25^{42} Ne 6^{17} 2C 9^{21} (1S 25^{42}, however, is doubly defective in many texts, e.g. Snaith, Letteris).

Among adjectives the plural of *gadol* furnishes a good example: גְּדֹלֹת is thus written at Nu 13^{28} Dt 1^{28} 6^{10} 9^1 (28^{59} also in some texts), all without the article, plus Dt 7^{19} 10^{21} 29^2 with the article; the termination is spelt with waw in Dt 27^2 28^{59} (so BHS spelling and Masora). The spelling גְּדוֹלֹת is found at Ne 9^{26} 12^{31}. Outside the Torah and Nehemiah there is a long run of examples, all written with waw of the ending. Similarly *g^{e}bohot* 'high' is with waw in BHS at Dt 28^{52} but without it in other texts (e.g. Snaith), and the three cases in other books have the waw.

Particularly interesting are the plurals of nouns and adjectives which in the singular have a vowel *o* normally marked with waw. Such words are in the singular predominantly plene but this may be altered with affix effect (discussed with the example of *qol* 'voice' above, p. 29). The plurals of such nouns are commonly with –*ot* and their spellings tend to vary in a similar way, and the absolute tends to be identical in form with the construct, so that they can be displayed together. Here is a map of *qolot* 'voices':

A	קֹלֹת	Ex $9^{23,28}$		34		12^{18}	
B	קוֹלֹת				20^{18}		
C	קֹלוֹת		$9^{29,33}$		1S 12^{17}	Ps 93^4	Jb 28^{26} 38^{25}

Fig. 18: *qolot* 'voices, sounds', absolute and construct, with or without article or other prefixes

Note the rapid alternation in Exodus and also in 1 Samuel. The doubly plene writing *קוֹלוֹת does not occur.

The word 'sign', singular and when 'alone', is אוֹת plene; but with the definite article it is thrice הָאֹת in Exodus, Ex 4[8,8] 8[19]; there is one exception in this book, הָאֹת Ex 3[12], the first in the book. The others with article, one in Deuteronomy, two each in Samuel, Kings and Isaiah, and one in Jeremiah, are all plene. After l^e-, in the phrase 'for a sign', which occurs about fifteen times, including two in Genesis, three in Exodus, two in Numbers, three in Deuteronomy, two in Isaiah and three in Ezekiel, the short spelling לְאֹת appears only at Ex 12[13]. Our interest here, however, is in the plural:

A אֹתֹת Gn 1[14]		4[17,28,30] Nu 2[2]	Dt 4[34] 7[19]	29[2]	
B אוֹתֹת			6[22]		
C אֹתוֹת	Ex 4[9]	14[11]		26[8] 34[11]	
A					Ne 9[10]
C Jos 24[17] 1S 10[7,9] Is 8[18] 44[25] Jr 10[2] 32[20,21] Ps 74[4] 135[9]					

Fig. 19: *'otot* 'signs', all cases in the Bible

The shortest spelling, אֹתֹת, is dominant in the earlier part of the Torah. The post-Torah books are agreed throughout except for the striking reappearance of the shortest spelling in Nehemiah.

Dor 'generation' is a complicated case, and the singular will be discussed shortly (below, pp. 58ff.). When it has the plural *dorim* all cases are דּוֹרִים doubly plene (Is 51[8] Ps 72[5] 102[25]). At Gn 9[12] we have the short spelling לְדֹרֹת (construct), but the other cases of *dorot* have waw in the termination.

To this we may add the feminine plural of the adjective טוֹב 'good', again always plene when without affix, i.e. in the masculine singular.

A טֹבֹת Gn 6[2]		26,26,35 Dt 6[10]			
B טֹבוֹת	41[5,22,24]		2K 25[28]	24[2,3,3,5]	
C טוֹבוֹת			Jr 12[6]		
B			Jr 52[32]		
C				Est 2[2]	

Fig. 20: *ṭobot*, 'good', feminine plural, absolute and construct, with or without article

Notice how Genesis 41 shifts after v. 24 from the longer spelling טֹבֹת to the shortest. The spelling *טוֹבֹת does not occur.

We need not pursue other cases except briefly: עוֹר 'skin, leather' is always plene in the singular without suffix; suffixed forms are without the waw in the Torah, thus עֹרוֹ etc., but with waw in the non-Torah books, e.g. עוֹרוֹ. The plural is found only in the Torah and the shortest form עֹרֹת is used twelve times in Genesis and

Exodus, the only exception being עורת Ex 39[34a], which is immediately followed by the shortest form again in the same verse.

Of words with a central vowel other than o, the most important is רוּחַ 'wind, spirit'. The plurals are not numerous. In the Torah we have two, Nu 16[22] 27[16], written (with article) as הָרוּחֹת, and Jr 49[36b] has הָרֻחוֹת. The other cases, all in the Latter Prophets and the Writings, all have the doubly plene except for Zc 6[5] רֻחוֹת which in any case is doubly plene in some texts.

Monosyllabic nouns with vowel i can seldom be usefully compared, since many of the words never vary in spelling, as אִישׁ 'man', or are like עִיר 'city' which in the plural has the a vowel; that עָרִים appears, in spite of its many cases in a wide variety of books, to be spelt always with the yod of the termination confirms what we have said (above, pp. 45, 49) about cases like *banim*, *banot*. Among relevant cases with i vowel we may cite *sir*, whether meaning 'cooking-pot' or 'fishing-hook': this seems to be always spelt with yod in the singular, but in the plural we have סִירֹת Ex 38[3] 2K 25[14], סֻרֹת Jr 52[18], while the following verse 52[19], along with 1K 7[45] and the other non-Torah instances, has the double plene form סִירוֹת.

C. THE TERMINATION –OT WITH PRONOUN SUFFIXES ADDED

That the plural termination *-ot*, though very commonly written with waw, tends to be written without waw when pronoun suffixes are added after it, is one of the best-known and most familiar manifestations of what we have called 'affix effect'. The examples of *banot* 'daughters' and of *'abot* 'fathers' were already cited in this connection above, p. 30. It would be too complicated to attempt to furnish many examples of the working of this phenomenon. As a very rough generalization one may say that *-ot-* with following suffix will commonly be short in the Torah with occasional exceptions, similarly but less regularly in the historical books from Joshua to Kings, with Kings particularly favouring the shorter spelling in this respect; while some other books like Psalms, Ezekiel, some Minor Prophets and Chronicles will favour the spelling with waw. A few examples follow:

The expression *tol^edotam* 'their generations' (in which, for present purposes, we ignore the o of the first syllable) seems to be solidly defective in its *-ot-* in all its cases in the Torah. Chronicles has seven cases all of which have the waw in this suffix. Even Chronicles, however, has 1C 26[31] לְתֹלְדֹתָיו. מִשְׁפָּחָה 'family' generates a long series of the expression *l^e-mišp^ehotam* in several books, 83 in total. Nu 4[38] is the sole case with waw out of the numerous Torah cases; in Joshua, on the other hand, which book is the other main user, there are seven with waw, still a small minority but nevertheless a larger proportion; cf. Mm 859. Chronicles has only two, but both are with waw. 'Their names', $\check{s}^e motam$, without prefix is dominantly without waw in the Torah (four cases) but is plene שְׁמוֹתָם at Ex 28[12] Nu 13[4] and in the non-Torah cases; with prefixes we have short spellings only in the Torah, Gn 25[13] בִּשְׁמֹתָם and the like, four cases, while non-Torah books are with waw. The noun 'altars', when made into 'your altars' or 'their altars', tends to be defective in the Torah and Kings but with waw in Ezekiel and Hosea. With the third singular masculine suffix even Chronicles sticks to the defective מִזְבְּחֹתָיו, 2C 23[17] 32[12]. These instances are perhaps sufficient to give an impression of the common tendencies.

2. Nouns and adjectives of the pattern *qatol*

The pattern *qatol* is extremely important in Hebrew. It includes familiar nouns such as *šalom* 'peace', *kabod* 'honour', *yatom* 'orphan', and adjectives like *gadol* 'great', *qadoš* 'holy' and *ṭahor* 'clean (ritually)'. First we look at some of the nouns.

שָׁלוֹם is a central and important word, and most readers would expect to see it written with waw. It occurs 237 times in all and of these only a small handful are suffixed or plural. There are in fact eight cases spelt שָׁלֹם without waw, and these are: Gn 37[4] 1S 16[4] 1K 2[5,6] 5[26] Jr 15[5] Ezk 13[16,16] — cf. Mm 1614. Four of these eight, we should note, have prefixed elements: לְשָׁלֹם Gn 37[4] Jr 15[5], and בְּשָׁלֹם 1K 2[5,6]. Sometimes proximity with another occurrence may be a factor, especially in the Ezekiel case, for in it the entire phrase *šalom w^e-'en šalom* 'peace, but there is no peace' appears at 13[10] with *šalom* twice plene, at 13[16] with it twice defective.

Contrary to the generalization that the Torah prefers a short spelling, it strongly prefers the spelling with waw: out of about 24 cases, it has only one written without waw. Kings is more evident as a centre of short spellings, having three out of about thirty cases in all, and these are concentrated at the beginning of the book, where they make a pattern as follows:

A שָׁלֹם 1K 2[5,6] [26]
B שָׁלוֹם 2[13,13,33] 5[4] — and all those that follow

Fig. 21: *šalom* 'peace' in 1K 1–5

For *kabod* 'glory, honour' the figures have been already given above (p. 13). The only one in the Torah written without waw is the first one in the Bible, Gn 31[1] (but the Torah has rather few in the absolute anyway); other defective spellings are in remoter books, Na 2[10] Pr 25[2,2].

With words of this kind the short-spelling tendency of the Torah is often to be seen primarily in the suffixed forms. Thus, to take *kabod* again as our example, we find *k°bodi* 'my glory' written כְּבוֹדִי at Gn 45[13] but כְּבֹדִי defective at Gn 49[6] Ex 29[43] 33[22] Nu 14[22]; similarly כְּבֹדֶךָ Ex 33[18] Ne 9[5] (note the agreement with Nehemiah, which depends however on the Masora, against nine or ten in other books); with כְּבֹדוֹ, this short spelling in the only place in the Torah, Dt 5[24], shared also with Is 10[16] and (after *min*) Ezk 43[2], as against about seventeen in other books. Outside the Torah the majority of spellings of *kabod* plus suffix will be very strongly with waw, with only occasional exceptions.

Another simple illustration is provided by צָפוֹן 'the north'. All cases without suffix appear to be thus, plene, including eight in the Torah. But with the local suffix –*a, sapona*, all eight occurrences in the Torah are צָפֹנָה without waw, and all outside the Torah, 45 in number, are צָפוֹנָה with waw. Not all examples are so simple.

Another typical word is *yatom* 'orphan'. In the singular this is universally יָתוֹם plene in all sources, including a dozen in the Torah, though only one in Exodus (22[21]), and including those with article affixed. The absolute plural has nine occurrences, and of these two are יְתֹמִים short, Ex 22[23] Jb 22[9] (cf. Jb 24[3] plene). Plural with pronoun suffix is twice without waw.

To sum up, then, in nouns of the pattern *qatol*, if these examples are a good guide, the Torah prefers the long spelling in the singular when alone, but strongly tends to write without the waw in suffixed forms, while the non-Torah books will often, though certainly not invariably, write the waw even there.

An adjective like *gadol* 'great' follows a similar pattern. The basic distribution for the singular has already been described above (pp. 29f.). With the feminine singular affix, however, the Torah massively prefers the short spelling גְּדֹלָה, both with and without article (eighteen cases), but the longer גְּדוֹלָה begins to appear in the latter part of the Torah and has four cases, Nu 22[18] Dt 4[36] 25[13,14], the last two being the last two cases of this form in the Torah (Mm 1193). As the same Masoretic note makes clear, this long spelling is greatly dominant in the non-Torah books (over 100 cases) as against only seven of גְּדֹלָה, which are at Jud 15[18] Jr 11[16] Ezr 9[7,13] Ne 1[3] 2[10] 9[37]. Dn 10[8] is also defective in BHS but is not counted by this Masora, and Ne 9[37] is plene in BHS against it.

In the masculine plural g[e]dolim the short spelling גְּדֹלִים is consistently followed in the Torah, with or without article, and is dominant also in the other books with occasional exceptions: גְדוֹלִים Jud 5[16] (contrast 5[15], cf. above, p. 38) Jr 25[14] Qo 10[4] Ne 11[14] 12[43] 1C 17[8]. The feminine plural, which in the Torah is dominantly spelt גְּדֹלֹת doubly defective, has already been described above (p. 50). The last two cases in the Torah, Dt 27[2] 28[59], have גְּדֹלוֹת, which is the only spelling in the non-Torah books until we come to Nehemiah, which varies this with two cases of גְדוֹלֹת, Ne 9[26] 12[31].

The common adjective *ṭahor* 'clean' seems to follow a similar pattern. All cases of the masculine singular without the article (58 cases in the absolute) seem to be טָהוֹר long; but the definite article seems to favour variation:

A	הַטָּהֹר		11[47]	14[57]	20[25] 24[6]	Nu 19[19]
B	הַטָּהוֹר	Gn 8[20]	Lv 10[10]		15[8]	
B		Dt 12[15,22]	15[22]	Zc 3[5]	Qo 9[2]	2C 13[11]

Fig. 22: *ṭahor* 'clean (ritually)', masculine singular with definite article, all cases in the Bible

The Torah is very equally balanced, but the long spellings are mainly at the beginning and, in Deuteronomy, at the end.

The feminine singular, *ṭ[e]hora*, prefers the shorter spelling טְהֹרָה, but, rather differently, we twice have the longer spelling with definite article, at Gn 7[2,8]: in both these verses we have הַטְּהוֹרָה followed by טְהֹרָה in the same verse but without definite article. The spelling with waw is found also in the only two cases of the feminine outside the Torah, Mal 1[11] Ps 19[10].

The common *qadoš* 'holy' has already been mentioned in respect of its singular (above, pp. 27f.). The masculine plural (there is no feminine of this word) achieves a much simpler pattern than was to be found in the singular. The greatly dominant spelling is the shorter, קְדֹשִׁים, which is used in all the nine cases in the Torah and eight cases in other books; the long spelling קְדוֹשִׁים occurs only at Ho 12[1] Ps 16[3] 2C 35[3].

Somewhat similar patterns can be seen with other adjectives, such as *qarob* 'near' and *raḥoq* 'far', and these again illustrate the importance of affix effect. Thus when alone קָרוֹב is thus spelt with waw (six in the Torah and plenty elsewhere) but with the article is solidly short, הַקָּרֹב, in the Torah (four cases) and even in a normally long-spelling source like Esther (Esth 1[14]); similarly also after the preposition *min* (short Dt 32[17] Jr 23[23], long Ezk 7[8] Jb 20[5]).

Again, רָחוֹק plene is normal for the word alone (exceptional defective וְרָחֹק Pr 31[10]) but the phrase מֵרָחֹק is thus defective in all seven cases in the Torah, and in the other books there are five cases of the same out of about 35: 1S 26[13] Is 25[1] 57[9] Jr 23[23] Ps 38[12] (Mm 1681); BHS text is against Masora at Dt 28[49] Is 25[1].

The above is sufficient to characterize the general features of the spelling of major groups of nouns and adjectives of the pattern *qatol*. It remains to observe that another group exists which has quite different spelling characteristics, in particular in that they seem *never* to be spelt with waw.

Thus *gaboah* 'high' occurs seventeen times in the absolute singular masculine, and every single case is defective, גָּבֹהַּ, although the occurrences are spread over books where some long spellings might be expected: Isaiah, Jeremiah, Ezekiel, Qoheleth, Esther. Nor is there any waw in any of the plural or feminine forms. Similarly, *ʿamoq* 'deep' occurs ten times in the masculine singular, and all are defectively written, עָמֹק: the seven cases in Leviticus are not surprising, but the same short spelling in Ps 64[7] Qo 7[24,24] is more striking. And the same tendency is most obvious of all with the common *qaton* 'small', of which all spellings that use the *o* vowel are written without waw (the feminine, of course, has the form *qᵉtanna* with the *a* vowel). קָטֹן occurs about 52 times and none is written with waw in MT (2C 15[13] is defective against Mandelkern's registration).

Now this in itself is not, perhaps, so very original an observation: perhaps the facts have been noted before. But within our own discussion they have a special context. Our subject is the variable spellings, and here suddenly we find a group of words in which spelling seems to be more or less invariable; yet they have, in the Masoretic pointed text, exactly the same *qatol* pattern. The most natural explanation is that, at the time represented by the consonantal writing, these words did not have the same vowel as words like *šalom* or *tahor*, and that they were thus not eligible for the variable spelling with or without waw. A simple way to express this is to say that they did not then have the long vowel which qualified for writing with waw; or else, in some cases, that they did not have the *o* vowel at all, but an *a* vowel, or a short *u* vowel. These thoughts are much confirmed when we look at the construct, feminine, or plural forms, which can have a short *u* vowel as in עֻמְקָה or a short *a* vowel as in קְטַנָּה or גְּבַהּ.

If we are right in this, it has important implications for our subject as a whole. For it means that, at least in certain cases, the absence of variable spelling is not a matter of scribal convention or of

Masoretic technique but goes back to actual differences that existed in the language as spoken; and these differences existed in the language at earlier times but by Masoretic times no longer existed, for by the Masoretic pointing עָמֹק 'deep' has just the same vowels as קֹדֶשׁ 'holy', whether the latter is written with waw or without. In this respect therefore these features of the spelling corresponded, or came near to corresponding, to a state of the language that by Masoretic times had ceased to be observed. And this in turn would seem to confirm that the spelling, in these respects, had not changed much over a considerable period of time, for it means that, although by Masoretic times עָמֹק had the same vowels as קֹדֶשׁ, that fact had not yet had the effect of producing in the former the plene spelling that was widely used in the latter.

In this particular aspect, then, we seem to have detected something that connected the spelling with older states of the spoken language. Even if this is correct, however, we should beware of supposing that something similar will prove to be true for every one of the many phenomena of biblical spelling.

And even in this case, even if we are right in identifying a group of words that belonged to a distinct philological group and that continued to retain the spelling that reflected that position, it would be premature to conclude that this happened always and universally, premature therefore to suppose that we could automatically read back from the spelling of the Masoretic text to the pronunciation and morphology of an earlier time. For the fact that *some* words of this kind retained their characteristic spelling intact, and can as a consequence be identified from that fact, does not prove that *all* words of the same kind avoided alteration in their spelling. There is evidence that makes it likely that this is not so. Thus I would think it very likely that ʿagol 'rounded' belonged to the same class as עָמֹק 'deep', as witness the feminine plural form עֲגֻלוֹת at 1K 7³¹; and of the five cases of ʿagol singular four are written עָגֹל short (so also 1K 10¹⁹ against Mandelkern), but the fifth case 2C 4² is עָגוֹל plene. If this was a word of the same class as עָמֹק, its spelling has, in one case out of five (and two out of five in some texts), moved to the plene. The same is the case with 'adom 'red': feminine אֲדֻמָּה Nu 19², and plural אֲדֻמִּים 2K 3²² Zc 1⁸ 6², strongly indicating a short u vowel. But the spellings of the singular are: אָדֹם Gn 25³⁰,³⁰ Is 63² Zc 1⁸, but וְאָדוֹם Ct 5¹⁰. Once the word came to be spoken as 'adom, especially if with a long vowel, that generated the plene spelling.

If this happened at all, it could have happened a lot more than is at first sight visible. Other words that now have the pattern qatol could have moved into it at a later stage, and could in earlier times have belonged to a different pattern. It is very likely of *qaton*, already mentioned; and if that is so, one must consider it for *gadol* also (note the abstract גְּדֻלָּה 'greatness'), and it must be considered also for *qadoš* 'holy', the unusual distribution of which was already pointed out above, pp. 27f. Some cases of קָדֹשׁ defective could possibly have been in origin not adjective forms but a noun like קֹדֶשׁ. I would suspect that קָרוֹב 'near' and רָחוֹק 'far' may also have belonged to the same category; cf. the evidence above, pp. 55f.

We therefore come, for the moment, to the tentative conclusion: the cases of words with non-varying spelling, like עָמֹק, form very powerful evidence leading back to earlier states of the language; but that does not remove the possibility that other words of the same original type have undergone substantial change of spelling, along with increase of variability.

3. Monosyllabic and related nouns

Monosyllabic nouns such as *'ot* 'sign', *qol* 'voice' and *dor* 'generation' have much of interest to tell us. Some aspects of their spelling distribution have already been discussed (e.g., their plural forms, pp. 50ff. above; their relation to affixes, p. 29 above; the repetition of *dor*, pp. 38f. above). But it is appropriate to bring together some general aspects of these words at this point.

Perhaps it will be useful to begin with the case of *dor*, commonly translated as 'generation', for the study of this word can disclose some rather fundamental principles about spelling. Certain points have been made already above (cf. pp. 38f.) but more must now be said if we are to elucidate the complicated spelling patterns of this word. It should be said in advance (a) that the choice of patterns, and the conditions governing them, are complicated, and (b) that there is more than the usual degree of disagreement between manuscripts and editions. The usage of the Leningrad Codex will be followed here except where otherwise stated. The main points are:

1. *Dor* alone is *always* דּוֹר plene, about 40 occurrences.
2. In the Psalms, which are the main source for reiterated *dor*, the dominant spelling pattern is double defective, דֹּר וָדֹר: so Ps 10⁶ 33¹¹ 45¹⁸ 49¹² 61⁷ 77⁹ 79¹³ 85⁶ 89² 90¹ 100⁵ 102¹³ 106³¹ 119⁹⁰ 135¹³ 146¹⁰, sixteen pairs in all.
3. The Torah has three such pairs, and both words are short, דֹּר דֹּר, at Ex 3¹⁵ 17¹⁶; at Dt 32⁷ however the Leningrad Codex has both

words long, דּוֹר וָדוֹר, though both are short in some editions, e.g. Letteris, Snaith.

4. The plural *dorim* occurs only thrice and is spelt דּוֹרִים, doubly plene; it is always in the phrase דּוֹר דּוֹרִים (Is 51[8] Ps 72[5] 102[25]).

5. The plural *dorot* without suffixes never has the waw of the first *o*. It is written four times דֹּרוֹת (Jud 3[2] Is 41[4] 51[9] Jb 42[16]) and once, in the construct, has the short spelling דֹּרֹת Gn 9[12].

6. Where pronoun suffixes are attached to the plural, they are attached to the form *dorot*. This is a very common combination (43 cases). Almost always (only exception Jos 22[27] דֹּרוֹתֵינוּ) *dorot* before suffixes is doubly defective, giving forms like דֹּרֹתֵיכֶם etc.

7. All cases in the prophets (Isaiah, Jeremiah, Joel) which repeat *dor* twice have both forms plene. This combination occurs also at a few other places: Ps 145[4,13] Pr 27[24] Est 9[28].

8. The sequence דֹּר וָדוֹר occurs at Ps 89[5] La 5[19]. The reverse sequence never occurs.

9. *Dor* with the article always remains plene, הַדּוֹר, but there are not many cases, nine in all, six of them in the Torah; and with pronoun suffixes, as in 'his generation', there are also very few cases, and the spelling is plene, Is 38[12] דּוֹרִי 53[8] דּוֹרוֹ.

One must apologize for the presentation of these complicated data, but the case of *dor* is a highly instructive one: for it, more perhaps than any other word in the Bible, enables us to see the effect of *repetition in proximity*. The word is a common one and its use extends through a good variety of books and types of usage.

That *dor* 'alone' is always דּוֹר plene is not a surprise, for we have seen this to be the case in a very large number of words, or sometimes to be the case but with a very small number of exceptions. But why is *dor* so often spelt *without* waw? The probable answer must be: because it occurs so often in close repetition. We have already seen the presence of affix effect: words with affixes will commonly have more defective spelling. Repetition in close proximity can have the same sort of effect.

Let us restate this as a suggestion of what may have happened. Let us suppose that the text at an earlier stage always or usually had דר defective. When the word was 'alone' its spelling shifted, slowly or quickly, into the plene דור. With the article it did so too, but there are not many instances. The very common plural before suffixes was *dorot* and it was written doubly defective, דרת. 'Affix effect' is no more than a constatation of the fact that, in these circumstances, waws did not come to be added as they did to *dor* when alone. But repetition in close contiguity had the same sort of effect: waws were commonly not added at all, or they were added to one of the *dors* and not the other; in the Prophets, and in a few other places, they were added to both. But a very large proportion of *dor* when repeated in close proximity remained without waw.

Enough of *dor*. And a number of other monosyllabic terms have already been discussed under the heading of plural terminations (above, pp. 50ff.). Some other examples will be noted in the remainder of this section.

Somewhat similar to *dor* is the word or words *dod*. One may (or may not) distinguish as different senses, or as different words: (a) 'friend, beloved one' (b) 'love', in the plural *dodim* (c) 'uncle' (specifically, father's brother). It is not clear that these differences are correlated with spelling differences; perhaps the entire series can be taken together anyway.

Where the meaning is clearly 'uncle' in a kinship sense, commonly *dod* construct followed by a personal name, we have דֹד defective at Lv 10[4] Est 2[15] but דוֹד plene at 1S 10[14,15] 14[50] 1C 27[32]. With suffix, *dodi* 'my uncle', *dodo* 'his uncle' etc., all cases are without waw in Leviticus (3), Numbers (1), Kings (1), Jeremiah (4) and Esther (1); but there is a plene spelling דוֹדוֹ at 1S 10[16] Am 6[10].

Where *dod* is 'beloved', all cases are written with waw, whether with or without suffix; all in fact are in Song of Songs except for one at Is 5[1]. The plural *dodim* 'love', when without pronoun suffix, is דֹּדִים defective at Ezk 16[8] 23[17] Pr 7[18], but דוֹדִים plene Ct 5[1]. All cases with suffix are in Song of Songs and all are without waw, thus דֹּדֶיךָ etc., Ct 1[2,4] 4[10,10] 7[13].

In addition one may mention the feminine *doda* 'aunt': this occurs only thrice and all with suffix, and is always defective, דֹּדָתוֹ or the like; all three are in the Torah.

It seems that these different usages nevertheless conform in a general way to the pattern we have sketched. Song of Songs used a plene spelling throughout on its key term *dodi* when in the singular, but in the plurals affix effect kept the spelling short. Incidentally, it may be interesting that the personal name *Dodo* is defective in both its occurrences in Samuel (2S 23[9,24]) but דוֹדוֹ plene in the corresponding places in Chronicles (1C 11[12,26]).

Other monosyllables with vowel *o* can be described more briefly. A common experience with many is that the word alone has plene spelling, so also mostly with the article, but with a very occasional defective spelling in one of these cases, and a somewhat more common defective spelling with plural terminations and other suffixes. Thus *bor* 'pit' (64 cases in all forms), when 'alone' (25 cases) has one defective בֹּר at Ex 21[33], and here in close proximity to the בוֹר four or five words before it; Gn 37[24] has הַבֹּרָה with the local suffix (and

וְהָבוֹר the very next word); 2K 18³¹ should have בְרוּ defective by the Masora, which contrasts it with Is 36¹⁶ which has the same form plene, but BHS is plene at 2K 18³¹ against its own Masora. Plurals are usually בֹּרוֹת and at Dt 6¹¹ וּבֹרֹת.

'*Ob* 'ghost, necromancer' is אוֹב plene in the singular and אֹבוֹת, אֹבֹת in the plural. Although '*odot*, used in the phrase עַל־אֹדֹת 'because of', is plural only, we may include it here, since it follows similar patterns to other monosyllables (e.g. pp. 50f.): it has thrice the spelling אוֹדֹת (Gn 21¹¹ Ex 18⁸ 2S 13¹⁶), and the spelling אֹדוֹת at Gn 21²⁵ 26³² Nu 12¹ 13²⁴ Jud 6⁷ Jr 3⁸, and so two cases with suffixes. אוֹן, whether 'strength' or 'grief', is almost entirely with suffix in the singular, and alternates quite a lot: Gn 49³ אוֹנִי but Dt 26¹⁴ בְאֹנִי, and Dt 21¹⁷ Jb 18¹² אֹנוֹ against several plene; the plural is אוֹנִים, five cases. כּוֹס 'cup', with 31 cases in all, is plene except for 2S 12³ וּמִכֹּסוֹ and the sole plural Jr 35⁵ וְכֹסוֹת. *Šor* 'ox', a common word, with many cases in the Torah, is plene throughout the singular, including suffixed cases, with the one exception of Ex 22²⁹ לְשֹׁרְךָ (on which more later, see p. 64).

Of monosyllables with the vowel *i* there is less detail to report. Some such words simply never vary in spelling. Of the common אִישׁ 'man' Levita said that there was a Masoretic tradition of three defective spellings,[1] but there is none such in our present text. Ezk 8² כְּמַרְאֵה־אֵשׁ, LXX ὁμοίωμα ἀνδρός, could well have been a case, and some consider that אִישׁ is the correct text, but it is the Masoretic reading that concerns us here. The common עִיר 'city' is always plene, and in the plurals the *i* vowel disappears anyway. Many other words are either always plene, or else they do not occur often enough to give us useful runs for study. It is therefore all the more interesting to find in *rib* 'lawsuit, quarrel' the short spelling Ex 23² רִב and, with *wᵉ-*, Jb 29¹⁶. Thus we have two short spellings out of about 35 cases without suffix, and to these we should add Pr 25⁸ לָרִב and, with suffix, Jb 31¹³ בְּרִבָם. These last two might be taken, indeed, as infinitives of the verb, rather than as noun forms, but this is a distinction without a difference, for monosyllabic infinitive forms, as could easily be shown, have similar spelling tendencies, and it is only for our own convenience that we separate the two categories. Thus, unlike the common אִישׁ or עִיר, *rib* displays an interesting degree of spelling variation, with the short forms distributed in Exodus, Proverbs and Job. Under infinitives of the same root we may note לָרִב Am 7⁴ Pr 25⁸, the latter with רִיבְךָ רִיב in the following verse.

---

[1] Levita, ed. Ginsburg, p. 164.

A few other examples with the *i* vowel: Pr 21[4] has נֵר, apparently a short spelling of נִיר 'light', which occurs four times elsewhere. For שִׂיחַ, supposed to mean 'meditation' or 'sigh' or the like, Jb 23[2] has the short spelling שִׂחִי with suffix, one in twelve out of all books; cf. also the שִׂחוֹ of Am 4[13] with the *e* vowel. Finally, with קִיר 'wall', a fairly common term occurring about 74 times, Is 22[5] has the short spelling in the phrase מְקַרְקַר קִר, another case where something like close repetition may have favoured the short spelling.

With the vowel *u*, we have טֻרִים 1K 7[20] against all others plene out of over 25 cases; this one is one in a series of the same within the same chapter. The frequent term חוּץ 'open space, outside' has a greatly dominating plene spelling, but with local suffix we have Is 33[7] חֻצָה and a number of plurals such as Jr 11[13] חֻצוֹת, 1K 20[34] וְחֻצוֹת by the Masora (contrast 2S 1[20] בְּחוּצֹת) and several cases of וּבְחֻצוֹת Jr 7[17] etc. If we may include *mul* 'other side, opposite' (36 cases), its sole occurrence with suffix, Nu 22[5], is מֻּלִי defective.

צוּר 'rock' is another frequent word (over seventy cases), and in the singular with article there is 1C 11[15] הַצֻּר, and in addition all seven cases of the plural צֻרִים are thus without waw. The one case of the other plural form, however, is doubly plene, Jb 28[10] בַּצּוּרוֹת.

The monosyllables that have been discussed in this section so far have been mostly ones in which the plene spelling is dominant, and especially so in the singular absolute and similar forms. Defective spelling comes in with affixes and is often a small minority. The average person would take the plene spelling as 'normal'. Monosyllables with the vowel *e* (sere), incidentally, are being left aside at this point, because they contain some further complications.

These monosyllables are easily distinguished from another group which have very different spelling characteristics. Although in the singular absolute they will commonly have the same Masoretic vowel point (mostly holem), their spelling will be very dominantly defective. With suffixes it will be obvious that the vowel of the root is a short one and in a closed syllable. Most such terms belong to the Double ᶜAyin class. The difference is elementary and requires no arguing.

Such words, however, do have in the Masoretic text very occasional and sporadic cases of plene spelling. Thus כֹּחַ 'strength' appears as כּוֹחַ at Dn 11[6], once out of 125 cases. חֹק 'statute' (129 cases) appears to have no plene spellings in the singular, but we have the one example in the construct plural בְּחוּקֵּי Ezk 20[18]. The extremely frequent *kol* 'all' has a trace of a spelling with waw in Jr 33[8] לכול K, which in the Q has become the normal לְכָל; and with suffix there is Jr 31[34] כֻּלָּם. Another common word, *rob* 'multitude, many', has several cases: Jb 33[19] וְרוֹב K ורב Q; 1C 4[38] 2C 31[10] לָרוֹב, out of a long run of this phrase in Chronicles. The presence of large numbers of such spellings in the Dead Sea Scrolls is well known. In the Masoretic text they are rare and sporadic. Few will dispute that they show the very occasional intrusion of a 'late' spelling style which is nowhere normal and nowhere even a serious minority option within the Masoretic text. The fact that such spellings exist at all, and the identity of the books in which they are found, may support the view that such spellings were beginning to exercise an influence at a late stage of development of the Masoretic text; they may also be a sign that the vowel of (say) *rob* was already being felt to be identical with the vowel of (say) *qol* by this time. But, since such unusual spellings do not present a serious or substantial sector within the traditional Bible text, we shall not do more than remark them in passing.

We return therefore to our main group of monosyllabic words surveyed in this section, and sum up with the following points. Firstly, the short spellings of the words surveyed extend over a wide variety of books and not confined to one or two or to a small group. As has been seen (pp. 29, 50f.) קֹל short is mainly in the Torah but also in Jeremiah; אֹת short is in Exodus; דֹּר short extends widely, especially through the Psalms; רֹב short is in Exodus, but also in Job and Proverbs; קָו short is in Isaiah. Others are found in Kings, in Chronicles, and elsewhere. A plural like אֹתוֹת is in Nehemiah.

Secondly, there seems to be a roughly similar distribution whether the vowel in question is *o, i* or *u*. More of our examples have the *o* vowel, but that may be because there are more such words in the language. Moreover, it is clear that, speaking very generally, the *o* vowel is the one that shows the highest degree of variability in Hebrew spelling. Some of the major words of *i* vowel have no variation of spelling at all. The high variation of a word like *dor* is explained through the special degree of repetition in close proximity. Apart from such special cases, the general pattern is: plene spelling in the singular with some slight degree of defective spelling, but a larger degree of defective spelling when affixed.

Thirdly, there is no clear evidence that suggests a difference of treatment as between words, in the case of the *o* vowel, that derive from an earlier diphthong *aw* and those that do not so derive. Naturally, it is difficult to prove beyond doubt which words came from an earlier diphthong and which did not. That *qol* 'voice' and *dor* 'generation' derived from earlier forms with diphthong seems fairly probable, and would be granted as a plausible supposition by most scholars.[1] בּוֹר 'pit' on the other hand very probably does not so derive, nor does כּוֹס 'cup'. Of אוֹת 'sign' one cannot be sure: perhaps there was a *w* in the original root, but there is little trace of an actual diphthong *aw* in the stage immediately preceding the Hebrew form.

In any case there are words in which we can be sure of the *aw* diphthong, or of the presence of the *w* as a consonant in Hebrew. One such is שׁוֹר 'ox', where we have the consonantal writing in Ho 12[12] שְׁוָרִים. It cannot be doubted that the word came from an earlier *šawr*, which in any case is confirmed by Arabic *thawr*. But if this *w* was still pronounced as a consonant, it would not have been possible to write a spelling such as Ex 22[29] לְשֹׁרְךָ. That word was so written because the vowel was pronounced as *o*, in all probability.

This, if right, is important, because it means that the short spellings of words like *qol, 'ot, šor*, especially in that zone of many short spellings that runs through the earlier part of the Torah and has its greatest concentration in Exodus, is a short spelling of a vowel that has already become *o*. In other words, it is a real short spelling, where the long spelling with waw would be a true alternative: it is not the spelling of some other vowel, in which there would be no variability and no choice. This, if right, has considerable importance for the interpretation of various other phenomena.

4. The *o* vowel of qal participles in triliteral and Lamed He verbs

The common qal participle with *o* as its first vowel, like שֹׁמֵר, דֹּרֵשׁ, raises a number of complicated problems of spelling. The first question is simple and clear: why is the dominant spelling of the qal participle defective, without waw of the *o* vowel? That this is factually so can easily be seen.[2] Nor is the shorter spelling a peculiarity of any one area such as the Torah: on the contrary, over the Bible as a whole, and over a large proportion of the relevant verbs, the

---

[1] The attempts by Cross and Freedman, *Early Hebrew Orthography*, pp. 50, 53 to show that *ql* in the Siloam inscription was *qal*, not *qol*, and similarly for *ym* 'day', alleged to be *yam* and not *yom*, seem to me quite precarious: they depend upon the assumptions with which these writers have approached the evidence, rather than upon the natural trends of the evidence itself.

[2] Andersen and Forbes give the total figures as: 4269 defective, 1040 plene, out of 5309. It is not clear exactly which items are included in these global figures and which omitted. See the table on their p. 193 and comment on p. 194.

dominance of the spelling without waw seems remarkable. In a book like Qoheleth, in which the *-ot* ending of plurals is overwhelmingly written with waw, is it not strange that the *o* vowel of the participle is still dominantly written without waw? In this book, if we count all *o*-containing participles, including plurals, suffixed forms and forms from Lamed He verbs, we find that the total number spelt without waw is still higher than the total number spelt with it. Is it not striking that books which habitually use waw in the writing of words like שָׁלוֹם or עוֹלָם nevertheless prefer not to use it in the spelling of the qal participle?

We shall not work from total overall numbers but will continue our policy of making an analysis of different lexemes separately; for, as we shall quickly see, there are very marked differences in the balance of spelling practices between the participle of one verb and that of another. We shall look first at the masculine singulars and come back to the feminines and plurals, where there is sufficient evidence, later on.

1. *'okel* 'eating' occurs 21 times, and the long spelling אוֹכֵל is found at four places: Gn 39⁶ Is 29⁸ Na 3¹² Ps 41¹⁰. Gn 39⁶ is the first case in the Bible; there are seven in all in the Torah.

2. *'omer* 'saying' occurs 36 times, including four in the Torah and eleven in Isaiah. All are defective except for Ne 5¹² 6⁸, which have the defective spelling sandwiched between them at 6⁶. Chronicles has the same word twice in the same verse, 2C 18¹⁹, both spelt short.

3. *holek* 'going' immediately introduces a startlingly different distribution. This is a common participle, occurring over 100 times in the masculine singular (in fact, 104, I think). Mm 1788 lists 27 cases that are plene, to which, they say, must be added all cases in Proverbs and Qoheleth except for one and four respectively. Since the details would be too many to provide a full map of the occurrences, we shall give a table only of the number of cases in each book:

	Gn	Ex	Lv	Nu	Dt	Jos	Jud	S	K	Is	Jr	Ezk
A הֹלֵךְ	6	2	2	1	5	6	2	10	1	4	4	5
B הוֹלֵךְ	3	1	3	3	–	1	2	3	1	1	–	–

	Ho	Jon	Mi	Hb	Zc	Ps	Pr	Jb	Ct	Qo	Est	Chr
A	2	–	1	–	1	2	1	1	–	4	–	1
B	–	2	1	1	–	2	11	–	1	5	2	–

Fig. 23: *holek*, qal participle active, masculine singular, numbers per book

In the Torah at least, the figures have to be qualified by the adding of the consideration of the definite article, for in the Torah *all* cases with the definite article are defective; this explains why all cases in Deuteronomy are defective, unlike the other Torah books, for, as it happens, all cases in Deuteronomy have the article.

It may be helpful therefore to add an exact diagram of the cases without article in the Torah:

A הֹלֵךְ 18^{16} 24^{42} 32^7 Ex 13^{21}
B הוֹלֵךְ Gn 15^2 25^{32} 28^{20} 19^{19}
A   Nu 14^{14}
B   Lv $11^{27,42,42}$ 17^{11} 22^{22} 24^{14}

Fig. 24: *holek*, 'going', participle masculine singular, without definite article, all cases in the Torah

There are many things of interest in this distribution. The effect of the presence of the article is just the opposite of what we found in several nouns in the Torah, such as אֲרוֹן 'ark' (p. 28) or adjectives such as גָּדוֹל 'great' (pp. 29f.); it is rather more like the pattern with קָדוֹשׁ 'holy' (pp. 27f.). There are enough cases in the Torah (eleven with the article) to make the uniformity in this respect very evident.

In the cases without article Genesis and Exodus are both equally balanced between the two spellings, but Leviticus and Numbers both prefer the long spelling and that makes it dominant in the Torah as a whole, in that zone of variation where the article is absent. In the non-Torah books the article seems to make no palpable difference. Samuel is dominantly short but there is one passage of long spellings, 2S $15^{12,20,20}$. The three Major Prophets are almost entirely short, the Minor are mixed. In the Psalms the long spellings come in the first part of the book, Ps 15^2 78^{39}, and the short later, 101^6 128^1. Proverbs is really solidly plene, for the one case registered as defective, 13^{20}, is a KQ with K הלוך: I doubt whether we can prove whether the Q would have been with waw or not, I would think with waw even if the Masora writes it without.

In any case the main point is the high ratio of long spellings in this very central and familiar participle, something quite different from our average experience with forms of this kind.

    4. *Yošeb* 'dwelling' is another participle that seems to have rules of its own. That it formed an exception was already known to Levita, who tells us[1] that, unlike other qal participles, which

---

[1] Levita, ed. Ginsburg, p. 151f.

were taken as dominantly defective and therefore counted by the Masoretes only when they were plene, *yošeb* was marked if plene in the Torah and Former Prophets, if defective in the Latter Prophets, and variously from book to book among the Writings. Once again we present a table only of the numbers by book:

	Gn	Ex	Lv	Nu	Dt	Jos	Jud	S	K	Is	Jr	Ezk	12P
A יֹשֵׁב	10	2	1	7	2	1	6	9	14	7	7	1	2
B יוֹשֵׁב	3	3	0	7	4	5	6	9	–	10	20	3	8

	Ps	Jb	Pr	Est	Ezr	Chr
A	8	1	–	2	–	1
B	2	0	2	3	1	7

Fig. 25: *yošeb*, qal participle active, masculine singular, numbers per book

The Masora counts 17 plene for the Torah, implying that Nu 13[29c] is plene against text of BHS. In any case it fails to disclose the same point that we saw with *holek*, that all cases with the article are defective in the Torah, one of them in Genesis, two in Exodus, one in Leviticus, three in Numbers and two in Deuteronomy. The effect of this is to produce an even greater preference in the Torah for the longer spelling, if we exclude the cases with article:

	Gn	Ex	Lv	Nu	Dt
A	9	–	–	4	–
B	3	3	–	7	4

Fig. 26: *yošeb* in the Torah, numbers without article, counting Nu 13[29c] as plene

Only Genesis has a substantial preference for the shorter spelling when without the article.

Detailed book-by-book comparisons between *holek* and *yošeb* can often not be made, because a book that uses one of them a lot may use the other very little. Kings is solidly defective in *yošeb*, while Jeremiah shows a substantial majority for the plene spelling. Up to ch. 40 his spellings are roughly evenly divided (nine long to seven short), but thereafter all cases are long; from ch. 44 to the end there are eleven thus spelt. The long spellings in the Psalms are in the earlier part, Ps 2[4] 22[4]. Chronicles shows a strong preference for the longer spelling, but in its one exception, יֹשֵׁב 1C 20[1], it follows the short spelling, contrary to its own general custom, and here it is parallel to 2S 11[1] which has the long spelling יוֹשֵׁב.

5. *Mošel* 'ruling' shows a ratio of eighteen defective to fourteen plene. Since this is a rather even distribution, it may be worth while to display how the variations fall:

A מֹשֵׁל Gn 24[2] 45[8,26] Jos 12[2,5]   Is 16[1] Jr 22[30]
B מוֹשֵׁל   2S 23[3,3] 1K 5[1]
A   51[46,46]   Hb 1[14] Ps 22[29] 59[14] 66[7]   105[20,21]
B   Mi 5[1]   89[10]
A   Pr 6[7] 16[32]   29[12]
B   23[1] 28[15]   29[26]   Qo 9[17] 10[4]
B cont'd   1C 29[12] 2C 7[18] 9[26] 20[6]

Fig. 27: *mošel* qal participle, all cases
(I have registered Pr 28[15] according to the Masora against the BHS text.)

6. *Boged* 'treacherous' is an example of a word of the same pattern, not very frequent, that is dominantly plene: it is spelt as בּוֹגֵד at Is 21[2,2] 33[1] Pr 21[18] 25[19], but as בֹּגֵד at Pr 22[12] and, if we follow the Masora against the text of BHS, at Hb 2[5].

7. By contrast, *nośe'* 'carrying', which has over forty instances, seems to be solidly נֹשֵׂא short in almost every case: this includes one from Proverbs, one from Daniel, and five from Chronicles. Many of the cases, about twenty in fact, come in the one expression 'armourbearer' from Samuel, and this may have something to do with the high proportion of short spellings. The only long spelling is וְהַנּוֹשֵׂא Lv 15[10], and this is the last of four cases of that expression in that book.

8. *Nopel* 'falling' occurs eighteen times and the only spelling with waw is Jb 14[18]; two other spellings in Job are short, and so is the one case in Esther.

9. *Soper* 'scribe' will be considered here, though later we will have to ask whether words of the same pattern which have in effect become nouns ought to be considered separately. Its spellings have an unusual pattern of distribution. In the Prophets, both Former and Latter, there are a good number of cases, especially in Kings and Jeremiah, but all are סֹפֵר defective except 2S 8[17] Is 37[2]. The long lines of instances in Kings and Jeremiah are all spelt short. In the Writings, on the other hand, as Mm 2348 rightly notes, Ezra uses the short spelling in all its five cases and Nehemiah begins in the same way (Ne 8[1,4,9,13]) but at 12[26]

switches over to the long spelling, which is then consistently used until the end of Chronicles (three in Nehemiah and eight in Chronicles, all plene).

10. *ʿober* 'crossing over' occurs about 56 times; these are formed by 42 without waw, 14 with it. All in the Torah are without (the main locus is Deuteronomy, with eight cases; and only four of the Torah cases have definite article, so that is not the cause of the short spelling this time). Ezekiel, with seven cases, is an almost solid block of plene (one exception, 35^7). The other eight long spellings are: 2K 12^5 (the last of seven in Kings); Is 60^{15} (the last of five in the book); two cases out of seven in Jeremiah; both the two cases in Zephaniah (the Minor Prophets have four defective); Ps 144^4 and Est 3^3. See Mm 2429.

11. *Šomeaʿ* 'hearing' occurs forty times or so, including four with definite article. The long spelling שׁוֹמֵעַ occurs only at Pr 15^{32} 21^{28}, and Proverbs itself has four short spellings, and so also are all five cases in the Psalms, the two in Job and the one in Qoheleth. The proportion of plene spellings is very low.

12. *Šomer* 'keeping' has about fifty cases, and nine of these are שׁוֹמֵר plene. See Mm 3634. The long spellings include three out of eight in Psalms, two out of twelve in Proverbs, one out of three in Qoheleth, the last of four in Nehemiah, and one out of two in Chronicles. The distribution in the Psalms is interesting: the three long spellings come together in the group 121^4 127^1 145^{20}, while the three earlier examples 34^{21} 97^{10} 116^6 are short, and after our group of three we return to short in $146^{6,9}$. Note how strongly Proverbs supports the shorter spelling.

The participles studied so far, then, have have shown a wide variety of proportions between short and long spelling, the percentage of spellings with waw ranging from as low as 2% or 3% up to as high as 40% or more. As has been clear throughout, some of this depends on which books happen to use a particular word: a word that is common in Samuel or Kings may be likely to have many short spellings in the participle, one that is common in Proverbs may have many long. But we have also seen that these relations are not constant. Proverbs, though commonly favouring the long spelling, strongly favoured the short in *šomer*, somewhat less strongly in *šomeaʿ*, and in *mošel*, a word with a high ratio of long spellings in total, is equally divided.

Particularly striking have been the high ratios of plene spellings in the heavily used participle forms *holek* and *yošeb*. Both of these are verbs of a special class, with imperfects of the type *yelek, yešeb*, and it may be worthwhile to investigate further and to see whether other verbs of the Pe Waw class have unusual spelling patterns in the participle. The answer is quickly seen to be in the affirmative.

13. *Yodea[c]* 'knowing' immediately gives us an example of this, for in it the long spelling יוֹדֵעַ is massively dominant. There are 48 cases in all, and 34 are plene and only fourteen are defective, the highest ratio of plene spellings that we have found so far in participles that are really widespread in usage. A major factor, of course, is the high number of cases that come from Proverbs and Qoheleth (Proverbs has six, of which two, the last two, Pr 28[2] 29[7], are short; Qoheleth has ten, of which only one, Qo 8[7], is short). The chief areas for the short spellings are: Genesis (all three cases) and Samuel (four defective out of six). Also the three cases with prefixed *w[e]–* are all וַיֵּדַע defective (Nu 24[16] Na 1[7] 2C 2[6]). The Psalms have four plene and two defective.

14. *Yose'* 'going out' occurs 64 times in all, and 22 of these are plene. The Torah begins with defectives at Gn 2[10] Ex 4[14] 7[15], but turns to plene at Ex 8[16,25] 11[4]. Numbers has many examples, mostly in the phrase כֹּל יֹצֵא צָבָא in ch. 1, but all are without waw. Samuel has four of each spelling, Jeremiah has two of each; Ezekiel has two, both plene, Nehemiah has three, all plene, and Chronicles has four, all plene. Once again, those with definite article in the Torah, five in number, are all defective.

15. *Yoser* 'forming, creating' does not belong to quite the same class of verbs. Its spelling patterns, however, are similar to those we have been discussing, for this participle has the surprisingly high total of 21 plene out of 28, i.e. 75%. Jeremiah's long run of a dozen is uniformly plene; Zechariah has two long, Zc 11[13] הַיּוֹצֵר twice with article, and a short, Zc 12[1] וְיֹצֵר with affixed *w[e]–*. In the Psalms Ps 2[9] is the only plene out of four.

16. *Yored* 'going down', by contrast, gives us a very ordinary picture. This participle is not very frequent, eleven cases in all, and all are short spellings except for Jud 9[36] Jb 7[9] (Mm 3470). Five of the cases, however, have an affix, three having the article and two having שֶׁ; this may have made a difference.

Our suspicion that verbs of the Pe Waw type or similar to it tend to have long spellings in the participle seems to have been confirmed. In some cases, like *yodea[c]*, it may be that semantic content has caused this word to be located in the gnomic works like Qoheleth which are also long-spelling books; but no such explanation attaches to *yose'* or *yoser*, or of course to *holek* and *yoseb* from which we began. *Yored* may have too few relevant examples to count for much. One cannot but suppose that this class of verbs is, for some reason, favoured for plene spellings in the participle.

The special place of verbs beginning with yod is much reinforced, however, when we turn to the plurals of the same participles. Although it may well be generally understood that the dominant spelling of *qotel* participles is defective, it can be surprising to the researcher when he discovers how very sparsely spread the plene spellings are. Thus, to offer a few illustrations, אמר has the participle *'om'rim* over fifty times, but not a single spelling with waw, in spite of fair representation in books otherwise long-spelling like Nehemiah, Chronicles, and Ezekiel; עמד 'stand' also has a long run, over forty cases plural, and not a single one with waw; עבר 'cross over' again has close on forty cases, and all are defective in the absolute: the construct plural occurs seven times, all in 'late' books, but the long spelling עוֹבְרֵי is found only once, at Jb 21²⁹. In fact a long list of verbs can be given which have a number of participles in the plural but simply have no cases at all written with waw: such are בטח, דרש, הרג, זכר, חשב, כרת, כתב, לקח, מצא, עזב, קרא, רדף, שכן, שלח.

It is, in fact, only quite sporadically that most verbs occur with a plene spelling of the plural participle: for instance, we have (by the Masora, against text of BHS) מוֹכְרִים Ne 13¹⁶ (no other case; construct defective 13²⁰, and suffixed defective Zc 11⁵); הַמּוֹשְׁלִים 2C 23²⁰, the only case plene out of eight (or ten if we count the homonymic word 'uttering proverbs'; incidentally, 2C 23²⁰ is the only one with article among these ten); סוֹפְרִים 2C 34¹³, the only one among four (and the construct also defective, Est 3¹² 8⁹); פּוֹשְׁעִים Is 46⁸ Ezk 20³⁸, two long out of ten. These seem to be typical examples. Less typical is בּוֹגְדִים, a participle which, as we saw, was dominantly plene in the singular also: in the plural it is written with waw at Is 24¹⁶ᵇ Hb 1¹³ Ps 25³ Pr 2²² 23²⁸, five plene out of a total of twelve; moreover, the last three on this list are all prefixed either by *u* – 'and' (Pr 2²² 23²⁸) or by the article (Ps 25³), which means in this case that all affixed forms are with waw. Note that Is 24¹⁶ᵃ has the same word also spelt defectively.

One case in which the long spelling of the plural is much more widespread is:

17. *Šo⁽ᵃ⁾rim* 'doorkeepers', a term beloved of Nehemiah and Chronicles: out of a total of 32 or so, ten are thus spelt plene, all of them in Ezra-Nehemiah-Chronicles but especially in Nehemiah, where there are seven of them, it seems, against three of the short spelling (7⁴⁵ 12⁴⁵,⁴⁷); cf. Mm 3889. This heavy preference for the long spelling is thus unique to Nehemiah in this

word: Chronicles, though it has many more examples, strongly prefers the short spelling and has only two of the long (2C 23[19] 34[13]). The strength of this long spelling must be ascribed, therefore, to the special tendencies of Nehemiah. But why does Nehemiah spell שׁוֹעֲרִים long, seven times out of ten in his book, when he spells אֹמְרִים thus short, all the four times he uses it (Ne 5[2,3,4] 6[19])? Is there not an element of lexicalization, that is, a purely arbitrary preference for *this* spelling for *this* word, quite independently of the fact that other words that are of the same pattern are spelt in another way?

To take another illustration, why is it that Ruth, which book has two favourite participles, writes גֹּאֵל thus short in all of its eight occurrences (Rt 3[9,12,12] 4[1,3,6,8,14]), both with and without article, but writes הַקּוֹצְרִים plene with article four times out of six (Rt 2[4,5,6,7]; the first and the last, 23,14, are without waw; 2[14] is with waw in BHS but against the Masora, Mm 3663)?

On the whole, as we have seen, the plene spelling of the participle in the plural is rather rare, at least in many verbs. But when we come back to the situation of verbs the first consonant of which is yod, we find a striking contrast:

18. The plural *yoš°bim* occurs 71 times and there are ten spellings as יוֹשְׁבִים plene: Jud 6[10] Is 10[13] Jr 36[12] 44[13] Ezk 3[15] 8[1] 1C 9[2] 2C 18[9a] 30[25] 31[6]. This is a much higher incidence than we have found in some other common verbs, as in עמד, עבר, אמר, studied above. Nor is it to be explained through heavy use in one particular book, like שׁוֹעֲרִים in Nehemiah: paradoxically, Nehemiah is always defective, יֹשְׁבִים, in this word (four cases), and the shorter spelling is preferred by Chronicles also (six short as against four long) and by Ezekiel (four to two; interestingly, at 3[15] he has הַיֹּשְׁבִים defective and יוֹשְׁבִים plene in the same verse; his two cases with article are both defective). All cases in the Torah and Kings are short.

With the construct plural the proportion of the plene spelling יוֹשְׁבֵי rises still higher. The form *yoš°be* occurs about 180 times, and the Masora counts 34 plene, plus two with prefix *min* (Mm 1518). The Leningrad text has some discrepancies from this but Figure 28 gives a good idea of the distribution, with latitude for one or two different here and there. It shows that the fairly high ratio of plene writings, about 20%, is not a result of concentration in one or two long-spelling books. On the contrary, all books seem to prefer the shorter spelling. Judges is the one that comes closet to an even balance between teh two. Its highly varying distribution in ch. 1 has already been displayed, p. 24 above. After the first chapter it

		Torah	Jos	Jud	S	K	Is	Jr	Ezk
A	יֹשְׁבֵי	10	19	12	2	–	13	33	10
B	יוֹשְׁבֵי	–	1	10	1	1	1	7	2

	12P	Ps	La	Dn	Ezr	Ne	Chr
A	11	9	1	1	1	3	18
B	5	2	–	–	–	–	8

Fig. 28: *yoš°be*, plural masculine of qal participle, construct, numbers by books

has a plene spelling at 2^2, and then all are defective until ch. 21, which has three plene ($21^{9,10,12}$). Though Chronicles has a good number plene, it prefers the defective much more.

Other verbs of the class also display unusual configurations of spelling. With יצא the plural absolute יוֹצְאִים appears thus, with waw, four times out of 25 (Ezk 14^{22} $47^{8,12}$ Zc 6^8), and the construct יוֹצְאֵי four times out of fourteen, but these four are all in Chronicles and in that book form four out of six. With *yod°°im* 'knowing' the long spelling יוֹדְעִים is very strong, four cases out of nine (Qo 4^{17} $9^{5,5}$ 2C 2^7), but this may be explained through concentration in late books. The construct plural, however, has יוֹדְעֵי plene at Am 5^{16} Ps 9^{11} 1C 12^{33} 2C 8^{18} (Mm 4068), four out of fourteen, which is quite a high proportion. With יצר we have only a couple of cases, not enough to go on. But ירד 'go down' provides a remarkable set of ratios. In the absolute, indeed, we have the long יוֹרְדִים only twice out of nine, at Jud 9^{37} 1S 9^{27}; but the construct is overwhelmingly יוֹרְדֵי plene: out of nineteen cases (plus a possible one in the K of Ps 30^4), the only exceptions are three, Ezk 32^{29} Ps 115^{17} 143^7. On the other hand, these are in a limited series of books (three in Isaiah, nine in Ezekiel, and six in Psalms), and most are in the stock phrase יוֹרְדֵי־בוֹר 'those that go down to the pit' or, in some, 'those that go down to the sea'; this may have something to do with the matter. Nevertheless the high percentage of יוֹרְדֵי plene remains a striking fact.

Early in this section we had reason to notice that the participle of הלך 'go' had more plene spellings than most others; and it is proper to return to it when discussing the plurals. The masculine plural, however, yields only one case of הוֹלְכִים out of 35 cases, and it is situated, surprisingly, at Gn 37^{25}. Plural constructs are few, and all defective. The feminine singular has a writing with waw at Ne 12^{38} הַהוֹלֶכֶת. The feminine plural has only four examples altogether, and the doubly defective הֹלְכֹת appears at Ex 2^5 and the doubly plene הוֹלְכוֹת only at Ne 6^{17}.

Something must now be added about the important class of Lamed He verbs. As with the triliteral verb, one is probably aware in a general way that the dominant spelling for this type is defective in respect of the *o* vowel; not until one examines the evidence does one realize that the defective spelling, in this class of verb, is commonly even more dominant than in others. Yet against this must be set a number of striking plene writings in certain verbs.

19. With עשה 'do, make', for instance, out of between eighty and ninety cases, the plene form עוֹשֶׂה occurs only once, in Pr 21^{24}; and, out of another number close to fifty, the construct עוֹשֵׂה appears only once, 2C 24^{12}. The plural absolute is always עשׂים defective, with many occurrences; the construct plural, out of about 25 cases, is עוֹשֵׂי plene only thrice, 2C 26^{13} 34^{10,17}. These various forms have considerable numbers in 'late' books like Esther, Nehemiah and Chronicles but all are defective except those named, and even in Chronicles these are a small minority.

We may add a simple listing of some of the more common and obvious verbs of this class:

20. *Boke* 'weeping' is וּבוֹכֶה plene at 2S 15^{30}, once out of seven cases, and in the plural we find 2S 15^{23} Ne 8^9 בּוֹכִים, two out of five; there is also the more unusual feminine form בּוֹכִיָּה La 1^{16}.

21. *Bone* 'building' is plene at Ne 6^6 2C 2^{3,4,8}, and with definite article at Am 9^6, a total of five out of twelve. This means that all cases in Nehemiah and Chronicles are plene. The plural is also בּוֹנִים plene in a large number of cases, Ps 118^{22} Ezr 4^1 and all six cases in Nehemiah. Chronicles, however, at 2C 34^{11} has the defective spelling of the plural.

22. *Gole* 'uncovering' has one of each, short at 1S 22^8, long at Pr 20^{19}.

23. *Hoze* 'seeing, seer' occurs about twenty times including both singular and plural, and all are spelt without waw except 2C 35^{15}, the last of ten cases in Chronicles. Heavy use of this word in Chronicles has not led to much long spelling of it.

24. *Hone* 'encamping' has fourteen plural cases, including a notable series of seven in Numbers. Among these we find the unusual spelling Nu 2^{12} וְהַחוֹנִם, plene in respect of the *o* vowel but short in the plural termination. At Na 3^{17} we have the full plene form הַחוֹנִים.

25. *Note* 'inclining' has eleven cases without suffix, and four of these are נוֹטֶה with waw: Is 40^{22} 51^{13} Ezk 25^{16} Ps 104^2. To these we add the suffixed form Is 42^5 וְנוֹטֵיהֶם. Three of the five cases in Isaiah are thus plene. Job with two, and Jeremiah,

Zechariah and Chronicles with one each, have only defective spellings.

26. *'Ole* 'going up' has a total of 21 cases singular masculine, and five of these are עוֹלֶה plene: Jos 11[17] 1S 17[23] (one out of six in Samuel) Is 24[18] Ezk 40[40] Jb 36[33]. The plural has eighteen cases, of which עוֹלִים occurs only at Ne 7[5,61] (defective between them, 7[6]). There is one case of the feminine with waw, עוֹלָה 1C 26[16]. The feminine plural *'olot* of this occurs seven times in Gn 41, four of them as עֹלֹת and three as עֹלוֹת, but none with waw of the first syllable. I keep the spellings of עוֹלָה 'burnt offering' separate: whether we think that it belongs to this root or not, its spelling distribution is greatly different from that of the participle, especially in its much greater use of waw. The Masora however sometimes lumps these together as one form for enumeration: Mm 297 is a good example.

27. *'One* 'answering' is עוֹנֶה plene in Is 50[2] 66[4] out of nine cases without suffix.

28. *Pone* 'turning' has strong plene representation in the singular, all with article: Ezk 8[3] 11[1] 47[2] 2C 25[23]. These are four out of a total of eleven singular, and three out of seven in Ezekiel, who is the main user of this word. The plural has nine cases, all defective, and one feminine plural, also defective; 2C 4[4] follows 1K 7[25] in the short spelling, twice repeated.

29. *Ro'e* 'seeing' is a common word. The masculine singular participle is found about forty times, but all cases are defective except 2S 15[27] הֲרוֹאֶה with the interrogative particle. Instances in long-spelling books like Ezekiel, Qoheleth (2) and Esther are all without waw. The plurals, though again distributed through a variety of books, are all without waw of the first syllable.

30. *Sote* 'drinking' is almost entirely defective: six in the singular plus one feminine, all defective, and in the plural eight, of which only 1C 12[40] has the plene spelling with waw, וְשׁוֹתִים, plus one construct out of four, Ps 69[13] שׁוֹתֵי.

It would be tedious to pile up further examples. A few final cases of interest may be added. חוֹטֵא 'sinful, sinning' is one participle that is dominantly plene: out of thirteen cases ten are with waw — all five in Proverbs, three in Qoheleth and Is 65[20] Hb 2[10], against one in Isaiah and two in Qoheleth defective. By contrast, *noten* 'giving' is a very common form, with over 100 cases of the masculine singular and over forty in Deuteronomy alone. Of these only six are with waw: Is 37[7] Ps 37[21] 145[15] 147[9] Pr 26[8] 28[27] (one of three in Isaiah, three out of seven in Psalms, two out of three in Proverbs).

With the article, however, it occurs ten times and four of these are plene, both the two cases in Isaiah and two out of the three in Psalms (taking 144¹⁰ as long).

One thing that I have noticed is that the participles of verbs of the Double ʿAyin class appear to be more often spelt with waw than the average of verbs of other classes. In the Psalms, for instance, *ṣorer* plural with suffixes is spelt six times with waw out of ten, צוֹרְרַי and the like. The same is true of *šorer*, also meaning 'enemies' or the like: five cases in all, and three of them שׁוֹרְרָי plene, Ps 5⁹ 27¹¹ 56³. Again, שׁוֹדֵד 'destroying' seems to be plene in all five cases in Isaiah and in Jb 15²¹ but only in one out of ten or so in Jeremiah plus one in the plural (Jr 51⁴⁸), and the plural construct שׁוֹדְדֵי Ob 5.

The prevalence of the waw in this type of formation may give some kind of hint of the reasons behind the choice of spelling. Another case that should be mentioned is *sobeb* 'going around': the participle סוֹבֵב appears at Gn 2¹³ 2K 6¹⁵ (8²¹Q?) Qo 1⁶,⁶ 2C 21⁹ as against the defective סֹבֵב Gn 2¹¹ Qo 1⁶. In general, if it is true that the Double ʿAyin class tend to have more plene spelling than others, that tends also to support the idea that some difference of pronunciation lies behind the preference for one spelling over another.

We have said enough to indicate the high complexity of the spellings in the qal participle, and the interpretation of these complexities remain difficult and obscure. Why is there so much difference between one lexeme and another, when their vowel patterns are the same? And why did the defective spelling remain far the dominant one? And why, when the defective spelling was so dominant, did the plene spelling find entry into some lexemes so very much more than others?

One consideration that should be discussed before we go farther is the following: it would be possible that some words of the same vowel pattern as participles might be classified effectively as nouns, and that this classification might lead towards a certain spelling preference. It is doubtful, however, whether this idea leads anywhere. As we have already seen, סֹפֵר 'scribe', certainly more like a noun in practice than a participle, is dominantly short over a long series, and becomes consistently plene only at the end of Nehemiah and in Chronicles. שׁוֹעֲרִים 'doorkeepers', on the other hand, has a remarkably consistent plene spelling in Nehemiah; but then Chronicles prefers the defective. זוֹנָה 'harlot', another 'professional' sort of term, is strongly plene, against the usual tendency of many Lamed He verbs, and this applies even to the Torah, Gn 34³¹ 38¹⁵ Dt 23¹⁹, though defective in Leviticus. A particularly striking case is אוֹיֵב 'enemy', doubtless to be counted as a noun. Taken over all books, this word has a large dominance of the writing with waw except where suffixes are present; in the singular absolute, out of about 55 cases, it is without waw only at three: 1S 18²⁹ Jr 6²⁵ 15¹¹. In the Torah, where participles are very dominantly spelt short, all seven cases of 'oyeb are with waw. On the other hand, as we have seen (above, p. 34ff.), kohen, which is of participial pattern but is certainly a noun, is always defective in spelling in all sources and periods. A sort of intermediate position is occupied by רֹעֶה, which is sometimes more like a noun, 'shepherd', and sometimes more verbal, 'pasturing, caring for (a flock)'. It has plenty of occurrences and in a good variety of books. In the singular it has the plene רוֹעֶה Ezk 37²⁴, which seems to be like the noun, 'one shepherd', and Ct 6³ רֹעֶה (but plene in some texts), more verb-like, 'he who feeds among the lilies'; in the plural there is Ezk 34²ᵃ, רוֹעֵי plural construct, in the sense 'the shepherds of (Israel)'. These three seem to be the only cases with waw out of something like 100 in all. Ct 2¹⁶, incidentally, has the same phrase as 6³, but with רֹעֶה clearly defective.

To sum up this point, I do not find any clear correlation between verb-like participles as against participles that are really nouns, and the difference between plene and defective spelling. There may be some factor in this that has had an effect, but it is far from obvious what it is.

There are various ideas that attempt to relate the spelling patterns of the participle to processes in the history of the language. One such idea is that the Canaanite sound shift from ā to ō had not yet taken uniform effect in Hebrew.[1] This could suggest that some participles were still in effect of the form qātel or qātil and that the ā was not marked by a vowel letter because ā in this position never came to be normally so marked. As against the older idea that a sound shift like this took place simultaneously over all words alike, the newer linguistic opinion suggests that such shifts took effect gradually: in the end they affected all like vowels in the same way, but the speed of change differed over different items. Many Hebrew participles were written without waw because their first vowel had not yet become o. Yet it is difficult to suppose that the shift in question was still incomplete as late as this hypothesis would demand. Nor would it easily explain why so many participles, and in late books, are defective.

---

[1] This is hinted at by Andersen and Forbes, p. 194.

Another idea, somewhat similar, is this: that in earlier times a larger proportion of Hebrew verbs were of the 'stative' type. A stative verb does not have, in Masoretic Hebrew, an *o* vowel in the participle, but an *a* vowel, written as qamets. Thus, by accepted grammar, שָׁמֵעַ would be a qal participle type (it occurs Jr 36[13] Ps 22[25] 34[7,18], but is often ambiguous, since the same form is also the third masculine singular perfect). It would be conceivable that 'hearing' in earlier times was often שָׁמֵעַ; this would then be the reason why the participle of this verb is so seldom written with waw. Later, people came to treat the form as analogous to the dominant 'active' type, and thus pronounced it as *šomea*ʿ; but the dearth of waws was a sign that the older pronunciation had been different.

A case where this could have happened is the verb אָהֵב 'love'. Of its participles only a few examples are actually vocalized in the Masoretic text as *'aheb*, perhaps half a dozen in all. A far larger number, about 64 or so, including those with suffixes and terminations, are vocalized as *'oheb* and have the *o* vowel. Yet out of these numerous cases only one is written with waw, Pr 27[6], and there marked as unique by the Masora. It is a reasonable hypothesis that many of these participles were earlier *'aheb* and that that is the reason why they were written without waw. Similar arguments might apply to a verb like שכן 'dwell' and still more to נפל, where the participle may mean 'fallen' or 'falling'; of this latter there are eighteen cases of the participle in the masculine singular and the only spelling with waw is Jb 14[18]. Some other plausible cases could be suggested.

But, though this is a reasonable and indeed a likely explanation for some of the many participles that are dominantly spelt defectively, it is most unlikely to be the general explanation, or indeed to cover more than a small proportion of the material. It does, however, suggestively indicate the sort of linguistic change that may have acted in the transmission of the text in certain of its elements.

However, a verb which might seem to point in a different direction is שׂנא 'hate'. From many points of view this seems to be exactly the traditional 'stative'. Where the form is *sane'* we cannot be quite certain as between participle and perfect, but the cases are few, only five or so in number. Where we can be sure that the form is a participle, we also find that it is vocalized as *sone'*, and in the masculine without suffix there are about eighteen cases. All in the Torah are without waw; the main group are in Psalms, Proverbs and Job, and these have many with waw: Ps 106[10] 120[6] Jb 34[17] Pr 13[24] 15[10,27] 26[24] 27[6] 29[24], all שׂוֹנֵא. This is quite a large number written with waw, compared with what we have seen in some other verbs. The example shows that there were indeed verbs of 'stative' type, with probable original participle pattern *śane'*, which came to be grouped with the 'active' qotel participles and given the vowel *o*, and, this being so, were spelt with waw in books like Proverbs, which book however has also some cases without waw: שֹׂנֵא Pr 11^{15} 12^{1} 28^{16} Q. It is worth noticing that in four of these examples in Proverbs שׂוֹנֵא comes immediately after, or in parallel with, another participle that is also written with waw: 13^{24} חוֹשֵׂךְ 15^{27} בּוֹצֵעַ 27^{6} אוֹהֵב 29^{24} חוֹלֵק. This might be taken to mean that the vocalization and spelling of שׂוֹנֵא was influenced by juxtaposition and analogy. And, on the other hand, the suffixed forms and plurals of this participle, not few in number, seem never to have the writing with waw. The case of שׂנֵא may, then, be a difficulty for our argument; or, equally, it may be an illustration of how a participle that began as qatel came to move into the qotel type and, perhaps just because it had so moved, came to be marked with waw to a high degree.

Another aspect is this: in the participle the *o* vowel was the penultimate and was, at least according to the stress patterns of the final text, unstressed. It might be possible to maintain that plene spelling was most likely to be applied to the stressed syllables of words. If the stress was on the last syllable as it came to be later on, then this might explain why participles were so often written defectively. This might be the simplest explanation. Yet it is not without its difficulties. There are certain types of words that have *o* in the penultimate syllable and yet are commonly written with waw: we have seen the example of עוֹלָם 'eternity' (above, p. 27). שׁוֹפָר 'trumpet', of the same vowel pattern, has indeed some spellings as שׁפר without waw (two in Exodus, some in Samuel, one in Job, etc.) but is very dominantly plene on the whole in the singular and in a wide variety of books. Again, גּוֹרָל 'lot' is almost entirely plene over a wide variety of forms, with only very sporadic representation of the defective writing, as in Nu 36^{3} Dn 12^{13}. For the explanation through the penultimate place of the *o* vowel of the participle to work, it might be necessary to suppose a difference of stress between the participle and nouns such as those just quoted. But, in general, the suggestion that stress in the participle was the cause of the distribution of spellings is a suggestive and creative one, that should be followed up.

The peculiarity of distribution in verbs which have yod as their first letter might have to be explained as having some phonetic grounds: the yod of such words had derived from an older *w* and this might be thought to have given a colour to the following vowel that caused it to be more often so marked. This is no more than a speculation, but is the only suggestion I have to offer other than pure scribal convention.

These various explanations are attempts to explain the distribution of spellings in the participle on the basis of differences that existed within the spoken language at some earlier time. The alternative is to explain them as a matter of scribal habit or scribal convention. This latter approach might take a more systematic or a more arbitrary form.

A more systematic approach might be to say that scribal habit favoured the nouns more than the verbs for plene spelling. That plene spelling appeared more extensively in nouns than in verbs was always one of the traditional and partly true axioms of the matter; if we follow this principle, all we are doing is to turn this observation around and make it into a causative account: the scribes, shall we say, noticed the nouns, emphasized the nouns, and tended more often to spell with vowel letters those of their elements which might be so spelt. This would help with some of the cases we have discussed. It would explain why the waw is generally there in עוֹלָם, שׁוֹפָר and גּוֹרָל but absent from most cases of אָמַר 'saying' or נֹשֵׂא 'carrying'. It would explain why אוֹיֵב 'enemy' is dominantly plene and the same for זוֹנָה 'harlot' by contrast with, say, עֹשֶׂה 'doing'. Unfortunately, it does not work at all well with סֹפֵר 'scribe', dominantly defective, and particularly not with כֹּהֵן 'priest'. It would help with עוֹלָה 'burnt offering' as compared with עֹלֶה 'going up', and it might make a difference with some other cases, for מוֹשֵׁל might often be taken as a noun 'ruler', and יוֹשֵׁב often as 'inhabitant' and thus a sort of noun, but it would hardly help us with the numerous plene spellings in יוֹצֵא 'going out' or יוֹרֵד 'going down'. Moreover, the whole general idea that verbs were ranked lower than nouns as candidates for plene spelling is highly dubious: for there are all sorts of verb forms to which it clearly does not apply, e.g. forms like הֵבִיא, הוֹצִיא, תִּירָא, or הִקְרִיב.

The more arbitrary sort of explanation would follow the idea of 'lexicalization', in the sense that it simply came to be accepted that, at least within the circles from whom the Masoretic text emanated, such and such a word should be spelt with waw, while another word was spelt without it. The fact that these words had the same vowel pattern did not matter. A particular spelling was the 'proper' spelling for that word. It was proper to spell כֹּהֵן defectively, just as it was proper to spell אוֹיֵב plene. Spelling differences were not conditioned solely by facts of pronunciation, whether present or past;

that a spelling might be felt as proper does not mean that no exceptions to it will ever occur. It is very likely that it was felt proper that
אֱלֹהִים should be without waw, even if one or two cases with waw
eventually crept in. Some aspects already noticed have made it
probable that lexicalized spelling preferences did exist. They
existed in some of the great unvarying cases like כהן, and they are
extremely probable in many personal names. That they existed in
some of the participles we have mentioned, such as Nehemiah's
שׁוֹעֲרִים, seems extremely likely, and similarly in Ruth's קוֹצְרִים.

In conclusion, some attention should be drawn to the rare but
striking occurrence of exceptional long spellings in unexpected
places. For most qal participles, as will be clear from the above, the
Torah steadily supports the short spelling. Leviticus thus surprises
us with וְהַנּוֹשֵׂא plene Lv 15[10], the only example in the entire Bible.
Genesis in particular has a number of such instances: as we saw, it
has אוֹכֵל 'eating' at Gn 39[6], the first case in the Bible. It gives us רוֹמֵשׂ
'creeping' at Gn 1[30] 8[19], but with the shorter רֹמֵשׂ in between at 7[8],
and (as so often) all cases with article in the Torah are defective. It
gives us הַסֹּבֵב at 2[11] but הַסּוֹבֵב at 2[13]. As so often, Genesis gives a
certain impression of trying out a variety of spellings, a kind of
experimentation that in Exodus will be more restricted. Or, to express it in another way, someone at some stage began from the
beginning of Genesis to introduce some additional waws, but did
not persist very long in doing so, nor did he do it very systematically. Did Deuteronomy do the same with רוֹצֵחַ 'murderer'? It is not
surprising to find this plene spelling at Jos 20[3,6] Jb 24[14] but it is
more surprising at Dt 4[42], the first in that book, especially after
Numbers has used it in the defective spelling a good number of
times.

To sum up, then, the spelling distribution of the qal participle is
one of the most complicated and difficult areas of our study, and
hence the number of pages we have had to devote to it. Taken in
itself it does not seem to lead to any one totally satisfying solution,
and we have to take it together with other phenomena in the
approach to a final interpretation.

5. The *i* vowel of hiphil in the triliteral verb

By traditional grammar, as we all know, many hiphil forms in
triliteral verbs have a long *i* vowel, as in the second syllable of הִקְדִּישׁ
'he consecrated', and this vowel is written in great preponderance
with yod. Indeed, so great may this preponderance seem to many

that they are scarcely aware that this vowel in hiphils may be written without yod, and many grammars fail to acquaint their readers with the fact that this may be so. Few people would naturally think of writing a hiphil form without its yod.

In fact, however, hiphils written without yod are far from uncommon. They can be divided into two groups: the first group is where there is some kind of additional termination, a plural ending most commonly, or some other suffix. Examples are: Zp 2[10] וַיַּגְדִּלוּ, Lv 9[9] וַיַּקְרִבוּ. This first group might perhaps be accounted for through affix effect; i.e. because the affix is there the yod of the hiphil syllable is not written. This might be argued, but in fact we probably have to take these defective spellings more seriously than that, and consider them as probable real features of the hiphil, because of what we find in the second group. The second group is formed by triliteral hiphils where there is no suffix or plural termination, etc., and nevertheless the *i* of the final syllable of the hiphil is written without yod. Examples are: Nu 7[19] הַקְרִב, Lv 2[4] תַּקְרִב, 1S 12[24] הַגְדִּל, Ps 18[51] מַגְדִּל.

According to Andersen and Forbes, the total numbers of hiphil forms in respect of this vowel are: defective, 719; plene, 4,935; total, 5,654.[1]

Our approach here will not be to try to give an exhaustive account of the matter, but to give a representative set of examples to show the general character and scope of the problem. As a first instance, consider the waw consecutive form *way-yamliku* 'and they made king', in which we have a fairly good run of occurrences:

A   וַיַּמְלִכוּ   1S 11[15]   16[16] 2K 8[20] 11[12] 14[21]
B   וַיַּמְלִיכוּ Jud 9[6]   1K 12[20]   17[21]
B   (cont'd)   2K 21[24] 23[30] 1C 29[22] 2C 21[8] 22[1] 23[11] 26[1] 33[25]

Fig. 29: *way-yamliku* 'and they made king', waw consecutive, all cases in the Bible

Cf. Mm 1584. Kings is equally divided: its first is plene, then there are four without the yod, then three at the end with it. All six cases in Chronicles have the yod. Some of the Chronicles passages are parallel with passages in Kings: so 2C 21[8]//2K 8[20], 2C 23[11]//2K 11[12], 2C 26[1]//2K 14[21], and 2C 33[25]//2K 21[24]. In the first three of these Chronicles has the longer spelling, as against the shorter in Kings; in the last they are identical in this respect.

---

[1] Andersen and Forbes, p. 166. These figures look high to me; it depends on exactly what is included, which is not made clear. It may include types like הָקֵם, הֲקִמוֹתִי etc., which I am not taking into account here.

In this verb, which is a fairly common one and has about 37 *i*-containing hiphil forms, the great majority have the yod written. Apart from the five defective as shown above, we have only 2S 2⁹ וַיַּמְלִכֵהוּ with object suffix, and perhaps 2K 10⁵ נַמְלִךְ (plene, נַמְלִיךְ, in Leningradensis but against its own Masora; defective in Snaith, Letteris).

Another verb that belongs to much the same milieu is *hirkib* 'make to ride, mount'. The same imperfect with waw consecutive is without the yod, וַיַּרְכִּבוּ, at all cases outside Chronicles: 2S 6³ 1K 1³⁸,⁴⁴ 2K 9²⁸ 10¹⁶. The one case in Chronicles, 1C 13⁷, is parallel to 2S 6³ but has the yod written. With object suffixes we have Ex 4²⁰ וַיַּרְכִּבֵם, Dt 32¹³ יַרְכִּבֵהוּ, 2K 23³⁰ וַיַּרְכִּבֻהוּ, as against Esth 6¹¹ וַיַּרְכִּיבֵהוּ, 2C 35²⁴ וַיַּרְכִּיבֻהוּ.

A good case from the Torah is *hiqdiš* 'consecrate'. Lv 27 has six cases of the imperfect *yaqdiš*, and the first of these, Lv 27¹⁴, is יַקְדִּשׁ without yod; all the others have it, יַקְדִּישׁ. Various other forms are without the yod before terminations; for example, the participle מַקְדִּשִׁים is so written in all three places where it occurs (Lv 22² Ne 12⁴⁷,⁴⁷).

But the Torah is not by any means the main centre for short spellings in this type of word: perhaps books like Samuel and Kings have them more often. הִקְטִיר 'burn (a sacrifice)' is a frequent hiphil verb with many occurrences in the Torah, over thirty with the *i* vowel; but none of these are defective. The only forms written without the yod are the participle וּמַקְטְרִים 2C 13¹¹ (plene at 1C 6³⁴ 2C 29¹¹) and יַקְטִרוּן 1S 2¹⁵ (the same plene in the next verse, 2¹⁶).

An even commoner hiphil in the Torah is הִקְרִיב 'offer'; the total number of relevant cases in the Torah seems to be high, well over 100. Out of these we get a handful of short spellings: Nu 7¹⁹ הִקְרִב and Lv 2⁴ תַּקְרִב were already cited above, p. 82. The imperfect 3rd singular masculine *yaqrib* occurs nine times in the Torah, but its only short spelling יַקְרִב is at Ezk 46⁴. The plural וַיַּקְרִבוּ with waw consecutive is twice thus defective, Lv 9⁹ Jos 8²³, out of a total of nine, seven of which are in the Torah. There are also Dt 1¹⁷ תַּקְרִבוּן, Nu 3⁴ בְּהַקְרִבָם. But the spelling of the Torah seems distinctly to favour the writing of these forms with yod in this word.

A few more examples: the infinitive בְּהִכְרַת and the imperfect תַּכְרִת, both 1S 20¹⁵, and the waw consecutive form וְאַכְרִתָה 2S 7⁹. From הִשְׁלִיךְ 'throw', וָאַשְׁלִךְ Dt 9²¹. From Exodus, the participle הַמַּבְעִר 'he who causes to burn', Ex 22⁵; another participle, מַבְרִחַ Ex 26²⁸. From Genesis: וְהֶאֱמִן Gn 15⁶, an important place. From the Psalms, the unusual infinitive form לִשְׁמֹעַ Ps 26⁷.

Some verbs seem to lack examples of defective spelling. A verb like *hizkir* 'remind', with about 37 or 38 relevant cases spread over a wide range of books, has no cases without yod at all. On the other hand, the hiphil of נפל 'fall', though it is dominantly plene in this respect, when it does have defective spellings, they tend to be in places where we might expect a long spelling: it is not so surprising to find the unusual writing וְלָנֻפֵּל at Nu 5²², but it is more striking to find תִּפְּלוּ at Ezk 47²² and especially so to find the rare short spelling וְהִפֵּל at Est 9²⁴ (the Leningrad Codex has the yod here, but against its own Masora); other short forms of this verb at Jos 13⁶ Jon 1⁷ Ps 140¹¹.

The writing of the *i* of hiphil again raises the question: is this merely a scribal variation, one of two optional ways of writing the same vowel, or does it go back to something that was different in the older grammar of the language? Considering how stable is the yod of the *i* vowel in some other word-types, such as the pattern of בְּרִית 'covenant', is it not surprising that quite a large number of hiphils should omit it, especially when it is clearly the dominant practice to write this yod?

Here again an explanation in terms of an older grammar may suggest itself. Was there always a long *i* vowel in the hiphil? Possibly not. Some indications suggest that at an earlier stage there was a short vowel, and that it was an *a* vowel rather than an *i* vowel. Other Semitic languages have an *a* vowel in the corresponding place: so Arabic, Aramaic and Ethiopic. And even in Hebrew itself, though by traditional grammar we say הִקְדִּישׁ, with person terminations we say forms like הִקְדַּשְׁתָּ 'you consecrated', with short *a* vowel.

Historical linguists, seeking to account for the long *i* vowel of traditional Hebrew, have said that it spread by analogy from the hiphil of verbs like קוּם: הֵקִים, יָקִים.[1] Perhaps so; though it does not sound highly convincing, there may be no better explanation. But, if the vowel spread by analogy in this way, it would be possible that some of the biblical spellings go back to a time when it had not yet spread so very far. But, if this should be true, then it might follow that the spellings without yod, a smallish minority in our present text, are a residue from what was once a majority, and that the great

---

[1] So Brockelmann, *Grundriss* i. 292; Bauer and Leander, § 46a–b, pp. 329f and note; cf. Andersen and Forbes, p. 166. Bauer and Leander say that this development into an *i* vowel had already taken place in the Amarna period, with *hi–ih–bi–e* 'he has hidden' (Hebrew הֶחְבִּיא). If this is so, then our explanation, suggesting that the shift was still in progress in latish post-biblical times, becomes less likely.

majority of hiphil forms came to have the yod added as the pronunciation with long *i* became normal. But the survival of so many without yod suggest that it was not a systematic and careful revision, but an informal and haphazard copying tendency, for a systematic revision would surely have left fewer forms unrevised. In thinking of such a revision, of course, the cases of Chronicles, several of which have been cited in this section, are highly suggestive.

6. The *o* vowel of hiphil and niphal in the Pe Waw verb and related nouns

As is well known, verbs of the Pe Waw class, like ילד 'bear (a child)', generate an *o* vowel in the first syllable of the hiphil, and also of the niphal in the perfect, as also in the participle. Nouns from the same roots commonly have the same *o* vowel. Speaking very generally, this *o* vowel is dominantly spelt plene, with waw.[1] There are nevertheless numerous exceptions in which the waw is not written. Here again the common generalization that the Torah is the locus for short spellings has to be qualified: in this type of word the Torah has a high proportion of spellings with waw, and only certain rather limited exceptions. We shall begin with some prominent examples.[2]

1. ידע 'know' has a good number of *o*-containing hiphils and niphals, nearly 100, but almost all have the waw marking the vowel. Exceptions are: Nu 16[5] וַיֵּדַע; Jud 8[16] וַיֹּדַע; 1C 17[19] לְהֹדִיעַ; הֹדַעְנִי Jb 13[23]; יְדִיעוּ Jb 32[7]. In the Torah the majority spelling is long: Exodus has at least four hiphils, Ex 18[16,20] 33[12,13] and three niphals, Ex 2[14] 6[3] 21[36], and all these are with waw. (The imperfect and imperative of the niphal are of course not relevant and are not counted, since the waw in these groups is consonantal.) Nu 16[5] seems to be the only case in the Torah without the waw. Jud 8[16] may, semantically, not be the same verb 'know', but this makes no difference to our question. The group of short spellings of this word, not a large group in any case, comes from books that in other respects often count as long spellers.

2. יכח 'argue' is normally written with waw. The total number of

---

[1] Andersen and Forbes, p. 191, give the figures as: defective, 260; plene, 1,443; total, 1,703. But again it is not quite clear exactly what cases they include.

[2] I have covered much of this ground in my article in *JSS* 30, 1985, especially pp. 2–22, and some of the detail there included will be covered only generally here.

occurrences of the verb is 60, but we subtract from this the hithpaels and imperfects of the niphal and that leaves the relevant, o-containing, cases at 57. Writings without waw include: Gn 20[16] וְנֹכָחַת; 24[14] הֹכַחְתָּ; 24[44] הֹכִיחַ; Jb 22[4] יְכִיחֶךָ, four in all. Here, contrary to what was said above, the Torah has a substantial number of writings without waw, for Genesis is equally divided, having three also with waw, Gn 21[25] 31[37,42], and Lv 19[17,17] are also plene. Job has sixteen cases of the verb, and one of these is without waw. Proverbs, also a large user of this 'Wisdom' term, has ten cases, all with waw. The derived noun *tokaḥat* occurs 24 times and all are written with the waw of the first syllable except for the plural Ezk 5[15] וּבִתֹכְחוֹת.

3. ילד 'bear (a child)' has already been mentioned. The hiphil 'beget' is a common word, and its waw consecutive form וַיּוֹלֶד 'and he begat' is spelt thus, with waw, in every one of its numerous occurrences (46 times, mostly in Genesis and Chronicles). Genesis has a succession of cases of the infinitive with suffix, הוֹלִידוֹ, seventeen in all, and every one thus plene, with three vowel letters. The third person perfect *holid*, however, has a more surprising spelling distribution. Of the four cases in the Torah the last, Nu 26[58], is written הוֹלִד, a unique spelling, but we pass it by since it is not directly relevant to our question, which is the spelling of the o vowel. There are a number of cases in Ruth and Nehemiah, all הוֹלִיד plene, and this is also the dominant spelling in Chronicles, which is much the largest user of this form. Chronicles begins with a series of the plene spelling, eleven cases down to 1C 2[22], and then there follows an intermittent series of eleven or so of הֹלִיד, starting from 1C 2[36] and continuing, sometimes in small blocks and sometimes intermixed with the plene spelling, down to 5[30], after which again only הוֹלִיד is used. Although the plene is the dominant one in the book as a whole, there is a portion of text within Chronicles, 1C 2[36]-4[2], in which it is equalled or exceeded by the defective spelling of this word.

As for the noun from this root, we have already noted (above, p. 2) that the construct *tolᵉdot* 'the generations of' was written in four different ways within Genesis, and four out of eleven occurrences in that book spelt it without the waw of the root. The same word with suffix, especially in the form *tolᵉdotam*, is written with waw in the first syllable throughout the many cases of Genesis and Numbers. The spelling without waw, לְתֹלְדֹתָם, appears in Ex 6[16,19] (contrast 28[10] with waw), and Chronicles has nine cases that consistently write without waw.

4. הוֹצִיא hiphil 'bring out' has a clear dominance of plene spelling in the Torah. The third person masculine singular of the perfect has twenty-five instances, fourteen of them in the Torah, and all are הוֹצִיא except for the solitary exception וְהֹצִיא (by the Masora, against text of BHS) Dt 22[14]. The Torah uses only forms like מוֹצִיא, הוֹצֵאתִי, לְהוֹצִיא, even with suffixes. In Judges and Jeremiah, however, we find the short וְהֹצֵאתִי (Jud 6[18] Jr 51[44]), and Job has הֹצֵאתָ Jb 10[18] וְהֹצֵאתָנִי 15[13].

The most common other form is the waw consecutive, third person masculine singular, *way-yoṣe'*, which occurs 25 times, seven of these in the Torah. In the Torah the last two of the seven are וַיֵּצֵא without waw (Nu 17[23,24]), while in the non-Torah books one out of two in Judges, all three in Samuel, three out of four in Kings, three out of five in Jeremiah, the one case in Job, and one out of two in Chronicles are spelt short. Over the Bible as a whole, the proportions for this form are: defective fourteen, plene eleven. Since the Torah prefers plene by five to two, the rest of the Bible strongly prefers the defective spelling.

It would be tedious to catalogue all the forms of the imperfect and other parts of this verb, especially the plurals and those with suffixes. We shall cite only a few of those written without the waw of the first radical: Gn 19[16] וַיֹּצִאֻהוּ, Nu 20[16] (Dt 6[21]?) וַיֹּצִאֵנוּ, Dt 5[15] וַיֹּצִאֲךָ (contrast Dt 4[37] וַיּוֹצִאֲךָ with waw); Jr 32[21] וַתֹּצֵא; Jb 28[11] יֹצִא. Thus writings without waw, though a minority taken over the verb as a whole, are by no means exceptional, especially in the imperfects with affix. Even in the Torah we quickly note half a dozen: Gn 19[16] Nu 17[23,24] 20[16] Dt 5[15] 6[21]. If we count all forms, Judges has three spellings without waw out of eight, Samuel has three or four out of nine or ten (the doubt is because 2S 18[22] might be from this verb or might conceivably be from מצא 'find'), Kings has six out of twenty, Jeremiah has five out of eighteen, Job has five out of six. A substantial number of spellings without waw exists.

The noun מוֹצָא 'exit' appears as מֹצָא at Jb 38[27] Dn 9[25], twice out of fourteen unsuffixed cases, and with suffix two or three cases (Ps 107[33,35] and Ho 6[3] if we follow the Masora against the text of Leningradensis). Another noun form, *toṣa'ot*, occurs mainly in the construct and with suffixes, and most cases are in lists in Numbers and in Joshua; in Numbers it is solidly plene in respect of the first *o*, but in Joshua all fourteen examples are without this waw, תֹּצְאֹתָיו etc.

5. ירד hiphil 'bring down' seems to have the waw in all forms of the perfect. In the waw consecutive imperfect we have forms without waw in Gn 24[18] וַתֹּרֶד (contrast Gn 24[46] וַתּוֹרֶד plene)

and Pr 21^{22}, the only case in Proverbs. Plurals written without waw include 1K 5^{23} יְרְדוּ, similarly Jos 8^{29} 2K 11^{19}. There are also the participle 2S 22^{48} וּמֹרִיד by the spelling of the Masora and the Aleppo Codex, and suffixed forms like 1S 30^{16} 1K 17^{23} וַיֹּרִדֵהוּ. Of all forms containing the o vowel, Samuel has three defective out of eight, Kings has four defective out of nine, and Joshua has two of each.

6. ירש 'drive out, dispossess' has about thirty cases in the perfect, הוֹרִישׁ and the like, and all are with waw except for 2C 28^{3} הֹרִישׁ, one of two cases in that book. Infinitive and participle are with waw. In the waw consecutive imperfect *way-yoreš* the two Torah cases are וַיּוֹרֶשׁ plene but Joshua and Judges both have one וַיֹּרֶשׁ defective and one plene; the defectives are Jos 15^{14} Jud 1^{19}, the latter followed by the plene in the very next verse. With suffix Jos 13^{12} has וַיֹּרִשֵׁם.

7. ישב hiphil 'settle (someone)' seems particularly rich in short spellings and particularly in an unusual place, namely Ezra and Nehemiah: Ezr 10^{14} הֹשִׁיב; Ezr 10^{18} Ne 13^{23} הֹשִׁיבוּ, similarly Ezra 10^{17}; Ne 13^{27} לְהֹשִׁיב; Ezr 10^{2} וַנֹּשֶׁב in waw consecutive; 10^{10} וַתֹּשִׁיבוּ. These examples in Ezra and Nehemiah are a slightly anomalous usage, with the sense 'marry (give a dwelling to)' (BDB, p. 443b) but this, even in conjunction with the unusual spellings, is no adequate reason for supposing that these come from some different root than ישב: the derivation as 'make to dwell' is perfectly reasonable, and there is the analogy of the Ethiopic 'awsaba 'marry' (Dillmann, p. 904), clearly cognate with ישב. In any case spellings without waw occur in other books and in places where the unusual sense 'marry' is not present: Jr 32^{37} וַהֲשִׁבֹתִים (on this case see again p. 189); 1K 21^{12} וְהֹשִׁיבוּ (but plene 21^{9,10}); וַיֹּשֶׁב 2K 17^{6,24}; וַיֹּשִׁיבֵם Jb 36^{7}; וַיֹּשִׁבוּם 1S 12^{8} and וַיֹּשִׁיבֵם 1S 30^{21}. There are only a few Torah examples and they seem to be all plene.

The corresponding noun מוֹשָׁב is usually with waw except for Gn 36^{43} לְמֹשְׁבֹתָם and 1C 7^{28}. There are numerous occurrences in the Torah, mostly plene apart from Gn 36^{43}, cf. Ex 35^{3} Lv 23^{14,31}. *Tošab* also is always plene except in the plural construct מֹתְשָׁבֵי 1K 17^{1}. In the verb, again, the niphal is also relevant, and here we have Ezk 36^{10} וְנֹשְׁבוּ.

An interesting feature of the group in Ezra and Nehemiah is that they not only have so many short spellings but also appear to lack any spellings with waw at all: such consistency even in two books is exceptional rather than normal.

8. ישע hiphil 'save' is a widely used word, found in many forms,

especially in the Prophets and Psalms. Once again forms with waw are greatly dominant, and some common forms, e.g. the participle מוֹשִׁיעַ without suffix, appear only so (22 occurrences). Samuel is the particular locus of short spellings, e.g. מֹשִׁעִי 2S 22³, תֹּשִׁעֵנִי also 22³. We have וַיֹּשַׁע 1S 23⁵ 2S 8⁶, and also Jb 5¹⁵, a total of three defective for this form against eight plene; all four in Chronicles are plene. In one of these, incidentally, 2S 8⁶ is without waw and the parallel וַיּוֹשַׁע 1C 18⁶ is plene, while at 2S 8¹⁴//1C 18¹³ both are plene. Other books provide a few short spellings: וְיֹשַׁע Pr 20²²; וְיֹשַׁעֲכֶם Is 35⁴; וַיֹּשַׁע Jud 3³¹. In Samuel there are nine or so writings without waw.

9. We have left until the end ידה hiphil 'praise' because it belongs also to the Lamed He class. Like others, it is commonly plene in respect of the first *o* of the hiphil. In the infinitive *hodot*, however, which is a rather common form occurring eighteen times, the short spelling is actually dominant: (לְ)הֹדוֹת Ps 92² 106⁴⁷ 122⁴ Ne 12⁴⁶ 1C 16⁷,³⁵,⁴¹ 23³⁰ 25³ 2C 5¹³ 7⁶ 31², twelve in all. No doubt much of the basis for this lies in affix effect, i.e. in the presence of the *o* written plene in the infinitive termination –*ot*. The fact remains, however, that the *o* of the first syllable could be, and was, written defectively in dominant proportions in this word, and this in books where the doubly plene spelling הוֹדוֹת would not be surprising and was in fact present (Ps 119⁶² 142⁸ Ne 12²⁴ 1C 16⁴ 2C 7³). Ezr 3¹¹ has הוֹדֹת.

10. Yet another verb is taken out of its alphabetical order because, as will be shown, its spellings have a quite special pattern. This is the verb יסף hiphil, 'add' or, in most cases, 'repeat' or 'do again'. This common verb is usually registered as having 174 occurrences belonging to the hiphil, six to the niphal, and 32 to the qal. It is the hiphil that mainly concerns us here.

The peculiarity of this verb is its much higher proportion of defective spellings of the *o* than we find in other verbs of the Pe Waw class. The perfect is written without waw at 2K 24⁷ הֹסִיף and 2K 20⁶ וְהֹסַפְתִּי, two out of three cases in Kings and two out of six in the entire Bible. In the non-waw consecutive imperfects, if we take together the various forms without suffix, such as *yosep, yosip, tosep, 'osep* and so on, we will find that the total number written without waw is almost as great as that written with waw; and in particular we will find a substantial preference for the writing without waw in the Torah.[1] Most of all, however, is this the case in the very

---

[1] Details in *JSS* 30, 1985, 5 ff.

common waw consecutive forms: in the commonest of all, *way-yosep*, there are seven cases in the Torah, and six of these are וַיֹּסֶף short, the only exception being the last of seven, וַיֹּסֶף Nu 22²⁶. In the same form, moreover, Samuel is equally constant in the short spelling, and out of a total of eleven cases nine are defective, with the two long spellings coming in the middle of the book at 1S 20¹⁷ 23⁴ and all before and after being short. All four cases in Job are also short. In the first singular *'osip* all three cases in Chronicles are short (2C 10¹¹,¹⁴ and 33⁸ if we follow the Masora). The plurals also have a high degree of spelling without waw: so Ex 14¹³ Dt 4² in *tosipu*, in the form with –*un* ending תֹּסִפוּן Gn 44²³ Ex 9²⁸ Dt 17¹⁶, i.e. all cases found anywhere (except Ex 5⁷ תֹאסִפוּן written with aleph); with the third person, *yosipu*, all five cases in Judges are וַיֹּסִפוּ.

In this case it is appropriate to suggest a special explanation for this word alone. Although it is customary to take יסף as 'do again' and the different verb אסף as 'gather, remove', few would doubt that the two are closely connected, and forms that would appear to belong to the one are found with the meaning of the other: thus we have just cited Ex 5⁷, meaning 'do again' but written with aleph, and the same is true at 1S 18²⁹; and conversely forms with no aleph are found with the meaning 'collect', e.g. 2S 6¹ וַיֹּסֶף, Ps 104²⁹ תֹּסֵף. Related also are first person cases like Mi 4⁶ 1S 15⁶. What we suggest is that in earlier times many of the cases which in the Masoretic text appear as belonging to הֹוסִיף and having the vowels of Pe Waw were not of this class and had an *a* vowel, most probably, where there is now an *o*. Hence the abnormal frequency of writings without waw. Eventually the force of analogy, working, I would guess, from the perfect and the infinitive, brought almost all cases into the Pe Waw type of formation, but many defective spellings remained as a sign of what had been there earlier. It is not certain but it is a reasonable supposition and accounts for the anomaly. If it is right, it confirms the view that the spellings of the Masoretic text reach back behind the actual grammar of the Masoretic period and — at least at times — reveal aspects of an older morphology.

Further listing of the details is unnecessary. Of greater interest is the interpretation of the distribution of spellings in this type.

It is well known that the *o* vowel of this class of verbs came from an earlier diphthong *aw*. At first sight it might seem easy to explain the dominance of spellings with waw, especially in the perfect, in this way, and particularly so in the Torah, which writes waw so commonly and, in this respect, appears to go against its own common liking for short spellings. According to this supposition, the writing with waw went back to a time when the diphthong was still pronounced in such forms: people still said something like *haw-lid* or *hawlad* 'he begat', or *tawra* rather than 'Torah', and so on. The waw was therefore written because it was still a consonant. Many texts had the waw, therefore, because they were very old. Some other books like Job and Chronicles, being historically much later, used the defective spelling more because by that time, or in the region of their provenance, they no longer spoke the diphthong but said *o* as we still do today.[1]

A moment's thought, however, indicates that this interpretation of the evidence is impossible. It seems to me that we do not know exactly when, or even roughly when, the diphthong *aw* was last used by Jews in words like 'Torah'. But our argument is not built upon historical evidence about such matters but upon the distribution of spellings in the biblical text itself.

If a text, let us say the text of the Torah, has been written upon the basis of a pronounced *aw* diphthong in words of the kind surveyed in this chapter, there would have been no exceptions: the waw should have been written because it has consonantal character, and this would have happened throughout the series. But this is just not the case. Though the plene writing of hiphils and niphals from Pe Waw words is greatly dominant, exceptions are far from negligible. One of our first examples (fig. 2, p. 2 above) showed that Genesis had *tol'dot* four times out of eleven without the waw of the first radical: if the pronunciation had been *tawlidat* or the like, this would have been impossible. The fact that in this one word spellings alternate, with or without waw of the first radical, with or without waw of the plural termination, all in one probable source of one provenance, make it highly probable that the text as we have it was built upon a pronunciation as *o*. The same applies to forms like *tol'dotam* (above, p. 86), spelt without waw twice in Exodus and consistently in Chronicles.

And so with the verb forms. We do not find long runs of any one verb form spelt without waw apart from some special cases like *hodot*, but spellings without waw are recurrent and are found in the Torah as in other texts: Genesis with יכח thrice defective, with יצא ;וַתֹּרֶד hiphil with several cases in the Torah, and so on. The

---

[1] D.N. Freedman in particular tried to use the spelling patterns of Job, and especially in this type of verb, to date and localize that book; see his 'Orthographic Peculiarrities in the Book of Job', *Eretz-Israel* 9 (Jerusalem, 1969), pp. 35–44, and my criticisms in *JSS* 30, 1985, 1–33. Freedman does not actually say that the waw of older texts was consonantal, but he implies it: 'diphthongs were not contracted at all in pre-exilic times' in Judah (his p. 36).

spellings of the Pe Waw series without waw are not the prerogative of a particular group of books: on the contrary, they run through the great majority, in all cases as a minority spelling, but only differing in smallish degree from book to book in the major cases.

It is possible, of course, that some words were moved from a plene spelling to a defective in the course of transmission: not only possible, but I am sure of it, and consider it an important principle that this must have happened. Some of the short spellings in Job, for example, may well have come about in this way. But it is difficult to account for the longer runs, say of הליד or תלדתם in Chronicles or of השיב in Ezra and Nehemiah, or of ויספו in Judges, in this way. The existence of a doubly short spelling like תלדת in Genesis suggest that the older spelling was defective, and defective not only in the plural termination –ot but also in the o of the first syllable, and that the longer spelling of the o grew from this base. There are no real signs that the Masoretic text was created on the basis of the pronunciation as the diphthong aw.

It is of course true, in terms of historical philology, that this vowel had at some past time been aw; and this fact no doubt generated the idea that the spelling with waw was a good one. But this does not mean that a w was actually used in pronunciation, and, actually, rather few scholars seem to have supposed that it was.

The problem here is not so much a historical one, more a terminological and philosophical one. Customarily spellings of o with waw have been regarded and described as 'historical spellings': they derived, historically, from an earlier diphthong containing the consonantal w, and after the sound had changed to the vowel o the spelling with waw was kept because it had been there in earlier times. But this, we suspct, was not the real reason. Why would anyone spell with waw simply because it had been so done some centuries before? It was done for another reason, because it had become the *convention* to spell in this way, and this convention was followed, as everyone knows, in lots of words which had never had a consonantal w anyway. In the case of Pe Waw verbs, and sometimes of derived nouns, this convention was followed, most of the time, for a quite different reason than the historical one. It was followed because it gave a *morphological* signal which represented the fact that this word came from a root that, in other forms, had a consonant in this position.

This may seem surprising, but it is confirmed by a number of other aspects uncovered in the present study. One is the influence of affix effect. By no means all, but a large proportion, of the cases with o spelt defectively are in affixed forms. If the w had been consonantal there could have been no affix effect, for a consonant had to be written, affixes or none. It was because it was an *o* vowel that affix effect was relevant. The vowel was already *o* and, if there had been no affix, would have been likely to be written with waw; the presence of affix, as seen in many hundreds of examples, means that this is not so likely to be done.

7. Some forms, mainly imperfect, from Pe Yod verbs

It was suggested earlier that differences in the variable spellings seldom if ever made a semantic difference (p. 8 above): an ephod spelt with waw was the same article as one spelt without waw, Absalom spelt with waw was the same man as Absalom without it, שָׁלֹם was the same condition of peace as שָׁלוֹם. But there may be, or may seem to be, some exceptions to this, some cases where the presence or absence of a waw or yod makes a significant difference of meaning.

One such possible exception that might come into mind is constituted by the imperfect of a verb like ירא 'fear'. It would be felt that יִירְאוּ with two yods, by contrast with יִרְאוּ with one yod, signals identification as the verb ירא 'fear' as distinct from the verb ראה 'see'. And in a way this is true, but it is not, strictly expressed, a case of variable spellings in our sense. It is only apparently that the forms are similar, and closer grammatical analysis shows that they are not identical. It is not, therefore, parallel to the difference between שָׁלֹם and שָׁלוֹם; it is not a matter of two different graphic representations of one phonological form. For by accepted phonological analysis יִירְאוּ 'they will fear' is *yir^e'u*, the first syllable being an open syllable with a long vowel; while יִרְאוּ 'they will see' is *yir'u*, with the first syllable being *yir*, a closed syllable with a short vowel.

It is true therefore that the spelling may give a semantic indication of one verb as against another; but it is not a case of variable spelling in the sense we have been studying, it is rather a case of two rather similar writings, which however stand for quite different forms within the language itself, the spoken language.

Moreover, it will be observed, variability in this case applies on one side only, i.e. with *yir^e'u* 'they will fear', for it *could* be written with two yods in the first syllable, but that would not be admissible for *yir'u* 'they will see'. But this means that our original statement was correct: the variability of the spelling does not make the semantic decision. For the only variability is between the two spellings of 'they will fear', יִירְאוּ and יִרְאוּ. The former of these cannot be from ראה 'see', and so there is no decision to be made; the latter, if read for its vowel and consonant signs only (for usually the Masoretic accents and in particular *ga῾ya* will make the decision), can be either, but if it is written thus it makes no decision.

The way it works in the actual text is as follows. Imperfects from ירא 'fear' are invariably plene when the preformative is aleph, *t* or *n*, thus תִּירָא, נִירָא etc. In the third person masculine, however, whether singular or plural, i.e. where the preformative is *y*, there is variation between the two spellings. *Yira'* 'he will fear' is always יִירָא plene, four times; but the consecutive form *way-yira'* 'and he feared' varies: out of a total of twelve cases seven are defective:

A וַיִּרָא   18¹² 21¹³ 28⁵,²⁰ 2S 6⁹
B וַיִּירָא Gn 28¹⁷ 32⁸ Ex 2¹⁴ 1S 12¹⁸
A   Jr 26²¹   2C 20³
B   1C 13¹²

Fig. 30: *way-yira'* 'and he feared', all cases in the Bible

Note the dominance of the long spelling in the Torah and of the short in Samuel. There is one case with suffix, Ml 2⁵ וַיִּירָאֵנִי plene. To this we should add Jr 10⁷ יְרָאֲךָ, which seems to be the only case of the simple imperfect, with suffix, written defectively.

In the plural again the simple imperfect occurs only with two yods, יִירְאוּ or (pausal) יִירָאוּ. This is without affixes; there are six in all. With the prefixed *w͒͑*-, not consecutive, there is a total of eleven, but these may be divided between with the two forms *w͒͑-yir͒͑u* and (pausal) *w͒͑-yira'u*. The former occurs five times: Dt 2⁴ Is 59¹⁹ Mi 7¹⁷ Ps 67⁸ 102¹⁶, and it is plene וְיִירְאוּ in all of these but Mi 7¹⁷ וְיִרְאוּ. The pausal form is found at Dt 17¹³ 19²⁰ 21²¹ Is 41⁵ Ps 40⁴ 52⁸, and of these all the cases in Deuteronomy are defective, וְיִרָאוּ; moreover, they are all in the identical phrase יִשְׁמְעוּ וְיִרָאוּ. The other three are plene, וְיִירָאוּ.

Particularly interesting is the situation with waw consecutive, *way-yir͒͑u* 'and they feared' (the pausal form only Gn 42³⁵ וַיִּירָאוּ). There are 24 occurrences in all. The six cases in the Torah are all plene, וַיִּירְאוּ (except for the pausal vowel in Gn 42³⁵). Joshua has one of each, 4¹⁴ defective and 10² plene. Samuel again is striking, for it has our word six times, and all are וַיִּרְאוּ defective except for the sole 1S 17²⁴, the fourth in the series. Kings has the defective spelling twice out of three (1K 3²⁸ 2K 10⁴ defective, 2K 17⁷ plene). Four in the Minor Prophets and two in the Psalms are all plene, but the one remaining example, Ne 6¹⁶, is again defective.

There are a few other cases in various forms, which it is not necessary to list in detail. 1K 8[40] has the short יְרָאוּךָ with second person suffix; Dt 13[12], with the –un termination, has the short spelling וְיִרְאוּן (again after יִשְׁמְעוּ); Qo 3[14] has שֶׁיִּרְאוּ. Others have yod in the first syllable, and the Torah tends to long spellings even with suffixes: Ex 9[30] Dt 1[29] תִּירְאוּן; Ex 1[17] וַתִּירֶאןָ; Nu 14[9] תִּירָאֻם.

Thus, to sum up, the Torah has no short spellings of this word except for a group in Deuteronomy, four in all, all of which are pausal cases closely following יִשְׁמְעוּ. Yet Deuteronomy has the long spelling also (Dt 1[29]), and like all other sources used it in all the forms with preformatives t and n. In Samuel, which has many cases, the defective spelling is overwhelmingly preferred, yet never without one or two exceptions.

One might well ask (a) whether there is any relevance in proximity to forms of the verb ראה 'see' which might make a difference, or (b) whether there might be some uncertainty of identification, especially in unpointed script, which would leave it uncertain whether an unpointed form belonged to 'fear' or to 'see'. The collocation of 'see... and fear' is not uncommon, e.g. Gn 42[35] Ex 14[31] Ps 40[4] 52[8]: and all these have two yods, which should make the word 'fear' unmistakeable even in unpointed script: here, for instance, is the phrase from Ps 40[4]: יִרְאוּ רַבִּים וְיִירָאוּ. But it must be considered doubtful that the plene writing was used for the express purpose of avoiding confusion here or elsewhere. The evidence points in the reverse direction: it is just where confusion could easily happen that the extra yod is *not* put in. Thus at Dt 17[13] we have the phrase וכל־העם ישמעו ויראו which in unpointed text could easily be taken for 'and all the people will hear and see', but no yod is provided to remove the possibility. Dt 19[20] 21[21] are just the same. Of course, since all these three are pausal forms, if the text is pointed, or if it is read with the reading tradition, the pause form makes it clear anyway that the form is from ירא, since this form could not be from ראה 'see'. At Mi 7[17] in the phrase יִפְחֲדוּ וְיִרְאוּ, the presence of an immediately previous 'fear' term makes it highly likely that both verbs will be so understood. The same might be said for 1S 17[11], but the rest of the Samuel cases point strongly in the opposite direction, since the defective spelling is strongly dominant in that book anyway: thus 1S 4[7] might conceivably be read as 'and the Philistines saw...' and no extra yod is inserted that would prevent that error. 2C 20[3] could also be confusing at first sight, and no yod is provided for guidance.

Given the possibilities of misidentification, it would not be surprising if textual difficulties had already risen in this connection. At

Ne 6¹⁶ וַיִּרְאוּ, the Masoretic provision of metheg makes it clear that the word is intended to be 'and they feared' — here again it comes almost immediately after שָׁמְעוּ 'they heard' — and many modern scholars have thought that this was actually 'and they saw' (so NEB; RSV margin; BHS annotation). LXX however had καὶ ἐφοβήθησαν (2 Esdr 16¹⁶), and took it as 'feared'. The scholars quoted could be wrong about Ne 6¹⁶ but it is a good illustration of the ambiguity that might exist.

To sum up our presentation of the verb 'fear', one might say this: the usage of *all* books is to write imperfects of ירא with a yod after all preformatives other than yod (i.e. aleph, *t* and *n*). The older way of explaining why it varies after preformative yod was to say that scribes disliked writing two yods together. But why should we say that they disliked doing this, especially when they in fact did it a good deal of the time? A reasonable explanation is that many more cases than we now have had, in an older stage of the text, no yod at all, or in third person one only. The defective spellings we now have survive from that stage. But yods were added, and where the preformative was other than yod, these yods came to be always there. Why was this same yod not added to every case which already had a yod preformative? Because there was already a yod there. One was enough. A factor, an important factor, in this kind of spelling is the consciousness of the morphological base upon which the word is built: in this case the yod is an essential part of that base. It was proper that it should be indicated. In third person masculine cases, however, there was a yod already there: a second one might be added, but might equally be omitted.

Other verbs of the same class display similar features. The verb 'dispossess, drive out', ירש, for instance, also has a yod written after the preformative consonants other than yod. In the third person masculine of the imperfects it varies. The great majority have two yods in the Torah, exceptions including Gn 22¹⁷ Dt 10¹¹ (but the latter plene in some texts). Outside the Torah we have spellings with one yod like Ob 20 יִרְשׁוּ and with waw consecutive Jos 12¹ 19⁴⁷ 2K 17²⁴ Jr 32²³. From יקץ 'be awake' all imperfect forms in the Torah (Gn 9²⁴ 28¹⁶ 41⁴,⁷,²¹) have the extra yod; outside the Torah Jud 16¹⁴ is also plene, but others in the qal are defective, Jud 16²⁰ 1K 3¹⁵ 18²⁷ Ps 78⁶⁵ and (plural) Hb 2⁷.

With the verb 'be good' the greatly dominant spelling is יִיטַב etc.: this seems to be almost universal in the Torah, but there are imperfects written יִטַב defectively at 1S 24⁵ 1K 21⁷ 2K 25²⁴ and the hiphil participle is found as וּמֵטִב Ezk 33³² וּמֵטִיב Ps 119⁶⁸. From this word, incidentally, we have the participle מֵיטִיבִים Jud 19²² with three yods, similarly several other forms (cf. above, p. 26). In the hiphil we also have the defective spelling וְהֵטַבְנוּ Nu 10²⁹,³².

In ינק 'suck' all imperfects qal seem to be plene, יִינַק etc., but there are occasional short spellings in hiphil like Dt 32¹³ וַיֵּנִקֵהוּ, and the participle *meneqet* 'nurse' shows in Genesis alone the very short מֵנִקְתָּהּ Gn 24⁵⁹ alongside the very long מֵינִיקוֹת Gn 32¹⁶. This shows variety in the spelling of *e* (ṣere) where there is no doubt that it has the consonant yod at its base, a point which can be important in discussing some other kinds of word.

And with this we may take leave of the Pe Yod roots.

8. The waw consecutive imperfect

The waw consecutive imperfect is one of the most important grammatical phenomena of biblical Hebrew, being the main narrative tense. Careful study quickly reveals some interesting phenomena in the spelling of these forms. According to traditional grammar, the waw consecutive imperfect is built upon the base of the jussive and, in the third singular of many forms, the stress shifts from the final syllable to the penultimate. This is to be seen especially in the hollow verbs such as קוּם 'arise', שִׂים 'put', מוּת 'die', and in the hiphils. Thus a typical form is *way-yáqom* 'and he arose', written וַיָּקָם; and this ends in a 'short' unstressed vowel in which therefore there is no question of choice between long or short spelling. But, where there is a further termination, and that means especially in the plurals with –*u* ending, there is by traditional grammar a 'long' vowel in the same position, thus *way-yaqúmu* 'and they arose'; and so *way-yásem* but *way-yasímu*, *way-yámot* but *way-yamútu*, hiphil *way-yáqem* but *way-yaqímu*, *way-yámet* but *way-yamítu*.

It is somewhat odd, however, that a vowel which was short and unstressed in the singular should in this way become long, stressed and identical in form with the pattern of the imperfect from which in the singular the jussive had been so precisely distinguished. Why should this be so? Now when we look at the spellings of verbs that occur with sufficient frequency we note that it is exactly these cases, in which by traditional grammar a long vowel is to be found, that have a high proportion of defective spellings, such as to make a striking contrast with the same vowel in the straight, non-waw consecutive, imperfect. Thus take the proportions for a typical frequent verb form, *yaqumu* 'they (will) arise' and contrast it with the same form as it stands within waw consecutive, 'and they arose':

		Torah	Samuel	Is	Jr	12P	Ps	Jb	Total
A	יָקֻמוּ	1	1	3	0	0	2	0	7
B	יָקוּמוּ	3	1	1	4	2	2	1	14

Fig. 31: *yaqumu* 'they (will) arise', plain imperfect, third masculine plural

Compare the proportions in the waw consecutive:

		Gn	Ex	Nu	Jos	Jud	S	K	Jr	Ezr	Ne	Chr	Total
A	וַיָּקֻמוּ	4	1	1	1	2	5	6	1	0	0	6	27
B	וַיָּקוּמוּ	1	0	1	0	1	2	1	0	1	1	1	9

Fig. 32: *way-yaqumu* 'and they arose', imperfect waw consecutive

The striking change of proportions is evident. But we must add to this the figures for some other frequent verb forms: here is the same table, made out for שוב 'return':

		Gn	Jud	Sam	Kings	Jr	12P	Ps	Ne	Chr	Total
A	יָשֻׁבוּ	–	1	1	–	2	2	1	–	–	7
B	יָשׁוּבוּ	1	–	–	1	4	3	7	1	1	18

Fig. 33: *yašubu* 'they (will) return', plain imperfect

If we include in this, however, the cases with prefixed w^e-, this increases the proportion of the defective spelling, for all eight cases with this prefix are defective:

		Gn	Ex	Jud	Sam	Kings	Jr	12P	Ps	Ne	Chr	Total
A	(וְ)יָשֻׁבוּ	–	2	1	1	–	4	3	3	–	1	15
B	(וְ)יָשׁוּבוּ	1	–	–	–	1	4	3	7	1	1	18

Fig. 34: *yašubu* 'they (will) return', plain imperfect, including those with non-consecutive w^e-

But consider the difference with the waw consecutive form *way-yašubu*:

		Gn	Ex	Nu	Jos	Jud	Sam	Kings	Jr
A	וַיָּשֻׁבוּ	5	2	3	8	–	5	7	2
B	וַיָּשׁוּבוּ	–	–	–	–	2	–	2	1

	Ezk	Zc	Ps	Ne	Chr	Total
A	1	–	–	–	5	38
B	–	1	1	2	4	13

Fig. 35: *way-yašubu* 'and they returned', imperfect waw consecutive

I do not pretend that the gradations between the different forms are the same for every verb, even of the same class. *Nus* 'flee', for instance, has an unusually high proportion of defective spellings, not only in the waw consecutive forms but in others also: this may, of course, be a function of the particular books in which this verb happens to be most used. Thus its infinitive construct is twice לָנֻס out of a dozen or so in all, at Nu 35[6] Dt 4[42] (the total in the Torah is six); with suffixes we have נֻסְךָ 2S 24[13] and בְּנֻסָם Jos 10[11]. Moreover, *all* the cases of the plural imperative *nusu* are נֻסוּ defective, four in Jeremiah and one at Zc 2[10]. The singular imperfects are plene as in most such verbs, but the plurals, without waw consecutive, show a high ratio of short spellings: Is 30[17] תְּנֻסוּ, Jr 50[16] יָנֻסוּ, Nu 10[35] וְיָנֻסוּ (each case one of two or three). But, in any case, the waw consecutive plural has a very high ratio of short spellings:

		Gn	Jos	Jud	Sam	Kings	Chr	Total
A	וַיָּנֻסוּ	1	3	4	10	5	3	26
B	וַיָּנוּסוּ	–	–	1?	–	1	3	4 (5?)

Fig. 36: *way-yanusu* 'and they fled', imperfect waw consecutive

The uncertain case is Jud 7[21]Q. The one long spelling in Kings is at 2 K 7[7], in the same verse with a short spelling of the same word.

Take the very common verb מות 'die'. The imperfects, taken alone, *'amut, tamut, yamut, namut* etc., are almost solidly plene over scores of cases: an exception is וְאָמֻת 2S 19[38]. The imperfect plurals with –u ending, as usual, show a strong rise in the use of the shorter spelling. In *yamutu* without waw consecutive, which occurs 29 times, all the nine Torah cases are defective, as are five of the six in Jeremiah, plus one out of three in Samuel, one of two in Job and the unusual שִׂימֻתוּ Qo 9[5]: as against this, the plene writing יְמוּתוּ is found at 1S 2[33,34] Jr 42[17] Ezk 5[12] 33[27] Am 9[10] Ps 49[11] Jb 4[21] Pr 10[21] 2C 25[4,4,4]. The totals are: defective seventeen, plene twelve. But, when we turn to the corresponding waw consecutive form, the defective spelling is even more dominant, only two plene spellings being found among a total of ten (וַיָּמוּתוּ is found only at 2S 11[24] Jb 1[19]).

This kind of pattern can be found in a long series of verbs. Consider verbs with the *i* vowel, like the hiphil of שוב. As in most such verbs, the imperfects 'alone' are plene: אָשִׁיב, תָּשִׁיב, יָשִׁיב, so long as it is the simple imperfect and without suffixes, over a long run of instances. Enter the plurals with –u ending, however, and we find a change: Dt 1[22] וַיָּשִׁבוּ as against several with yod. But then move to the waw consecutive imperfect *way-yašibu* 'and they brought back', and we have seven out of ten וַיָּשִׁבוּ — Dt 1²⁵ Jos 22³² 1S 5³ 2S 3²⁶ 1K 12¹⁶ 2K 22²⁰ (by Masora) Jr 34¹¹ — and the longer spelling וַיָּשִׁיבוּ only at Nu 13²⁶ 2C 10¹⁶ 34²⁸. Jr 34¹¹ is defective in the hiphil but plene in the qal in the same verse.

A series of such examples can hardly fail to provoke the suggestion: perhaps there was, in older times, no 'long' vowel here. If people said, in the singular, *way-yánŏs* 'and he fled', then perhaps they said in the plural *way-yánŏsu*, and the plural retained the shorter vowel, and the difference of accent, which was characteristic of the jussive and the waw consecutive formation from the beginning and which is still taught as doctrine in our grammars? If this were so, then the shorter spelling would correctly reflect the older morphological pattern, while the longer spelling would reflect the entry of the later grammatical pattern, which introduced a long vowel here on the analogy of the non-waw consecutive imperfects, and which thus began to influence the writing of the text but succeeded in doing so in only a limited number of cases. This, if right, would once again confirm that the Masoretic text reflected grammatical conditions of a time much earlier, conditions which had already been lost from sight by Masoretic times.

We may look at one or two other verbs in order to test the likelihood of this hypothesis. One of the commonest of all verbs relevant for this question is בוֹא 'come', hiphil 'bring'. In the qal, in the plain imperfect, third person singular, *yabo'*, the total figures for the Bible are: יָבֹא 59 times, יָבוֹא 97 times, total 156. When we move to the waw consecutive of the same, we find: the vast majority are וַיָּבֹא defective, only nineteen cases plene out of 263 in all. Against this, however, must be set one point: even in the simple imperfect, the Torah strongly favoured the shorter יָבֹא. Nevertheless, the difference is very striking.

In the corresponding imperfect plural with waw consecutive we have an even more sweeping victory for the short spelling: out of a total of about 186 cases, all are short, וַיָּבֹאוּ, except for the three lonely cases of וַיָּבוֹאוּ at 2K 11¹⁹ Jr 8¹⁶ 2C 29¹⁸ (Mm 2498). On the other hand we should recognize that the imperfect plural without waw consecutive has, in this particular verb, already gone some of the same way: out of 52 cases, only three are written יָבוֹאוּ, 1S 31⁴ Ps 86⁹ 2C 32⁴ (Mm 3344). So there may be something about this verb, something perhaps in the fact that, the aleph being quiescent, it has the very variable *o* vowel in its root syllable.

The idiosyncratic behaviour of בוֹא is increased when we look at the hiphil. The simple imperfect has an unusual configuration:

A   יָבֹא   Nu 6^{10}
B   יָבִיא   Lv 4^{32} 5^{25} 7^{29} 6^{13} Jos 23^{15} Is 7^{17} Jr 27^{11}
A   Ps 78^{29} Ct 8^{11} Qo 12^{14} Dn 11^{8}
B   2C 24^{11}

Fig. 37: simple imperfect hiphil of *bo'*, 'he will bring', third person, all cases

This is a remarkable pattern, very different from many that we have hitherto seen to be common. The Torah favours the long spelling, while the short spelling appears in out-of-the-way places.

The plural imperfect with waw consecutive, *way-yabi'u*, is even more striking. There are a total of 36 cases in all, and there is a ratio of thirteen defective to 23 plene. The Torah is uniformly long (ten cases) until we come to the end of Numbers; Samuel is entirely short (six cases); Chronicles has eleven cases and, like the Torah, prefers the long spelling, having only one, its first, short (1C 11^{18}). The high proportion of long spellings, the preference of the Torah for them, and the considerable agreement between the Torah and Chronicles, are all worthy of note.

And this is not the only case of the kind. From the verb שִׂים 'put', if we take the waw consecutive imperfect plural, third person, *way-yaśimu*, there are 35 occurrences over a wide variety of books, and only four have the short spelling וַיָּשִׂמוּ: Jos 10^{27} 1S 6^{11,15} 2K 11^{16}. The Torah has eight, and all have the long וַיָּשִׂימוּ; so have the six in Judges. The other verb 'put', שִׁית, does not have enough examples to tell us much.

Another important case in principle is the hiphil of מות, 'put to death'. Imperfects 'alone' are plene as usual: יָמִית, תָּמִית, אָמִית etc., without exception, but waw consecutive imperfects in the plural without suffix, which is the type we have used for comparison, are too few, in fact only one, 2K 21^{23} וַיְמִיתוּ. The best examples are those with the singular verb plus pronoun suffix *–ehu*, and with the plural verb plus pronoun suffix *–hu*. The form *way-y^{e}mitehu* has fifteen cases, with the greatest concentration in Kings (ten cases). By the text of BHS these divide as follows:

A   וַיְמִתֵהוּ   Gn 38^{7} 2S 21^{17} 1K 2^{34} ^{26} 15^{28}
B   וַיְמִיתֵהוּ   1S 17^{50} 13^{24} 16^{10}
B   2K 15^{10,14,25,30} 23^{29} 1C 2^{3} 10^{14}

Fig. 38: *wa-y^{e}mitehu* 'and he put him to death', all cases, spelling as in text of BHS

By the Masora, however, 1S 17^{50} 2K 15^{25} should be defective (Mm 2137). By BHS text we have five defective and ten plene, by the Masora seven defective and eight plene. In either case we recognize strong representation of the plene spelling here.

The corresponding form with plural verb, *wa-yᵉmituhu* 'and they killed him', has six occurrences, and they divide up easily, for the three in Chronicles (2C 22^9 25^{27} 33^{24}) all have the yod, וַיְמִיתֻהוּ, while the three in Samuel/Kings are וַיְמִתֻהוּ without it (2S 4^7 18^{15} 2K 14^{19}). 2C 25^{27} is a parallel of the same words in 2K 14^{19}. There are about four other imperfects of מות hiphil which are defective before other suffixes, but rather more with yod written; the most important is waw consecutive singular with suffix *-em*, four occurrences, once defective: Jr 52^{27} וַיְמִתֵם. In general it seems that מות hiphil had a larger degree of writing with yod than without, even in the waw consecutive, but not as large a degree as we saw to obtain with בוא hiphil.

These examples must suffice for the present discussion; we cannot go farther without a much more extensive presentation of the complicated spelling patterns of the hollow verbs. This being so, we should be careful not to claim too much as a conclusion from the limited data presented.

As usual, we face the question: do the phenomena go back to actual differences in an earlier form of the language, or are they graphic and scribal differences? The strikingly higher proportion of defective spellings in some verbs in the waw consecutive, as compared with otherwise identical imperfect forms, gives reasonably strong ground for the former conclusion. It is conceivable that the spelling reflects a stage when there was, in a phrase like *way-yaqumu*, a short vowel in the syllable *qum*, whether *o* or *u*, as there is, even in Masoretic Hebrew, in the singular. The plene spellings, on the other hand, may reflect the rising tendency to pronounce with a long *ū* vowel as is done in the simple imperfect. These ideas, it will be remembered, do not rest solely upon the evidence from the hollow verbs, some of which has been presented in this section: our studies of the *i* vowel of the hiphil in triliteral verbs, and of the forms of hiphil and niphal in Pe Waw verbs, both illustrated the importance of the waw consecutive imperfect as locus of short spellings. And the spelling patterns of בוא, one of the commonest of all Hebrew verbs (2,570 cases according to Jenni's useful table)[1] and certainly the most profitable to investigate in this respect, fit in very well at least as far as concerns the qal. Nevertheless we still have to consider the other series of possibilities:

---

[1] Jenni and Westermann, *Theologisches Handwörterbuch zum Alten Testament*, ii. 538–9, table of the incidence of the most frequent Hebrew verbs.

suffix effect of the ending –*u*, affix effect of the preceding waw, the general fact that, among the vowels subject to variation, *o* is in many forms the most volatile — all these may lead us still to consider explanations through graphic considerations and scribal convention.

But what about the dominantly plene spelling of the hiphil of this same verb? It might well be that *this* aspect could be accounted for under graphic, scribal procedures. Firstly, wide experience shows us that the *i* vowel is written plene in a much higher percentage of possible places than is the *o* vowel, which is much more likely to vary. The entry of the *i* vowel into a form like *way-yabi'u*, even if it was not 'original' there, might well be extensively marked with yod. Secondly, we have noticed that the *i* vowel tends to be marked with yod a great deal in terms that are frequent in the text — for instance, plurals like בָּנִים, עָרִים, common words like עִיר 'city', אִישׁ 'man'. Now בוא as has just been said is one of the most frequent of verbs. Its total number of hiphils is over 500. Its very frequency could well attract the attention of scribes and cause them to be more likely to add a yod where needed. Thirdly, semantically this could make a difference which would be noted. The writing יבא must have been a rather ambiguous group of signs. In effect a fairly good distinction appeared — one should not say 'was worked out', since one cannot say if this was deliberate or not; but in the qal of such a word a very large majority left the *o* vowel unmarked by waw. In the hiphil, both with and without waw consecutive, a large majority write the yod. The fact that this is so in the Torah in particular makes the explanation all the stronger. It should count, I submit, as having reasonable probability.

9. *O* vowel of imperfect qal in triliteral verbs

Some other phenomena characteristic of verbs will be dealt with only briefly. The same features are common to many lexemes, and we are forced either to give only bare numbers, or else to heap up many small details. Yet our subject would not be fully covered without some summary mention of features like the *o* of the imperfect qal. Imperfect forms like *yizkor* are common, but the spelling of the *o* with waw, taken over the Bible as a whole, is distinctly a minority spelling.[1] To take the verb we have just cited,

---

[1] Andersen and Forbes, p. 194, Type 40, give the figures as defective 1,356, plene 125, total 1,481.

in its various relevant parts (which include the first, second and third persons singular masculine, the first plural, and the third singular feminine), we have three cases spelt with waw, Ho 9⁹ יִזְכּוֹר, Hb 3² תִזְכּוֹר and (third feminine) the same La 3²⁰. These are three cases out of 24, not counting the waw consecutives. With the verb דרש we have Ezk 20⁴⁰ אֶדְרוֹשׁ, Jb 39⁸ יִדְרוֹשׁ, and Ezr 4² נִדְרוֹשׁ, three out of seventeen calculated in the same way. Many other verb lexemes will give similar results, and we can simply state some of the findings that will quickly emerge:

(a). Although spellings plene of this kind are to be found dispersed in many parts of the Bible, much the largest representation of them would seem to lie in certain books: the Minor Prophets, Ezekiel, Job and Proverbs, in particular. Even in these books it is not probable that the plene spellings reach majority status.

(b). Waw consecutives were not included in the figures given above, and for a good reason: even where verbs have some examples of this plene spelling, they very often have none in their waw consecutive imperfect. Waw consecutive cases do occur but are in proportion much more infrequent: examples include Rt 2⁷ וַתַּעֲמוֹד, Jb 15²⁸ וַיִּשְׁכּוֹן.

There are a few verbs that have a higher proportion of plene writings than we might have expected on the basis of the evidence of others. Sometimes this is because the verb happens to be a favourite of one of the books that uses, more than others do, the long spelling of this type of form. For example, חמל 'pity' appears in the first singular imperfect seven times: Jr 13¹⁴ Ezk 5¹¹ 7⁴,⁹ 8¹⁸ 9¹⁰ Zc 11⁶, and all of these except Ezk 8¹⁸ 9¹⁰ are written אֶחְמוֹל with waw. Another root that is strongly represented is עבר 'pass', with five cases of יַעֲבוֹר plus others in other persons.

One common verb that seems to be like this is נפל 'fall'. Out of about forty cases of the third person masculine singular *yippol* fifteen are יִפּוֹל plene; and to these we add תִפּוֹל, four times masculine second person and four times feminine third person. So this is a high proportion of the longer spelling. But there again a large number of these are in just the books that favour this writing with waw — Ezekiel, the Minor Prophets, Proverbs, Qoheleth, plus some from Isaiah, while the considerable number in the Torah, Samuel and the like are dominantly or entirely without waw, and so also the waw consecutive forms.

This fact that the waw consecutive imperfects very seldom shared in the plene spelling seems significant. Does it suggest something about the stress and vocalism of the period when these plene writings in imperfects came into existence? The *o* might be written plene because it was felt to be *long*; and, if so, it might mean that this long quantity was not perceived in the waw consecutives, which are after all a very common type. Or might it suggest that waw consecutives, even in the triliteral verb, had the stress on the penult rather than the final syllable, something that in traditional grammar happens only in certain circumstances, and which therefore would not apply by traditional grammar to a common regular form such as וַיִּמְלֹךְ? Might such a form have had penultimate stress, and therefore the final *o* was never spelt with waw?

Another possibility that was considered is that the matter of spelling imperfects with waw of the *o* in the final syllable was connected with stress within the sentence, with pausal position as the traditional grammar terms it. Surveys to test out this possibility proved to be inconclusive so far. Thus in the Minor Prophets, while a number of verbs thus spelt were in pausal position, others were not. Thus Mi 6[15] תִקְצוֹר is definitely in pause (athnach), but others such as Hos 2[20] אֶשְׁבּוֹר, 4[14] אֶפְקוֹד, 5[10] אֶשְׁפּוֹךְ, Am 2[3] אֲהֲרוֹג are all with conjunctive accents. Am 3[5] יִלְכּוֹד is clearly in sentence-final position. But in the Minor Prophets, far from it seeming that the long spellings go with pausal position, the reverse would seem easier to defend: consider again Ho 9[9] יִזְכּוֹר, יִפְקֹד both away from major pauses. Of course it cannot be taken for granted — this is an obvious qualification — that the present accent signs, which were placed by the Masoretes, perfectly represent the stresses and divisions of the text in ancient times. But, even allowing for this, it seemed difficult to find any correlation with sentence stress in the Minor Prophets. It would be easier to suppose that the longer spelling was simply an option of spelling which the scribes could apply wherever they thought fit to do so. Nor have I found a clear correlation in Ezekiel: for example, of the five cases of *'eḥmol* used by him and cited above, all are in pausal position, but two are written without waw and three with it. Further work, however, might produce more evidence on this matter.

Finally, there is one rare phenomenon that deserves recording, even if only as a curiosity: there are one or two imperfects with the plural ending –*u*, or the feminine –*i*, which are spelt with the previous vowel plene, but with that vowel realized as *u* rather than as *o*. Such an unusual writing is not so surprising in Rt 2[8] תַּעֲבוּרִי, but Ex 18[26] יִשְׁפּוּטוּ is strikingly out of the way. In general, plene spellings of the *o* of the qal imperfect in the Torah are few, and the historical books from Joshua to Kings seem to have them little also.

10. Vowel *o* of infinitive construct

In triliteral verbs the infinitive construct is commonly considered to be identical with the imperative, masculine singular, which is a type generally spelt defective but with some long spellings, e.g. Jud 6[20] שְׁפוֹךְ, Ps 132[1] זְכוֹר, Qo 12[13] שְׁמוֹר, which is just as we would expect. 'Eat' is interesting: in the imperfect this is not an o-containing verb, but it is so in the imperative. Here there are fifteen cases, and four of these are אֱכֹל with waw: 1S 28[22] 1K 19[5] Ezk 3[1,1], plus Pr 23[7] according to Mm 1692 and many texts (but defective in BHS).

Our subject, however, is the infinitive construct, and in it we have the advantage of much longer runs of examples for many verbs. The infinitive, however, rather seldom occurs alone, without prefixes or suffixes, and far larger numbers are found with prefixes k^e-, b^e-, *min* and most of all l^e-. Thus the commonest of all, לֵאמֹר, occurs over 900 times; and out of this large mass of material there emerge only three plene spellings לֵאמוֹר, and these at Gn 48[20] Jr 18[5] 33[19]. It is hard to see any sort of reason for the appearance of these unusual spellings at these particular places, and in books that might well be expected to favour a short spelling. The case is a little bit like the strange appearance of יַעֲקוֹב with waw, one case in Leviticus and four in Jeremiah out of about 350 examples (cf. pp. 40, 162).

Just above we noted the incidence of plene spelling in the imperative of אכל 'eat', and the infinitive with l^e- appears as לֶאֱכֹל plene in thirteen cases out of about 58. These are: 1S 20[5,24] 2S 13[9] 16[2] 17[29] 2K 4[40] Ezk 16[20] 44[3] Am 7[2] Mi 7[1] Hb 1[8] Qo 5[17] 2C 7[13] (Mm 1640). The five plene in Samuel are out of a total of twelve in that book; 2K 4[40] has both spellings of the same form in the same verse; all cases in Isaiah (three) and in Jeremiah (three) are short; the two in Ezekiel are the only ones in that book; all three in Psalms and the two in Job are short; Qoheleth has one long and two short; Nehemiah has two, both short; 2C 7[13] is the only case of the form in that book. Ezk 44[3] is long only in the K form, not in the Q. The three in the Minor Prophets are out of four in that book, and this fits well with the trend to long spelling that we have seen in the imperfects there.

A well-represented verb is דרש 'seek'. Its infinitive compounded with l^e- is short, לִדְרֹשׁ, in: the Torah (two cases), Kings (six), Ezekiel (one), Ezra (two). The long spelling appears in Samuel (one), Hosea (one) and Qoheleth (one). The most important book is

Chronicles, which is divided: ten with waw, five without it (Mm 4226).

These are enough to give a idea of what to expect: on the one hand very rare plene spellings of a frequent verb, which may turn up almost anywhere; on the other hand, for the most part, defective spellings in the Torah, Kings with some exceptions, Jeremiah with some exceptions; a very mixed picture in Joshua, Judges and Samuel; and a distinct trend towards the plene spellings in Qoheleth, sometimes Ezra and Nehemiah, and particularly Chronicles, but there also with a good number of defective spellings mixed in.

One famous passage is the sequence 'a time to...' in Qo 3. Here we have a good collection of infinitives, but not all belong to our class since some are piel or for other reasons do not have the *o* vowel. And I exclude the Lamed He class, for in them, as we shall see, the spelling with waw is greatly dominant in the Bible as a whole. Leaving these out, the list has twelve infinitives with waw: 3^2 לַחֲבוֹק, כְּנוֹס 3^5 רְקוֹד, סְפוֹד, לִשְׂחוֹק 3^4 לִפְרוֹץ, לִרְפּוֹא, לַהֲרוֹג 3^3 לַעֲקוֹר; לִשְׁמוֹר 3^7 לִקְרוֹעַ, לִתְפּוֹר 3^6.

Defective by contrast are: לִשְׂנֹא, לֶאֱהֹב 3^8; לִרְחֹק 3^5. Note that all these three are verbs that belong to, or come close to, the 'stative' category (cf. above, p. 78): might this confirm that their vowel was, at the time relevant for the Qoheleth text, still not the same as that of the others?

11. Infinitive construct of Lamed He verbs

These infinitives end in *–ot*, and their spelling pattern is quite different from that of the *o* vowel of regular triliteral verbs. In essence the position is simple: (a) the spelling of the *–ot* ending is overwhelmingly plene if all cases are numbered together[1]; (b) as we have seen already in the case of the verb עשה (above, p. 27), the infinitive, if it is 'alone' without prefix, is very commonly spelt plene, and indeed this can be said to be normal, although the numbers are not high, because most infinitives have an affix; (c) with prefix, the spelling without waw becomes an option, and tends to be found in the Torah, especially in Genesis and Exodus, but with some cases in other quarters, notably Ezra and Nehemiah; (d) even in those areas where the short spelling is found, it tends to be a minority spelling in comparison with the longer.

---

[1] Andersen and Forbes, p. 192, Type 37, give the figures with 'high' stress, which is what mainly concerns us in our approach, as 97 defective, 845 plene, out of a total of 942.

For the verb עשה the defective spellings have already been listed on p. 27. It remains to add that they form a minority in the relevant books: Genesis has one short spelling out of about thirteen; Exodus has six out of sixteen, and they all belong to the latter part of the book, after 35[1] (and even in this region they only slightly dominate, six cases defective as enumerated above, against five plene at Ex 35[29,33,35] 36[7] 39[3] — on this cf. our study of parallel passages in Exodus, pp. 174–77); Leviticus has two out of four; Numbers has two out of ten; cf. Deuteronomy, which has a large number of cases of לַעֲשׂוֹת, about 38, and every one of them plene. In Nehemiah, similarly, there are three short writings, and they are scattered among a considerable number (ten or so) of the plene spellings: all one can say is that they fall within the latter part of the book.

The incidence for the verb היה 'to be' may be suitably displayed. Without prefix the form is always written הֱיוֹת plene, including one case each in Genesis and Exodus. With prefixes, l^e-, b^e- and min, however, all cases in Genesis (five) are plene, but there are six defective, לִהְיֹת etc. in Exodus and two in Leviticus, out of a total of nine in the former and six in the latter. The pattern is thus:

A	לִהְיֹת etc.		9[28]	19[16] 23[1]		36[18] 39[21] 40[15]
B	לִהְיוֹת etc. Ex 5[13]	12[4]		28[28]		
A		Lv 11[45]			26[13]	
B			20[26] 22[33] 25[38]	26[45]		

Fig. 39: infinitive construct of היה 'be', with l^e- or other prefix, in Exodus and Leviticus

Exodus after ch. 35 uses only the shorter spelling. Leviticus uses the longer increasingly, and after Leviticus there are no short spellings at all, though the term occurs in Numbers once and in Deuteronomy six times. Ex 12[4] Lv 26[45] are also defective in BHS, against Mm 725 which specifies eight defective. עלה 'go up' can be treated briefly. It is interesting in that Ne 3[19] עֲלֹת is one of the few cases where the infinitive without prefix is written defectively, another sign of the place of Nehemiah. Prefixed by l^e-, we have a simple pattern: לַעֲלֹת defective at Ex 19[23,24] Dt 1[26,41], that is, all cases in these two books, and לַעֲלוֹת plene at Nu 13[13] 14[44], the only cases in Numbers. All cases after the Torah are plene.

The hiphil of the same verb is also relevant. The total number of infinitive constructs, with or without prefixes but without suffixes, is about 34. Of these only the first three have the short spelling

הֶעֱלֹת, i.e. Ex 27²⁰ 30⁸ Lv 24². These are all the occurrences in the Torah, and all are defective, while all in non-Torah books are plene.

'To see' is, alone, רְאוֹת, but when prefixed there is an interesting pattern in Genesis and Exodus:

```
A   רְאֹת            11⁵  24³⁰  27¹  33¹⁰
B   רְאוֹת  Gn 2¹⁹ 8⁸                      34¹  42⁹,¹²  44²³,²⁶  48¹⁰
A                          10⁵      33²⁰
B              Ex 3⁴   19²¹
```

Fig. 40: infinitive construct qal of ראה 'see', with prefix but no suffix, in Genesis and Exodus

Genesis begins with the long spelling and ends with it; Exodus alternates. The remaining few cases in the Torah, and all in the other books, are plene.

Of שתה 'drink' the pattern is the same: the defective writing לִשְׁתֹּת appears at Gn 24¹⁹, the first of four cases in that book, and in Exodus it is defective at 7²⁴ 15²³ 17¹, the last three out of six cases in that book (the plenes are 7¹⁸,²¹,²⁴, and 7²⁴ contains the last of the plene, and the first of the defective only a few words after it). The two cases in Numbers that follow are both plene and so are all others in later books.

These examples do not constitute all the evidence, but enough to make clear a general pattern. The short spellings of the *-ot* of the infinitive are mainly to be found in the Torah but are not at all dominant in it and are often specially located in the first two books, and even within them are often a minority in comparison with the longer spelling.

12. Qal infinitive absolute of triliteral verbs

The average reader might well think that the infinitive absolute is one of the simplest cases: surely its spelling is plene, with perhaps some occasional exceptions? The standard grammars support this impression: GK § 45a, p. 122 says 'קָטוֹל, sometimes also קָטֹל', similarly Bauer and Leander, § 43k, p. 317; and grammars for learners tend, perhaps, to use plene forms throughout for this infinitive.[1] 'Sometimes' is in fact a serious understatement, for the infinitive

---

[1] Thus Lambdin, *Introduction to Biblical Hebrew* (London, 1973), p. 157, lists nine infinitives absolute of triliteral verbs and spells all of them with waw.

absolute is one of the types in which a very considerable degree of variation exists, for something over 40% of these infinitives are written defectively.[1] Moreover, unlike the case with many other types, the Torah tends to be a zone of considerable variation, while the centre for defective spellings tends to lie, for some lexemes at least, in certain non-Torah books, notably perhaps Jeremiah.

Variety in the Torah can be easily illustrated from one or two examples. In the verb שמר all cases are in Deuteronomy:

A שָׁמֹר 11^2 27^1
B שָׁמוֹר   Dt 5^{12} 6^{17} 16^1

Fig. 41: infinitive absolute of שמר, all cases in the Bible

With זכר the preference of the Torah for the long spelling is rather stronger:

A זָכֹר   Dt 7^{18} Jr 31^{20}
B זָכוֹר   Ex 13^3 20^8 24^9 25^{17} Jos 1^{13} La 3^{20}

Fig. 42: infinitive absolute of זכר, all cases in the Bible

That the two great cases of זָכוֹר and שָׁמוֹר in the two versions of the Ten Commandments are both plene will be familiar to anyone with a good knowledge of the Bible (Ex 20^8 Dt 5^{12}). But this long spelling is by no means inevitable; it might, conceivably, be a late spelling, influenced, perhaps, by the importance of these particular sayings. For a plot of infinitives absolute through this part of Exodus, noted for its ancient legislation, produces the following:

defective: 21^5 אָמֹר ^{20} נָקֹם
plene: Ex 20^8 זָכוֹר ^{22} עָנוֹשׁ ^{28} סָקוֹל
defective: 22^{11} גָּנֹב ^{12} טָרֹף ^{15} מָהֹר ^{22} צָעֹק, שָׁמֹעַ
plene:
defective: 22^{25} חָבֹל 23^5 עָזֹב ^{22}
plene: ^{22} שָׁמוֹעַ

Fig. 43: plot of infinitive absolute qal in Ex 20–23

Thus the Book of the Covenant, Ex 21–23, strongly favours defective spelling for this type but has two or more that are plene. Yet Torah spellings in general, as we have already shown from

---

[1] Andersen and Forbes, p. 193, Type 38, report a count of 179 defective, 245 plene, out of a total of 424.

small examples, tend often to favour the longer spelling. The Book of the Covenant is an area in which lie a number of the other short spellings that we have noticed. Might this be a case for some correlation between spelling and date? Or is it rather that this section of Exodus has been left out of a revision that affected some other parts of the Torah? Incidentally, we might mention also Ex 21^{19} רְפָא, which was not listed because it is not qal, but is another case which could have been plene but is in fact defective. Ex 23^{22} I have entered as plene against the Leningrad text, see BHS and Weil's note there. Dothan prints it as defective.

Among single verbs which have many examples of the infinitive absolute, so that we can trace it through a wide variety of books, the most striking is הלך 'go'. It will be useful to cite the evidence in full:

A	הָלֹךְ	31^{30}	Jud 4^9	1S 6^{12}
B	הָלוֹךְ Gn $8^{3,5}$ 12^9 26^{13}	Jos $6^{9,13,13Q}$	4^{24} 9^8 14^9	14^{19} 19^{23}
A				20^2
B	2S $3^{16,24}$ 5^{10} 13^{19} 16^{13} 18^{25} 24^{12} 2K 2^{11} 5^{10} Is 3^{16}		38^5 42^{24}	
A	Jr 2^2 3^{12} 7^9 17^{19} 19^1 23^{14}	34^2 35^{13} 37^9	41^6	
B	13^1	28^{13} 31^2 35^2	39^{16} 50^4	
A				
B	Zc 8^{21} Ps 126^6 Pr 13^{20K} 1C 11^9			

Fig. 44: infinitive absolute qal of הלך, all cases in the Bible

The Masora states the situation economically: there are four defective except in Jeremiah and all Jeremiah cases are defective except for six (Mm 1408, which also records that there is difference of opinion about Jr 19^1; it is plene in BHS, but I have taken it as defective with the Masora). The general situation is clear. The Torah is dominantly plene but there are no occurrences after Genesis, in which the last one is defective. In Judges and Samuel the first occurrence is defective but all thereafter are plene. Isaiah has one defective out of four. Samuel has the largest number of steady plene writings, nine in succession. Jeremiah, which is the largest user by far, prefers the defective spelling by a ratio of ten to six.

Here is the pattern for שמע:

A	שָׁמֹעַ	22^{22}	Dt 1^{16} 11^{13}	1S 23^{10}
B	שָׁמוֹעַ Ex 15^{26} 19^5	23^{22}	15^5 28^1	Is 6^9 55^2
A	Jr 17^{24}			
B		31^{18} Zc 6^{15} Jb 13^{17} 21^2 37^2		

Fig. 45: infinitive absolute qal of שמע, all cases in the Bible

Ex 23[22] is disputable for text, as indicated just above (pp. 110f.). If it is defective, Exodus has two of each spelling, as does Deuteronomy. Job favours the long spelling.

And here is the same for נתן 'give':

A נָתֹן		Nu 21[2] 27[7]	2S 5[19] Is 37[19]
B נָתוֹן	Gn 41[43]	Dt 15[10] Jud 8[25] 11[30]	
A	Jr 37[21] Ezk 23[46]		
B		Qo 8[9] Est 2[3] 6[9]	

Fig. 46: infinitive absolute qal of נתן, all cases in the Bible

A few more cases can be briefly described. With אכל 'eat' there are seventeen cases in all, of which six are defective: Gn 2[16] Lv 7[24] Jud 14[9] 1S 14[30] Is 22[13] Pr 25[27]. The Torah has two of each spelling of this form. Is 22[13] has two examples in the same verse, the first of them being the defective; Isaiah has two other occurrences, both plene. הרג has four cases: it is defective in Numbers, Deuteronomy and Isaiah, and (though not in all texts) at Est 9[16]. 'To know', ידע, has Gn 15[13] יָדֹעַ defective, 43[7] הֲיָדוֹעַ plene; these are the only Torah cases. There is another plene at Jos 23[13]. In addition we have three in Samuel, two in Kings, six in Jeremiah, and one in Proverbs, all defective; here again the dominance of the defective spelling is noticeable. יצא 'go out' has seven cases, three plene (Gn 8[7] 2S 16[5] 2K 5[11]) and four defective (Gn 27[30] Nu 35[26] 2S 18[2] Jr 38[17]). The Torah is divided but prefers the shorter spelling, which is maintained again by Jeremiah. לָקֹחַ 'take' is defective in its one Torah case, Dt 31[26], and לָקוֹחַ plene at Jr 32[14] Ezk 24[5] Zc 6[10]: Jeremiah here abandons his preference for the short spelling. פָּקֹד 'count, review, inspect' has five cases, two in Genesis, two in Exodus, and one in Samuel: all five are defective.

The infinitive absolute is commonly collocated with another form from the same verb, and sometimes this is also an o-containing form that might or might not have plene spelling. There is, however, no obvious correlation between plene spelling of the one and plene spelling of the other. Gn 37[8] first has both words defective, הֲמָלֹךְ תִּמְלֹךְ and then has the infinitive plene, אִם־מָשׁוֹל תִּמְשֹׁל. 1S 24[21] has the infinitive defective but the imperfect plene, מָלֹךְ תִּמְלוֹךְ. We may also have both words plene, as in Am 3[5] or La 3[20], זָכוֹר תִּזְכּוֹר לָכוֹד לֹא יִלְכּוֹד.

13. The type of the passive participle qal

The passive participle of the type *qatul* distinctly favours the spelling with waw, if we count all instances without distinction.[1] But there are some special factors with this type. One is that certain words of this type tend to occur in repetitive lists, and this may have tended to standardize their spelling. 'Blessed', בָּרוּךְ, is an obvious example: the masculine singular occurs 65 times, and all with waw; and indeed the waw is maintained in the (rather few) cases with feminine or plural terminations, except for the one case of בִּרְכִם at 2S 2[5]. 'Cursed', אָרוּר, is the same, with about 40 cases including the five that are feminine or plural. The effect of this standardization with some terms tends to obscure the fact that defective spellings of the passive participle are not uncommon and are widely spread over a variety of different books.

For example, *labuš* 'clothed', absolute masculine, occurs six times and is לָבֻשׁ defective in four of them: Ezk 9[2,3] Zc 3[3] Pr 31[21] — all of them books that, in some other forms, might have been expected to be long-spelling. The plene writings are at the opposite ends of the spectrum, in 1S 17[5] Dn 10[5]. Proverbs has some other short spellings, notably in its later chapters: Pr 28[17] עָשֻׁק, 25[11] דְּבֻר. In particular, the plurals, which with words like בָּרוּךְ and אָרוּר remained very often plene, in many other participles appear in good proportion as defective, even in books that might well be long-spelling, e.g. Qo 4[1,1] הָעֲשֻׁקִים, Zp 1[7] קְרֻאָיו 1[16] הַבְּצֻרוֹת. In the Minor Prophets Joel has פְּרֻשׂ defective Jl 2[2] in the same line with עָצוּם plene, and Amos has Am 6[4] סְרֻחִים 6[7] וּסְרֻחִים. Deuteronomy has Dt 32[34] כָּמֻס and חָתֻם in an (old?) poem, but many plene spellings, e.g. 28[29] עָשׁוּק וְגָזוּל and cf. 28[33].

The pattern *qatul* includes not only passive participles proper but also nouns and adjectives which, whether they are connected with passive participles or not, really function as something different. A common example is בָּחוּר 'young man', and this has a very high rate of standardization in the plene spelling: out of 44 cases all are written with waw including plurals with suffixes except for three (2K 8[12] Jr 31[13] 51[3]). It should be added that the same steady plene spelling attaches to a score or so cases of בָּחוּר which can be properly classified as passive participle 'chosen' (and are commonly entered under a different entry in concordances). These spellings extend

---

[1] Andersen and Forbes, p. 202, Type 61, give the total as 271 defective and 818 plene, out of 1,089; and for 'high' stress, i.e. the word alone and not construct or suffixed, 27 defective and 393 plene.

over a wide variety of books and seem to indicate a strong element of lexicalized standardization.

On one or two examples, however, such as that of לָבֵשׁ with its strong representation of defective spelling, one might reasonably consider the possibility that here again there had, at an earlier stage, been a stative qal participle of the pattern לָבֵשׁ, upon which later the pattern of the passive participle had been overlaid. The verb occurs in the stative form in Ps 93[1,1] לָבֵשׁ.

Another passive participle that strongly confirms what has just been said is כָּתוּב 'written'. The masculine participle is thus spelt in every one of its 38 cases. There are ten feminines, and everyone of these is כְּתוּבָה plene, including four in the Torah (all in Dt 29–30). Still more striking, the many plurals, most of them in the phrase 'are they not written?', are very largely spelt כְּתוּבִים plene. In Kings we have the short spelling כְּתֻבִים at the first occurrence of the phrase, 1K 11[41], where incidentally 2C 9[29] in rewriting the same spells it with waw. After this first case all the long run of examples in Kings are plene, and all the Chronicles cases are the same, including a plural feminine כְּתוּבוֹת at 2C 34[24]. The shorter spelling כְּתֻבִים is found at Ex 31[18] 32[15,15] Dt 9[10] 2K 23[3,24] Jr 51[60], the latter three with article, but the long spelling appears already in the Torah at Dt 28[58] (defective, however, in some texts). In this case standardization on the long spelling seems to have overcome affix effect very largely, at least in the case of the feminine and plural terminations, except in the Torah, although with article and in the plural it still has some influence. Once again it looks as if passive participles that were very frequent in use tended to attract standardization. If these very frequent participles are counted separately, then the proportion of defectively spelt passive participles becomes higher. It would be a reasonable supposition if one judged that the strongly dominant plene spelling in this type was the result of a rather late and fairly systematic extension, which spread over most portions outside the Torah and some within it. In addition one must consider the more general possibility that, not only in this type but in other word types also, words that were very *frequent in use* and in limited, standard, forms, tended to attract to themselves a more consistent spelling, and that often a plene spelling.

14. The second person masculine termination — *-ta* and *-ka* when spelt with he

The spelling of the terminations *-ta* and *-ka* is in many ways a special case and different from most of the others that have been discussed in this section. Most have been cases of the presence or absence of waw or of yod, but here it is he that is present or absent. We are interested in writings such as Gn 3⁹ אַיֶּכָּה 'Where art thou?', 3¹² נְתַתָּה 'you gave'. Spellings of –ta and –ka like this, with he, form in total a small minority among the thousands of second person masculine expressions in the Bible, and this makes it possible to provide a plot of their distribution (see pp. 125–27). We shall begin by offering some factual observations on the distribution, and later will pass over to some of the more uncertain and possibly speculative questions of a philological nature.

Firstly, it quickly emerges from a first glance at the material that the distribution of spellings with he is very unequally spread over the books. Genesis has four with –ta and eight with –ka, Deuteronomy has ten and four, respectively, Samuel has twenty and three; Isaiah, by contrast, has very few and the Minor Prophets have scarcely any. The Psalms, on the other hand, are one of the major books for this sort of writing, with about 25 for –ta and six for –ka. The rest of the Writings have only a small handful, except for five in Lamentations (of these, four are all in one passage, 3⁴³⁻⁶⁰), three in Nehemiah (and all of these in one place, ch. 9), and six or seven in Chronicles, again all but one of them in one place, ch. 6 of 2 Chronicles. (It should be added, before we go farther, that the figures cannot be of absolute exactitude and objectivity, since a small number of cases are disputable either textually or philologically: for example, is Ps 10⁸ חֶלְכָה really a case of the suffix –ka attached to a noun, or is it a noun of the stem h–l–k and thus nothing to do with that suffix, cf. the plural חֵלְכָּאִים Ps 10¹⁰?).

There is, then, a wide difference between book and book in the degree to which they use this spelling. The largest users, taken purely quantitatively, are Psalms, Samuel and Exodus but in none of these is it more than a tiny fraction of the second person terminations used. On the distribution as between one Psalm and another, see below. Genesis is the only book in which the spelling of –ka with he is more common than the spelling of –ta in the same way; in Isaiah the two are equal, but the figures for both are slight. In most books the spelling of –ka with he is very thinly represented.

Secondly, there is a distinct tendency for the spelling with he to recur with certain particular words. The first of these is the perfect of נתן 'give': in Exodus, for instance, there are long strings of wᵉ–nátattá 'and you shall put' in the instructions for the making of the tabernacle, and in Exodus this form is spelt with he 15 times, without it 16 times, in other words almost equally balanced. The fifteen cases with he thus form the great majority of the nineteen

	−ta	−ka
Genesis	4	8
Exodus	19	5
Numbers	10	1
Deuteronomy	10	4
Joshua	3	–
Judges	6	–
Samuel	20	3
Kings	10	4
Isaiah	2	2
Jeremiah	7	3
Ezekiel	11	1
Obadiah	1	–
Zechariah	1	–
Malachi	1	–
Psalms	25	6
Job	no real case	
Proverbs	–	2
Ruth	no real case	
Qoheleth	–	1
Lamentations	5	–
Ezra	1	–
Nehemiah	3	–
Chronicles	7	–
Totals	146	40

Fig. 47: Number of spellings of −ta and −ka with he, book by book

cases in all in which Exodus spells the −ta ending with he. Moreover, the prominence of natatta, with or without the preceding
w^e−, is maintained in other books. Six of the ten in Numbers are
spellings of this particular form, seven of the ten in Deuteronomy,
two of the three in Joshua, five of the ten in Kings, seven of the
eleven in Ezekiel, six of the 25 in Psalms, all of the three in Nehemiah plus the one in Ezra and all of the seven in Chronicles. This
extremely strong link between this particular lexeme and this
rather unusual mode of spelling is very striking, and cannot but be
a clue to be followed up.

The second such case is the equally striking conjunction of this
spelling, in the suffix −ka, with the verb form yakke 'he will smite
(you)'. In this form, perhaps uniquely, every case that occurs in the

Bible, seven in all, is spelt with he. The forms are יַכֶּכָה at Is 10²⁴ Jr 40¹⁵ Ps 121⁶, and יַכְּכָה at Dt 28²²,²⁷,²⁸,³⁵.

The two cases can hardly be a coincidence. The writing of –ta with he is found most conspicuously in a verb form, natatta, in which the consonant t is omnipresent; and the writing of –ka with he is universal in attachment to a verb form in which the consonant k is dominant. The question quickly arises: is this done for graphic clarity? Or does it suggest that there was in earlier times a difference of pronunciation between the two spellings, that the writing with he betokened a pronunciation with full final vowel, –ta or–ka, and that in these particular cases, and others like them, the final vowel was retained so as to provide a distinction as against the identical consonant of the root which immediately preceded? The question will be discussed shortly.

Another word that has a disproportionately high representation of the spelling with he is ʿaśita 'you have done', a common word. In Samuel it is found spelt עָשִׂיתָה with he no less than seven times, as against eight of the more 'normal' spelling עָשִׂיתָ, two of them in waw consecutive and the other six not so. Moreover, the same spelling of this form with he occurs in other books: Ezk 35¹¹.

Moreover, the verbs that are spelt with he in this form include not only עשה 'do, make' but also a rather large number of verbs from the same (Lamed He) class. We have for instance:

רָאִיתָה Nu 27¹³ 2S 18²¹ Ps 10¹⁴ (without yod) 35²² La 3⁵⁹,⁶⁰ plus the hiphil הִרְאִיתָה Ps 60⁵ — seven in all

צִוִּיתָה Nu 27¹⁹ Jr 32²³ Ps 119⁴ La 1¹⁰ — four in all

הָיִיתָה Jud 11⁶ (2S 5² perhaps not a real case) 2S 10¹¹ (one yod only)

הִכִּיתָה 1S 15³ 2K 9⁷ Jr 5³ — three in all

These are the cases where the same verb occurs several times with this spelling of the second person termination. There are seven or so isolated cases of this or that verb of the same class to be added, making over 20 cases in all. These cases include: 1K 9³ בְּנִתָה (note the absence of the yod); 2S 7²⁷ גָּלִיתָה; Ob⁵ נִדְמֵיתָה; Jr 38¹⁷ וְחָיִתָה (one yod only); Ps 31⁶ פָּדִיתָה; Jud 11³⁶ פָּצִיתָה; Rt 4⁵ קניתה is hardly a real case, since it is the spelling only of the marginal Qere note (K קניתי); Jr 25¹⁵ וְהִשְׁקִיתָה.

In some of these verbs the cases spelt with he thus make up a fairly large proportion of the second person masculine singular perfects. Thus in ra'ita 'you saw' there are six spelt with he out of a total of 28, or 21 if we exclude those preceded by the interrogative h ᵃ–, none of which have the spelling with he. In siwwita 'you commanded' there are four cases with he out of a total of thirteen in all.

With *hikkita* 'you smote' spellings with he amount to three out of a total of seventeen. There may be, then, some affinity between the Lamed He class and the occasional use of the spelling with he. As has been noted above, the spelling with he in this verb class is some-times accompanied by omission of the yod which is commonly written in the preceding syllable.

Thirdly, it seems as if there may be a certain tendency for the spelling with he to appear with *short* words such as particles, mono-syllables, and verbs of the 'hollow' type which in the perfect have only one syllable before the termination.

The most striking such case is *bo'ᵃka* 'your coming', which in Genesis appears five times as בֹּאֲכָה with he as against one without it (Gn 10^{19,19,30} 13^{10} 25^{18} as against בֹּאֲךָ Gn 19^{22}), and in Kings 1K 18^{46} (contrast 2K 19^{27} written without he). Notice in addition that, in these two books, the cases spelt with he coincide exactly with those that belong to the idiom meaning 'as you come to (a certain named place)', e.g. Gn 10^{19} 'from Sidon, as thou comest to Gerar' (AV): by contrast, Gn 19^{22} is in a conversation, 'I shall not be able to do anything until you arrive there', and similarly 2K 19^{27} 'I know your coming in, etc.', which is a different construction alto-gether. The cases of the idiom 'as you come to (a named place)' in other books, such as Judges and Samuel, are spelt without he. But the coincidence of the idiom with the uncommon spelling with he in both Genesis and Kings would appear to be significant.

And other cases can be added: כָּמֹכָה 'like you' is so written twice at Ex 15^{11,11} (the same line has the uncommon spelling אֵלִם 'gods'); or cf. בִּשְׁמְכָה Jr 29^{25}. Against this spelling of *kamoka* there stand about thirty cases of כָּמוֹךָ, in a variety of books (but no others in Exodus than the two quoted). There are three cases of בְּכָה 'in you', Ex 7^{29} 2S 22^{30} Ps 141^8 (Mm 964); this is against the normal spelling בְּךָ, found some eighty times. With *lᵉka* 'to you' we find a similar pattern: the spelling with he, לְכָה, is at Gn 27^{37} 2S 18^{22} Is 3^6 (cf. Mm 2214, which however includes also Ps 80^3; I would think this to be imperative with *-a* ending from *halak* 'go'. Mm 2214 adds that such imperatives are *normally* spelt לְכָה, only three exceptions being written as לֵךְ 'go').

For other 'short' forms written with he of the termination cf. Ex 13^{16} יָדְכָה, Gn 3^9 אַיֶּכָּה, Nu 22^{33} אֹתְכָה, Ex 29^{35} אֶתְכָה, 2K 7^2 הִנְּכָה, Ps 139^5 כַּפֶּכָה, Pr 24^{10} כֹּחֶכָה; and, among verbs, Ex 12^{44} וּמַלְתָּה, Gn 21^{23} גֵּרְתָּה, Jud 14^{16} possibly חַדְתָּה, Jr 12^5 רְצְתָּה, Ezk 28^8 מֵתָה, and Ps 90^8 שַׁתָּה.

One does not wish, of course, to exaggerate the extent to which the spelling with he goes along with 'short' forms: it is also found with longish words, as in 1K 9³ הִתְחַנֶּנְתָּה, Is 37²³ הֲרִימוֹתָה. Nevertheless the degree of coincidence with short words may have some significance, yet to be explored.

The distribution of spellings with he as between books had already been mentioned, but to that one should add some mention of the distribution within individual books. A look at the plot of all cases will show that this spelling tends to be widely scattered within the books in which it occurs, apart from cases of words like נָתַתָּה 'you gave' which often occurs in groups together and will be discussed further in due course. Apart from repetitions of one single word in this way, it is rather seldom that we find a large grouping of spellings with he in one place. Nu 27 has three cases; Jud 11 has two; 1S 15 has five, and if we include 14⁴³ that means a grouping of six in one fairly limited area. 1K 9 has three and so has 1K 18: the former are all of –ta, the latter all of –ka. The Psalms are a good area for study in this respect since the separation between units is fairly clearly defined. Ps 8 has two with –ta; Ps 10 has three spellings with he, but only if we count the uncertain cases of 10⁸,¹⁴; Ps 60 has three and so has Ps 139. La 3 has four cases. I have not found any sizeable unit that employs only the spelling with he: Ps 60 and Ps 139, for instance, both employ also the common endings תָ and ךָ without he.

The distribution reconfirms a point that has been made already in a different connection (above, pp. 21, 39): there is no sign of any connection between the less common spelling of –ta and –ka with he, and the date or provenance of the passage. The spelling with he occurs alike in what are doubtless very ancient passages like Ex 15 and in unquestionably latish sources like Lamentations and Nehemiah. In the Psalms it occurs alike in poems that look ancient like Ps 8 or Ps 60, and in others from the latter part of the Psalter which may well be later.

The facts of distribution having been thus stated, we may consider possible ways of explaining this particular set of variations; and here we may begin from certain well-known past controversies and certain valuable pieces of epigraphic evidence.

First of all, concerning the suffix –ka, it is well known that Kahle, following Sievers, maintained that the form which in Masoretic Hebrew is –ᵉka had earlier been –ak. Striking and influential as this theory was, it was much opposed, and the discovery of Qumran texts with –ka written plene as כה, many times, was hailed as proof that the ancient form had been, as the Masoretic tradition had it, –ᵉka or the like. This, however, was to claim too much: the Qumran texts which so spell prove only that in Qumran times some people *thought* that this was the pronunciation, they do not prove that it had always and universally been so. Indeed, the very fact of these writings at Qumran could be taken as an indication that opinion on the matter was divided and that efforts were then being made to induce the community to use the pronunciation –*ᵉka* or the like.[1]

Into this controversy, however, we would prefer not to go. But we have to touch upon it, for with the spelling of –*ka* (as likewise of –*ta*) with he we return to our recurrent problem: are the two writings, ךָ and כָה, merely variant *spellings* of the same phonetic substance, which is the way in which the Masoretic grammar takes them? Or are they perhaps in some way signs that point back to differences in the actual pronunciation and morphology of the language at an earlier stage?

It is not necessary to solve the problem by a simple one-way decision, as if all cases had been –*ᵉka* in ancient Hebrew, or as if all cases had been –*ak* or some other form. Possibly both forms existed, and Kahle reports a conversation with Murtonen in which this possibility was discussed.[2] Moreover, Kutscher's own demonstration that in Mishnaic Hebrew, doubtless under Aramaic influence, the pronoun suffix was –*ak* on the authority of the best manuscripts (the popular text of the Mishnah was in this respect made to conform to the biblical usage of the Masoretes) only strengthens the possibility that such an ending may have existed in the Bible text itself.[3]

There are two or three serious reasons why we should recognize that the common and normal writing ךָ, understood as –*ka*, presents a difficulty:

1. From the point of view of graphic structure, such a writing is peculiar, in that it seems to suggest a final vowel –*a* which is not marked by a following vowel letter. The general rule in Hebrew is that all final vowels are 'long' and are marked by a vowel letter, so with *e, i, o* and *u*. It is of course conceivable that *a* should be treated

[1] See P. Kahle, *The Cairo Geniza* (2nd edition, Oxford: Blackwell, 1959), pp. 171–9; this represents, however, a modification of his earlier views. For an example of repeated and concentrated opposition to Kahle's views on this matter see E.Y. Kutscher, *A History of the Hebrew Language* (Jerusalem, 1982), e.g. §§ 28, 30, 46.

[2] Kahle, ibid., p. 176; cf. also Cross and Freedman, *Early Hebrew Orthography*, pp. 65ff.

[3] Kutscher, ibid., §§ 196, 201–2.

in the opposite way, but why should this be so? The final *a* vowel elsewhere, e.g. in third person singular feminine of verbs in the perfect, is written with the vowel letter he, e.g. נָתְנָה 'she gave'. Might this not suggest that the writing כָה־ does imply a pronunciation -*ka*, but the writing ךְ־, even if later provided with the vowel point for *a*, was at an earlier time a suffix that ended in the consonant *k*, thus –*ak* or the like?

2. From the point of view of historical linguistics, one would expect that the short vowel *a* of a suffix –*ka* would disappear, as other final short vowels did, at an early date. If, by an alternative treatment of the same, it was preserved through being made into a long vowel, one would expect it to be marked with a vowel letter such as he.

3. It is difficult to dismiss the evidence from the Hexapla and other transliterated sources, suggesting that in the early centuries A.D. pronunciations as –*ak* and (for verb endings) as –*ath* were current.[1]

For our purposes, fortunately, it is not necessary to enter into controversies about what was the exact form of the second person masculine termination in biblical times themselves; but it is enough that we should see at least the possibility that the two writings of –*ka* and of –*ta*, with he and without, may go back to different phonetic and morphological realizations of this termination at some earlier time.

An analogy may perhaps be seen in the spelling of the free second person pronoun, normally 'atta אַתָּה. The normal feminine is 'att אַתְּ. But there are a number of cases where the masculine has been written את without he, and has been transferred into the usual masculine form אַתָּה only through the KQ system: so 1S 24[19] Ps 6[4] Jb 1[10] Qo 7[22] Ne 9[6]. What is more, there are three cases in which no KQ variant is found, and where the form אַתְּ actually acts, without modification of any kind, as the masculine pronoun: Nu 11[15] Dt 5[27] Ezk 28[14] (Mm 900). Since the –*ta* ending of verbs is clearly related to the ending of the pronoun 'atta, if the pronoun can exist also in the form 'att, then it is reasonable to suppose that verbs in the perfect, second masculine singular, might also at some times or places end in –*t* rather than in –*ta*; and this, if so, might reflect also on –*k* and –*ka*. We conclude, therefore, that we have to reckon with the possibility, at least, that the spellings with he and without he may reflect earlier forms of two different kinds: –*k* and –*t* without following vowels, and –*ka* and –*ta* with following vowels.

---

[1] See again Kahle, ibid., pp. 171, 178.

There is also epigraphic evidence that closely affects this matter.[1]
There is evidence from Arad and Lachish that the simple perfect
was written with he: כתבתה 'you wrote', ידעתה 'you knew'; while
the waw consecutive perfect was written without he: ונתת 'and you
will give', ולקחת 'and you will take'. This at once leads to several
consequences for our subject, namely:

a. If in inscriptions a systematic difference in spelling of this kind
   can be seen, it is all the more likely that these corresponded to a
   difference in pronunciation; and in Masoretic Hebrew a shift of
   stress made many waw consecutive perfects prosodically very
   different from the same perfect when not in that construction.
b. On the other hand it is a little surprising if the ending with he
   corresponds to the simple perfect, since by Masoretic grammar
   one might expect the ending with he to go with the waw
   consecutive perfect, since it has (in many forms) a main stress
   upon the –ta termination.
c. In any case the position revealed by these inscriptions does not
   agree in any simple way with the situation in the Masoretic text,
   for in it the writing with he is used in both types, the simple
   perfect and the waw consecutive.
d. On the other hand the position in the Masoretic text seems to
   vary from book to book. In Exodus the number of cases that are
   waw consecutive is very much greater, a result of the numerous
   occurrences of וְנָתַתָּה; and so in Deuteronomy, where out of ten
   cases eight are waw consecutive. But in the Psalms, which is a
   big user, out of 25 cases *all* are simple perfects, and the same is
   true of the five in Lamentations and the three in Nehemiah.
   Samuel, another major user, is mixed, but the waw consecutive
   cases are a distinct minority, about six out of 21.

It will be helpful if we give a table of the full figures for this:

	Gn	Ex	Nu	Dt	Jos	Jud	S	K	Is
Waw consecutive:	–	17	9	8	1	3	6	4	–
not waw consecutive:	4	2	1	2	2	3(4?)	14	6	2

	Jr	Ezk	12P	Ps	La	Ezr	Ne	Chr
Waw consecutive:	4	9	–	–	–	1	–	2
not waw consecutive:	3	2	3	25	5	–	3	5

It is possible that there is some correlation between the usage of
some books and the evidence reported from Arad and Lachish. The
Psalms are much the most striking material in this regard; the only
qualification is that in these poems the waw consecutive, being

---

[1] On this see Z. Levit, *Matres Lectionis*, pp. 31f.

largely a narrative tense, is not quite as common as in other literature. Samuel is divided, but shows a distinctly greater tendency to
use the spelling with he in non-waw consecutive constructions.
Some other books have the same preference but the numbers are
small: Genesis and Lamentations are sufficiently noticeable. The
other Torah books, and especially Exodus, lean heavily in the opposite direction. All we can say, then, is that, if there should be any
kind of systematic correlation between the spelling with he and the
simple, non-consecutive, perfect, that correlation is seen in some
books and completely obscured in others. It is possible, of course,
that the one verb *natatta* forms a special case because of its own
peculiar pattern of consonants; for if the cases of this verb were
separated out from the calculation, the position in the Torah books
apart from Genesis would be considerably changed.

The position in Exodus is peculiar because of the high degree to
which the two spellings of $w^{\,\varepsilon}$-*natatta* are interwoven. A diagram
will indicate this:

A	וְנָתַתָּ		16,21,26,30	34		23	30
B	וְנָתַתָּה	Ex 21²³ 25¹²	26³²,³³ 27⁵ 28¹⁴	24,25,27			
A		29³,⁶ ¹⁷	16,18,18	7,7,8		Total: 16	
B		¹² ²⁰ 30⁶	³⁶ 40⁵,⁶			Total: 15	

Fig. 48: $w^{\,\varepsilon}$–*natatta*, 'and you shall give (put)', waw consecutive perfect, all cases in
Exodus

Rapid alternation is well evidenced here. Within the same passages, of course, the large numbers of other verbs than נתן which are
also in the second person masculine perfect are *all* spelt without he,
so that, when seen within the totality of all verbs in this section of
Exodus, the cases with he are a small minority.

To this we must add an aspect of textual history. There are
distinct signs which lead us to suspect that the spelling of –*ka* and of
–*ta* with he was more prevalent at an earlier stage than it is in our
present text. There are not many cases at which we can trace this,
but where we have the information we can see that books that are
likely to represent a 'later' style of spelling have tended to eliminate
the spelling with he. Thus compare 2S 7²⁷ גָּלִיתָה with the much
more 'normal' spelling of the same, גָּלִיתָ, at 1C 17²⁵; similarly 2S
10¹¹ וְהָיְתָה and 1C 19¹² וְהָיִיתָ. 2S 22³⁰ בְּכָה has the spelling with he,
but Ps 18³⁰ בְּךָ has the vastly more common writing without it. (On
the comparison of this poem in its two parallel texts, see further
below, pp. 168–174). If we are right in this, the spelling with he for
–*ka* and –*ta* moved in the opposite direction from many other spell-

ing phenomena: they moved from the shorter towards the longer, at least according to common opinion, but this one moved from the longer towards the shorter. If so, the spellings with he that we now have may be the remnants of a larger number that were present at an earlier stage.

The case of Chronicles may be particularly instructive in this regard. Chronicles is unusual in that (a) its spellings with he, seven in number, are all spellings of the same word, *natatta* — two with waw consecutive, the others straight perfects; (b) *all* its spellings of *natatta* are alike in this — in this it differs from Nehemiah, which has three spellings with he but a slightly larger number without it, actually four (Ne 9[15] has the he in BHS but against the Masora and I have counted it as defective); (c) all but one of its instances fall within the one passage, 2C 6, which is closely parallel to 1K 8. Note that Nehemiah, having a roughly equal mixture of the two spellings (three to four or four to three) is once again close to the practice of Exodus.

But before pursuing the comparison between Kings and Chronicles we should note a literary point. 1K 8 and 2C 6 are alike versions of the long and solemn prayer of Solomon at the dedication of the temple. Now the place where Nehemiah also has the spelling with he is in the long and solemn prayer in a very similar style, and the one case in Ezra is in his prayer of the same kind. This *might possibly* be taken to support the idea that there was a difference of pronunciation, going along with a higher and more solemn style; and this in turn would fit with the many cases in Exodus in the speech of God giving instructions for the building of the tabernacle. We do not press this suggestion, however, and our following arguments do not depend upon it: it is simply an idea worth consideration.

We return to the parallel between Kings and Chronicles. Kings, as we have seen, is a book with a fairly wide distribution of spellings of *-ta* with he; Chronicles, by contrast, does not have any at all except in *natatta*. But in this particular chapter Chronicles has *more* cases with he than Kings has. Kings has *natatta* four times with he and twice without, while in Chronicles all the same cases, six in all, are with he. For ease of comparison, the parallels are set out below:

1K	8[34]	אֲשֶׁר נָתַתָּ	2C	6[25]	אֲשֶׁר־נָתַתָּה
	8[36]	וְנָתַתָּה מָטָר		6[27]	וְנָתַתָּה מָטָר
	8[36]	אֲשֶׁר־נָתַתָּה		6[27]	אֲשֶׁר־נָתַתָּה
	8[39]	וְנָתַתָּ לָאִישׁ		6[30]	וְנָתַתָּה לָאִישׁ
	8[40]	אֲשֶׁר נָתַתָּה		6[31]	אֲשֶׁר נָתַתָּה
	8[48]	אֲשֶׁר נָתַתָּה		6[38]	אֲשֶׁר נָתַתָּה

Kings, it may be added, has one other case of וְנָתַתָּ without he, at 1K 3[9], and one other of נָתַתָּה with he, 1K 9[13], so that there is a total of three without he and five with he in the book.

The position of Chronicles can be interpreted in two opposite ways. On the one hand, it could be only a graphic policy applying solely to this one word, that in all cases *natatta* should be spelt with he. If this is so, it is odd that Chronicles avoided spellings with he on all other words of any kind. On the other hand, it is possible that the older text of Kings, on the basis of which Chronicles was written, actually contained *more* cases of the spelling with he: this older text was copied in this respect by Chronicles, while later on the text of Kings drifted towards the more 'normal' spelling without he. Parallels to this process may be seen in various other kinds of words.

To sum up, it seems likely that the spelling of –*ka* and –*ta* with he was an older style which had been reduced in numbers in the later history of the text. Those which remain are remnants which have survived that process. As such remnants often are, they are a small minority, submerged by the enormous preponderance of the spelling without he. The survival of the longer spelling in certain words, especially in נתתה and יככה, may be reasonably explained in that this spelling materially assists clarity and identification in these particular words; but even in *natatta* the spelling without he came close to equal numbers in many books. Similarly Gn 27[7] has וַאֲבָרֲכֶכָה but the spelling אברכך without he remains dominant (Gn 12[2] 22[17] 26[3] (this with –*ekka* ending) Ps 63[5] 145[2]; and so also all the many cases of יְבָרֶכְךָ etc. with the verb in 3rd person).

We have mooted the question whether the two spellings went back to two different pronunciations in older times, and certain linguistic evidence that might favour this has been mentioned. The distribution of spellings of –*ka* and –*ta* in itself, however, does not seem to be decisive in this regard. It may become more decisive, however, when we consider the termination –*na* of the feminine plurals in imperfect and imperative, to which we turn next.

1. Plot of cases of –*ta* written with he

Gn	3[12] נִכְסַפְתָּה 31[30] גֻּרְתָּה 21[23] נָתַתָּה 15[3] נָתַתָּה
Ex	5[22] הֲעַדְתָּה 19[23] וְהִזְהַרְתָּה 12[44] וּמַלְתָּה 18[20] הֲרֵעֹתָה 21[23] 25[12] 26[32,33] 27[5] 28[14,24,25,27] 29[12,20] 30[6,36] 40[5,6] וְנָתַתָּה
Nu	3[9,48] 7[5] נָשָׂאתָה 14[19] וְהֵמַתָּה 14[15] וְנָתַתָּה 27[13] וְנָתַתָּה 31[29,30] 27[20] וְצִוִּיתָה 27[19] וְרָאִיתָה

Dt	וְחָפַרְתָּה 23[14] וְיָשַׁבְתָּה 17[14] וְנָתַתָּה 15[17] 14[25,26] 11[29]
	נָתַתָּה 26[15] וְנָתַתָּה 26[12] נָתַתָּה 26[10] וְקַצֹּתָה 25[12]
Jos	נָתַתָּה 17[14] וְנָתַתָּה 15[19] זָקַנְתָּה 13[1]
Jud	פָּצִיתָה 11[36] וְהָיִיתָה 11[6] מָאַסְתָּה 9[38] וְנָתַתָּה 1[25]
	הִגַּדְתָּה 14[16] חַדְתָּה in some texts, not BHS] 14[16]
	וְאָסַפְתָּה 18[25]
1S	וְהֻמַתָּה 1[11] וְהִכִּיתָה 15[3] עָשִׂיתָה 14[43] וְנָתַתָּה 1[11]
	מָאַסְתָּה 15[26] וְהַחֲרַמְתָּה 15[18] עָשִׂיתָה 15[6]
	עָשִׂיתָה 24[19] עָשִׂיתָה 24[20]
2S	עָשִׂיתָה 2[26] 3[7] יָדַעְתָּ 3[24] בָּאתָה 2[26]
	הָיִיתָה [5[2] not a real case — he belongs to next word מוֹצִיא]
	עָשִׂיתָה 12[21] וְהָיִיתָה 10[11] גָּלִיתָה 7[27]
	רָאִיתָה 18[21] עָשִׂיתָה 16[10] וְהֶפַרְתָּה 15[34] חָשַׁבְתָּה 14[13]
	תַתָּה 22[41]
1K	נָתַתָּה 9[13] בָּנִתָה 9[3] הִתְחַנַּנְתָּה 9[3] נָתַתָּה 8[36,40,48] וְנָתַתָּה 8[36]
2K	וְנָפַלְתָּה 14[10] וְהִכִּיתָה 9[7] וְנָסַתָּה 9[3]
Is	הֲרִימוֹתָה 37[23] נָטַשְׁתָּה 2[6]
Jr	וְנָתַתָּה 29[26] וְהִשְׁקִיתָה 25[15] וְשָׁמַטְתָּה 17[4] רַצְתָה 12[5] הִכִּיתָה 5[3]
	וְחָיִיתָה 38[17] צִוִּיתָה 32[23]
Ezk	עָשִׂיתָה 35[11] נָמַתָּה 28[8] וְנָתַתָּה 4[3] וַהֲכִינוֹתָה 4[9] וְנָתַתָּה 4[1,2,2,3]
	וְנָתַתָּה 43[19,20] הֵבֵאתָה 40[4]
Ob	נִדְמֵיתָה 5
Zc	זָעַמְתָּה 1[12]
Ml	בָּגַדְתָּה 2[14]
Ps	רָאִתָה 10[14] שַׁתָּה 8[7] כּוֹנַנְתָּה 8[4] נָתַתָּה 4[8]
	הֶעֱמַדְתָּה 30[8] נָתַתָּה 21[3,5] 18[41]
	נָתַתָּה 39[6] רָאִיתָה 35[22] פָּדִיתָה 31[6]
	הִרְאִיתָה 60[5] הִרְשַׁעְתָּה 60[4] סִפַּרְתָּה 56[9] הֵבֵשְׁתָה 53[6]
	אִמַּצְתָּה 80[16] הִצְמַתָּה 73[27] נָתַתָּה 60[6]
	שַׁתָּה 90[8] מִגַּרְתָּה 45 נֵאַרְתָּה 89[40]
	הִסְכַּנְתָּה 3 בָּנִתָה 139[2] צִוִּיתָה 119[4]
	סַכֹּתָה 140[8]
Jb	[יָדַעְתָּ הַשַּׁחַר not a real case: Q ידעתה שחר מקמו 38[12]]

Rt 4^5 K קְנִיתִי Q קָנִיתָה (not a real case?)

La 1^{10} סַכּוֹתָה 3^{43} צֻוֵּיתָה 3^{44} סַכּוֹתָה
      3^{59} רָאִיתָה 3^{60} רָאִיתָה

Ezr 9^{13} וְנָתַתָּה

Ne 9^{20} נָתַתָּה 9^{36} נָתַתָּה 9^{37} נָתַתָּה

2C 6^{25} וְנָתַתָּה 6^{27} נָתַתָּה 6^{27} וְנָתַתָּה 6^{30} נָתַתָּה
      $6^{31,38}$ נָתַתָּה 20^{10} נָתַתָּה

2. Plot of cases of –ka written with he

Gn 3^9 בָּאֲכָה $10^{19,19,30}$ אַיֶּכָּה 13^{10} 25^{18}
      27^7 וּלְכָה 27^{37} וַאֲבָרֶכְכָה 27^7

Ex 7^{29} כָּמֹכָה $15^{11,11}$ יָדְכָה 13^{16} וּבְכָה
      29^{35} אֹתְכָה

Nu 22^{33} אֹתְכָה

Dt $28^{22,27,28,35}$ יַכְּכָה

1S 1^{26} עִמְּכָה

2S 18^{22} בְכָה 22^{30} וּלְכָה

1K 18^{46} בָּאֲכָה 18^{44} יַעַצְרְכָה 18^{10} יִמְצָאֻכָּה

2K 7^2 הִנְּכָה

Is 3^6 יַכֶּכָּה 10^{24} לְכָה

Jr 7^{27} יַכֶּכָּה 40^{15} בִשְׁמְכָה 29^{25} יַעֲנוּכָה

Ezk 40^4 הַרְאוֹתְכָה

Ps 10^8 יַכֶּכָּה 10^{14} חֵלְכָה 121^6 לְחֶלְכָה
      139^5 יְבָרְכוּכָה 145^{10} בְכָה 141^8 כַּפֶּכָה

Pr 2^{11} כֹחֲכָה 24^{10} תִּנְצָרְכָה

Qo 2^1 אֲנַסְּכָה

15. Imperfects and imperatives with the 2nd/3rd person plural feminine ending –na

In the Masoretic text the suffix –na, found in feminine plural imperfects and imperatives, is dominantly spelt נָה with he. Nevertheless there is an important incidence of the shorter spelling without the he.[1] In this regard the most impressive single verb is the common היה 'be', and the following is a map of the distribution:

A תִּהְיֶיןָ Gn 26^{35} 41^{36} 49^{26} Ex 25^{27} 26^3 27^2 $28^{21,21}$
B תִּהְיֶינָה   Lv $23^{15,17}$
A   Dt 21^{15}
B   Nu $35^{11,13,14,15}$ $36^{3,4,6,6,11}$ Jos 21^{42} Jud 15^{14}
A   1S 25^{43}
B   2S 20^3 Is 16^2 17^2 Jr 18^{21} 44^6 $48^{6,9}$ 49^{13}
A   Ezk $7^{4,9}$ 29^{12} ^{10}
B 23^4 30^7 $34^{5,8}$ ^{22} 35^{10} 36^{38} Ps 130^2 1C 7^{15}

Fig. 49: 2nd/3rd feminine plural imperfect of *haya* 'be', all cases in the Bible

A few of these (Jr 18^{21} 48^6 1C 7^{15}) differ in that they write only one of the two yods, but this does not matter at the moment since here we are concerned with the termination. I have not marked those that are waw consecutive, partly to avoid cluttering up the diagram, partly because it does not seem to correlate with differences of spelling in any case, unless possibly in Ezekiel, which will be mentioned in a moment.

Apart from Ezekiel, books tend to have one constant spelling of this form. Genesis and Exodus use only the short spelling, Leviticus and Numbers only the long; Jeremiah with five cases uses only the long. Ezekiel is the main locus of variation; with eleven cases in all it has four of the short spelling and seven of the long. In it, all cases with waw consecutive (23^4 $34^{5,8}$) have the long spelling; but it is doubtful whether this is significant. In Samuel both cases are waw consecutive but they differ in spelling.

The example of *tihyena*, however, is not typical: there are few verbs that recur so often in the feminine plural of the imperfect. For most individual verbs, we have to be content with a run of a few examples, sporadically distributed. A few examples will be shown of verbs that have division of spelling in these feminines:

אמר 'say' has the short וַתֹּאמַרְןָ at Ex 1^{19} 2^{19} 1S 18^7 but the longer וַתֹּאמַרְנָה at Gn 31^{14} 1S 9^{12} Rt $1^{10,19}$ 4^{14}, and similarly, but not with waw consecutive, Ps 35^{10} Esth 1^{18}.

---

[1] Andersen and Forbes, p. 180, under Type 28, give the global figures as 41 defective and 301 plene.

זכר   'remember, mention', niphal, has תִּזָּכְרוּ at Ezk 3[20] but the spelling with he at Is 65[17] Ezk 18[24] 33[13,16].

ילד   'give birth', qal, has the short וַתֵּלֶדְן Gn 30[39] but the spelling with he at Jr 29[6] Ezk 23[4] תֵּלַדְנָה.

לבש   'wear' appears to have its only case תִּלְבַּשְׁן short at 2S 13[18].

מצא   'find' has its only imperfect תִּמְצֶאן short at Dt 31[21] and the imperative also short at Rt 1[9] וּמְצֶאן; none with he, but niphal with he Jr 50[20] תִּמָּצֶאינָה.

Some other verbs seem to have all cases written with he, so תִּקְרֶאנָה 'cry' (all cases in Ruth) except the imperative Rt 1[20], תַּעֲשֶׂינָה 'do, make', תַּעֲמֹדְנָה 'stand' (about six cases), תֹּאכַלְנָה 'eat' (four cases qal, including Gn 41[4,20], and four niphal, all in Jeremiah).

In this case, then, it is not very profitable to follow up the spellings within an individual verb, since by their nature they tend to be sporadic and to provide at best only short runs of examples. Another approach is to look at passages which contain a cluster of feminine plurals, imperfect and/or imperative, and count all instances together, whatever verb they belong to. Here are examples of such passages:

	Gn 19[33ff]	30[38ff]	33[6]	37[7]	41	Ex 1[17ff]	2[16ff]	Nu 27[1-2]
A ־ן	3	2	2	1	2	4	1	0
B ־נָה	0	2	0	1	9	0	4	2

	36[6-11]
A	0
B	3

	2S 1[20-24]	Is 3[16]	Jr 49[1-3]	Ezk 7	13[18-19]	16[50-56]	23[1-4]	34
A	0	0	0	2	0	2	0	1
B	3	3	5	3	5	4	3	9

	Rt 1[9ff]	4[14ff]
A	3	0
B	14	3

The most striking concentration on the shorter spelling is in Ex 1, the story of the Hebrew midwives; but its preference for the spelling without he is sharply reversed in the very next chapter, the story of the daughters of the priest of Midian. Genesis has several passages that prefer the short spelling but ch. 41, the story of the thin and fat cattle, strongly prefers the longer. The two Numbers passages cited use only the longer. Ezekiel has some passages which use a good proportion of the shorter, but others strongly prefer the longer. Ruth, a major locus for examples of this question, has in its first chapter three short spellings (1[9] וּמְצֶאןָ, 1[12] לֵכְןָ, 1[20] קְרֶאןָ) but the great majority are with he, and so all cases in the final passage 4[14ff].

Now, when we turn to our customary question, whether the spellings are merely graphic or whether they point to a difference of pronunciation and morphology at an earlier stage, we have some valuable additional evidence afforded in this case from within the Masoretic text itself. For, although the overwhelmingly dominant form is with *–na*, with final vowel, whether spelt one way or the other, we have some cases in the traditional text itself that end in *–an* or *–en* with no final vowel. Lamech tells his wives שְׁמַעַן 'listen', Gn 4[23], and not the normal שְׁמַעְנָה or שְׁמַעַן (in fact, apart from this case, all writings of this verb are with he, imperative Is 32[9] Jr 9[19] and imperfect Is 30[21] Mi 6[1] Ps 92[12]); and the priest of Midian says to his daughters קְרֶאןָ לוֹ Ex 2[20] (normal would be קְרֶאןָ, קְרֶאנָה cf. GK § 46f, p. 125). In these cases, then, the spelling that ends in nun indicates a termination *–an* or *–en*, and no final *a* vowel at all, whether marked by a vowel letter or not. This makes it quite plausible that in many other cases there had been the same kind of pronunciation, so that the words now written with ending ןָ had earlier ended with *–an* or *–en*. If so, taking the verb 'be', תהיין was *tihyen* and תהיינה was *tihyena*: later tradition, and Masoretic pointing, superimposed the latter upon the former. The difficulties about graphic structure and about historical linguistics which were mentioned above in connection with *–ka* and *–ta* (above, pp. 120f.) are equally a problem for the feminine *–na*. Perhaps, then, there were in the older traditions two pronunciations, one as *–an* or *–en*, written with nun and no he, and one as *–na*, written with nun and he. Within the Bible text the latter gained dominance and the writing with ־נה is vastly more common; the other is a survival, occurring sporadically and with some particular verbs such as היה 'be'. Masoretic pointing imposed the dominant pronunciation upon all, except for the one or two exceptions like Gn 4[23] Ex 2[20].

It is not claimed that this account of the matter is necessarily the right one: I do not feel sure of it myself. But it forms a *reasonable* hypothesis for the understanding of this group of phenomena.[1] If it is right to suppose that the two spellings go back to two different pronunciations of this termination, then that has the effect of supporting the same supposition with regard to the commoner and

---

[1] Note that Andersen and Forbes, p. 181, speak also of 'evidence of a variant pronunciation' in the phenomenon *–na*.

more central terminations –*ka* and –*ta*. In any case, both ended up with the same type of structure: consonant plus final vowel in open syllable, –*ka*, –*ta* or –*na*. But in the spelling to which this syllable was attached, the two went in opposite ways. For –*ka* and –*ta* were, in overwhelming dominance, planted upon the spelling that had the one consonant alone, ךָ or תָ, giving ךָ and תָ. The longer spelling was sporadic and much less frequent: כָה or תָה. With the feminine –*na* things went the other way: the consonantal base upon which –*na* was planted was, in a great majority, the spelling with he, נָה.

From what has been said it follows that we cannot measure off the antiquity of texts in their origins from the data of such spellings. For we have made it probable that these very spellings were in movement during the transmission of the text. Exodus might, at an earlier stage, have had נָתַתָה consistently, or feminines in ן con- sistently; we have at present no way of knowing. And movement need not have been in one direction only; if there were later people who were convinced of the rightness of one mode of writing (and pronunciation?), then this can have been so earlier also. Since movement in both directions is possible, there is no way of extrapo- lating back to the 'original' from the contours of the text we have worked with.

16. Yod before suffixes

A plural noun with a following suffix commonly has, in certain forms, an –*e*– vowel, ṣere or segol, which is normally marked with yod: thus אֱלֹהֵיכֶם, בָּתֵּיכֶם. We may add that, less commonly, some- thing similar applies in the singular with nouns belonging to Lamed He roots such as מִקְנֶה 'cattle'. This yod, however, is some- times omitted. Thus for example Ps 134[2] יְדֵכֶם is pointed as plural but has no yod. Many examples of such writings will be found.

With second person singular masculine suffix the full ending is thus, with segol, ־יךָ, as in דְּבָרֶיךָ 'your words'. At Jr 38[22] we have רַגְלֶךָ without yod, and the plural verb fixes this as plural (or, more strictly, dual) 'your feet'. Mm 1267 lists examples of this writing; but it thereby indicates another problem, for the same form רַגְלֶךָ may be the pausal form of the singular, and in fact seems likely to be so in the other cases listed there. This means that the presence or absence of the yod, though commonly an indicator, is not necessar- ily or always an indicator as between singular and plural (dual). דְּרָכֶךָ is found thrice: Ex 33[13] Jos 1[8] Ps 119[37] (Mm 605). As pointed, this must be plural, but no yod is present; the three cited are three out of about twenty cases of this form in all.

Sporadic instances of this occur. An important case is עֵינֶךָ 'your eyes': concord, or analogy with use elsewhere, makes the dual very probable at cases like Dt 15[18] (where many manuscripts are said to have the yod, confirming that they read it as dual) 1K 8[29] (concord with פְּתֻחוֹת makes the dual certain) Is 37[17] Jb 14[3] (the dual is normal with the verb פקח). Some others among those listed by Mm 1145 may well be singular in pause.

Another word sometimes affected is רֵעַ or רֵעָה 'friend', where the position is complicated by the existence of what appear to be two forms of the base word itself. רֵעֵהוּ seems to be clearly plural at 1S 30[26] Jb 42[10], both without yod. Conversely, רֵעֶיךָ with yod seems to be singular at 2S 12[11] Pr 6[3].

The case of בִּדְרָכֶךָ Ps 119[37] was mentioned just above, and this leads us on to a further topic, for, so far as I have noticed, this long and majestic Psalm is one of the most important areas in the Bible for the kind of dilemma as between singular and plural that we have been discussing. For instance, the Psalm has twenty cases of *miṣwo-teka* 'your commandments', and all of them are written with yod before the suffix except 119[98] מִצְוֹתֶךָ; and the same spelling, with prefixed *min*, is found at Dn 9[5]. Since the waw of the –*ot* ending is in any case not written with waw (after the waw of the stem), it would be possible to suppose that Ps 119[98] was actually singular: other cases in the Psalm are mostly plural, but the singular מִצְוָתֶךָ occurs just before (119[96]), and concord makes clear that it is singular there. If it is taken as plural, however, it shows that this poem may omit the yod before the suffix, in the midst of a long run of the identical form. Again, the same poem has a number of cases of *d⁰bareka*, either 'your word' (pause form) or 'your words': grammatically, there is some doubt whether these are singular or plural, and textually there are often traditions which add a yod where our texts lack one, just as there are cases which have a yod in our text but others do not have it. And the KQ system may remove a yod which was present in the K, converting a case from plural to singular: cf. such cases as Ps 119[9,25,28,57,65,74,81,114,130,139,147,161].

Take a case like Ps 119[41] חַסְדֶךָ וִיבֹאֻנִי חֲסָדֶךָ. חַסְדֶךָ should not be a pausal form, for it has a conjunctive accent (Munaḥ). By its vocalization, and by concord with the preceding verb, it should be plural. If so, it is another case of omission of the yod before the suffix. On the other hand, all the other cases of חֶסֶד in this Psalm are singular, חַסְדֶךָ or חַסְדֶּךָ (Ps 119[64,76,88,124,149,159]). The proof of the plural at v. 41 depends on concord with the verb, but the plural form of the verb itself depends on the pointing, for its *u* vowel of the plural is not marked by a waw. So the two words could have been a phrase in the singular, later understood as plural but without altering the consonantal text which fitted the singular rather better.

There are several such cases in Ps 119. Another is Ps 119[175] וּמִשְׁפָּטֶךָ יַעְזְרֻנִי. By the Masoretic text מִשְׁפָּטֶךָ must be plural written without yod. The consonantal text would bear the understanding, however, that both subject and verb had been singular at an earlier stage, וּמִשְׁפָּטְךָ יַעְזְרֵנִי, and a plural reading tradition had been imposed upon this without alteration of the written text. Cf. similarly Ps 119[149] כְּמִשְׁפָּטֶךָ חַיֵּנִי and 119[156] כְּמִשְׁפָּטֶיךָ חַיֵּנִי.

Ps 37[6] is another instance of the same question.

Ps 119 is thus a very important case in its own right, for it is an excellent proving-ground for questions of textual transmission. It appears, moreover, to have a quite exceptional number of dilemmas or abnormalities of this kind, which suggest that this particular poem has had a peculiar history of transmission in exactly this respect.

Another case that has been handled in detail by the author elsewhere and need be discussed only briefly here is that of מִגְרָשׁ, usually understood as 'pasture lands' or the like.[1] In the lists of the Levitical cities in Joshua, a typical expression like 'Yattir with its pasture lands' is written וְאֶת־יַתִּר וְאֶת־מִגְרָשֶׁהָ, with no yod in the last of these words. The phrase in this form occurs no less than 49 times in Jos 21, and the yod is absent in every single case. In Chronicles, however, where more or less the same list is given, every single example is written מִגְרָשֶׁיהָ with yod. Nowhere else in the Bible have I come across a comparable steady and unbroken run of such a defective spelling as this has in Joshua. It is very probable that in Joshua the word was originally a singular, which in Masoretic Hebrew would have been written as מִגְרָשָׁה 'and its migrash'. By the time of Chronicles, however, probably as a result of semantic changes in the use of the term, the word had come to be understood as a plural and was so written. That plural use, and the accompanying pronunciation, then spread back into Joshua, but without affecting the consonantal writing, which continued to be without yods although these would have been normal for the plural. If this is correct, it confirms that such spellings when lacking yod could at an earlier stage have been singulars, so that this may have happened, though less systematically, in other cases.

---

[1] 'Migraš in the Old Testament', *JSS* 29, 1984, 15–31

Mention was made above of nouns associated with Lamed He roots such as מִקְנֶה 'cattle', מַחֲנֶה 'camp'. When these have suffixes, it is understood that a yod of the original root reappears before the suffix, thus: מִקְנֵיהֶם 'their cattle' (Gn 36[7]) or מַחֲנֶיךָ 'your camp' (Dt 23[15b]), producing an appearance like the ending of the plural in other words. Some (e.g. GK § 93*ss*, p. 273) seem to want to take many cases as being really plural, but it seems better to take them mainly as singular (so Bauer-Leander, pp. 584–5, § 73 c). For our purpose it does not matter too much in any case, for if they are singular they appear with a large number of yods like that other-wise attached to the plural, and if they are plural they present us with a striking number of absences of the yod that is otherwise normally there. Consider for example the occurrences in the Torah of מִקְנֶה 'cattle' with the suffixes –*kem* and –*hem*, taken together:

A מִקְנֵכֶם or Gn 34[23]   47[17b] Nu 31[9] Dt 3[19]
   מִקְנֵהֶם
   without yod
B מִקְנֵיכֶם or   36[7] 46[6] 47[16,16,17a]
   מִקְנֵיהֶם
   with yod

Fig. 50: *miqne* 'cattle', with suffixes –*kem* or –*hem*, all cases in the Torah

Four cases without the yod to five cases with it. Not surprising, one might hastily say, considering the well-known tendency to short spellings in the Torah. But that would be a rash conclusion: for the yod, whether it comes from the verbal stem or from an old plural termination, is the philologically prior form. The short spelling, without the yod, here seen to be well represented in the Torah, is the philologically secondary form. This will be signifi-cant for something else that will be seen later in this section.

Note similarly Dt 23[15a] מַחֲנֶךָ, only a few words before the spell-ing of the same word with yod already cited. With *mar'e* 'sight, aspect' we have writings like מַרְאֵיהֶם Ezk 1[16] which are probably grammatically singular, but without yod מַרְאֶה as in Lv 13[4,20,25]. (It appears to me that the spelling practice with some of these words depends on which of the *suffixes* is appended: the suffixes like –*hem* and –*kem* tend to have a yod, those like –*hu* and –*ha* tend not to have it, and in that sense it seems more dependent on the identity of the suffix than on the question whether the noun is singular or plural).

A common instance of this sort of variation, so common that it is little noticed, is that with the two prepositions אל and על. When combined with second and third person suffixes, these undergo a high degree of variation in spelling, and this is especially so with the form from אל with third person plural suffix, *'alehem*. In all, however, there are four different forms that have to be considered, and these, in their respective plene spellings, are: אֲלֵיכֶם, אֲלֵיהֶם, עֲלֵיהֶם, and עֲלֵיכֶם.

Let us begin with אל when combined with third person plural suffix, which is the most important of the series:

		Torah	Prophets	Writings
A	אֲלֵהֶם	86	29	16
B	אֲלֵיהֶם	17	about 121	11

Fig. 51: אל with third person plural suffix

Mm 250 gives the numbers of אֲלֵיהֶם plene, the minority spelling, in the Torah; Mm 1954 gives those of אֲלֵהֶם defective in the Prophets; for the Writings see Masora at Jb 29²⁴.

The great preponderance of the spelling without yod in the Torah is immediately evident. But the significance of this cannot be seen until we break it down as between the different books. For the essential thing to know is that Exodus, out of 25 examples, *never* uses the yod, but always writes אֲלֵהֶם. Exodus is thus the centre of the defective spelling of this form. Genesis has eight cases with yod as against over twenty without it; Leviticus has two with yod as against about thirteen; Numbers has four with yod as against about eighteen; and Deuteronomy, with nine cases in all, has three with yod and six without.

In the Prophets, as our table shows, the proportions are dramatically reversed, and the spelling with yod is much more common. The areas in which the spelling without yod occurs are: Joshua (two), Judges (six), Kings (thirteen), Ezekiel (seven), and Zc 1³.

For the Writings, it will be sufficient to give a list of the places where the shorter writing אֲלֵהֶם is to be found:
Jb 29²⁴ Qo 8¹⁴,¹⁴ Ezr 6²¹ 8²⁸ 10¹⁰ Ne 2¹⁷ 13²¹ 1C 19¹⁷ 2C 10⁵,⁷,⁹,¹⁰,¹⁴ 18⁵ 23¹⁴.

Notice the degree to which the short spelling, dominant in the Torah and exclusive in Exodus, is supported in the Writings, where all cases in Ezra, two out of three in Nehemiah, and eight out of twelve in Chronicles follow it (spellings with yod in Chronicles only 1C 12⁴¹ 2C 8¹¹ 14⁸ 24¹⁷). The short spellings of the Torah are allied to the usage of these late books. (Ne 13²¹ has yod in BHS but in some other texts lacks it and this fits with the Masora at Jb 29²⁴: 16 defective in the Writings).

Strangely, the picture changes when we move to the similar form *ªlekem*, with the second person suffix:

		Torah	Prophets	Writings
A	אֲלֵכֶם	6	–	–
B	אֲלֵיכֶם	19	38	4

Fig. 52: אל with second person plural suffix

The six cases written without yod are: Gn 42^{14} Ex $7^{4,9}$ Dt $1^{9,20,29}$. In Genesis this is one out of four; in Exodus two out of eight; Leviticus has three, all with yod, and Numbers two of the same; in Deuteronomy the three spellings without yod are the first three in the book, out of a total of eight.

Even more striking, perhaps, is the comparison with the similar forms from על 'upon'. For *ªlehem* 'upon them' the gross figures are: without yod, thirteen times in the Torah (Mm 675); with yod, 28 times in the Torah. All cases in the Prophets and Writings are עֲלֵיהֶם plene. A breakdown for the Torah may be of interest:

A	עֲלֵהֶם			45^{15} 47^{20}	^{14} 9^{19}	^{19} 16^{20}
B	עֲלֵיהֶם	Gn 14^{15} 18^{8} 31^{34} 42^{24}		Ex 5^{8}	14^{3} 15^{16}	
A		^{21}	32^{34} Lv 4^{20}		^{27} 7^{9}	^{26}
B	18^{11} 28^{9}		10^{17} Nu 4^{8}		$8^{7,21}$ 10^{34} $11^{17,25}$ ^{29}	
A		^{14}				
B	14^{9} $16^{17,18,19,29,33}$ 35^{6} Dt $7^{16,25}$ 9^{10} 27^{5}					

Fig. 53: על with third person plural suffix, all cases in the Torah

Thus Exodus, which consistently writes אֱלֵהֶם defective, with 25 examples, in עֲלֵהֶם / עֲלֵיהֶם is almost equally split, with six of the short spelling to five of the long. No sort of block distribution is evident. Exodus was writing, apparently, עֲלֵיהֶם plene on the same page on which he was writing אֲלֵהֶם defective, e.g. 5^{4} אֲלֵהֶם defective but 5^{8} עֲלֵיהֶם plene. The same was true of Genesis, which wrote עֲלֵיהֶם plene throughout its chapters up to ch. 42, and in 42^{24} wrote עֲלֵיהֶם plene, surrounded by the cases of אֲלֵהֶם defective in $42^{7,9,12,14,18,24,36}$ (42^{7} has both spellings in one verse). In Numbers, on the other hand, by contrast with Exodus, we see something more like a block spelling, and finally it settles down with that long spelling which then continues unaltered to the end of the Torah and indeed of the Bible.

As for the corresponding second person, עֲלֵכֶם defective occurs only once, Ex 12[13], as against about seventeen plene in the Torah and many more in other books. With the feminine plural suffixes, אֲלֵהֶן defective occurs at Ex 1[19] (contrast plene 1[17]); with עֲלֵהֶן, the short spelling is found at Lv 3[4,10,15], as against two plene in Exodus, two in Leviticus, one each in Numbers and Deuteronomy and five elsewhere.

The exact details of every form need not be pursued further; we have already come upon something that is very significant for our whole understanding of the concept that the Torah, and especially Exodus, is the centre of short spellings, at least of certain kinds of words. The preference of the Torah for אֲלֵהֶם without yod, and the absolute consistency of Exodus in that preference, is very striking. But it leads in a direction that to many might be surprising. For in this form surely it is the long spelling, the writing with yod, that has philological precedence: the yod was original, cf. forms like the Arabic 'ilayhim, and the shorter spelling, favoured in the Torah, is the philologically secondary spelling, produced through the reduction of the diphthong –ay– to the vowel e. This particular short spelling, then, is far from being an indicator of early date; and in the light of these considerations the support of it from Ezra, Nehemiah and Chronicles becomes significant.

Why then did Exodus, and the Torah, not favour the short spelling of אֲלֵכֶם with second person suffix, or of עֲלֵהֶם, in the same way? I have to answer that I do not know. A fair hypothesis however would be that, since the favoured אֲלֵהֶם was actually a secondary and reduced form, such forms came to be more favoured when they were very frequent. As our tables show, אֲלֵהֶם was, at least in the Torah, much more frequent than these other forms were. Alternatively, we have to speculate that there was an actual difference in pronunciation, the –ay– having remained a diphthong longer in the forms from אל: which is possible, for these phonological shifts did not take place, as used to be supposed, simultaneously and instantaneously in every word, but gradually and with different speed for different words. Or should we suppose that אֲלֵהֶם goes back to an earlier form that had a different vowel here altogether, not an e or ay vowel but perhaps an a vowel, which would naturally not be marked with a vowel letter? One must doubt if there is any philological support for such an idea. For the present the question must be left without further answer.

17. The vowel ṣere and the zone of non-varying spellings

The vowel ṣere is like the vowel o (holem) in one important respect: it comprises elements which, we know by historical philology, have descended from different earlier antecedents. Hebrew o contains elements which in an earlier stage were long ā, others that were the diphthong aw, and others again that probably were the short vowel u. Similarly ṣere contains within itself elements which in some earlier stage were the diphthong ay, and others that were the short vowel i — perhaps others too, but these at least. This is an important structural similarity between these two vowels, but there is an equally important difference. The spellings that apply to o vary over a wider range than the spellings that apply to e. Thus a noun like קוֹל which may well derive from the diphthong aw is normally spelt with waw, but it can be spelt קֹל without waw, and when this is so it has the same spelling as a word like חֹק 'statute' which derives from short u. A qal participle like שֹׁמֵר in all probability has a first vowel that derives from an older long ā, but the actual spelling is the same as that of the vowel of חֹק. In other words, though the vowel o descends from these different earlier stages, the options of spelling do not definitely decide between one descent of the vowel and another.

With ṣere it is otherwise. Where words have a vowel descended from the diphthong ay, they are written with yod; where they are descended from the earlier short vowel i, they are written without yod. There may be some special and extra cases, and there may be some exceptions — we shall see that there are indeed. Nevertheless over a great mass of the vocabulary, including many very common and important words, a clear distinction applies, and applies both ways: one writes בֵּית 'house of', בֵּיתִי 'my house', אֵין 'there is not', all with yod wherever the e vowel is present. But, though the vowel is the same ṣere, one writes אֵם 'mother', בֵּן 'son', עֵץ 'tree', צֵל 'shadow', all without yod over hundreds of cases each.

On both sides a long list of such words can be given: with yod, in all e-containing forms, are written אֵיךְ 'how?', זֵית 'olive of', חֵיל 'force of', יֵין 'wine of', and similarly בֵּיצִים 'eggs' and other words. Without yod are written חֵן 'grace', חֵץ 'arrow', לֵב 'heart', עֵת 'time', קֵן 'nest', קֵץ 'time, end', שֵׁם 'name', שֵׁן 'tooth'. That the former come from an earlier ay diphthong can be seen from the presence in many of them of a consonantal yod in some forms, and from comparative evidence (e.g. Arabic bayt 'house'). That the vowel in many of the latter comes from a short vowel, commonly i, can be seen from suffixed forms like אִמִּי 'my mother', צִלּוֹ 'his shadow', where a short vowel in closed syllable reappears.

In words of these kinds that contain the vowel *sere*, then, we seem to have a fairly exact correlation between one particular spelling and one particular type of word. The clarity of this contrast is furnished by the fact that the spelling usual for one side is not permitted to range also over the other side (as, we saw, was the case with *o*). In that sense we have here something that we have seldom found in the course of this study, a zone of non-varying spelling. 'Shadow' is not found spelt as *צִיל, and 'my house' is not found written as *בְּתִי.

It is in the zone of unvarying spelling, such as we see here, that it is meaningful to speak of an 'orthography'. There is little sense in using the term 'orthography' where the word *tolᶜdot* can be spelt four different ways in one source within one book. The word 'orthography' is meaningful where the spelling of a given word is fixed and the differences of spelling can be read as differences in the word that is written. There is indeed, then, an orthography in the Hebrew Bible, and it applies over all that zone where the spelling is unvarying, or varies only in extremely rare and sporadic occasions. In the zone of variable spellings, which has been the subject of this study, there was no orthography, but a network of competing options.

On the other hand, where we have, as in this case, a very exact correlation between differences of spelling and differences of types of words, it is extremely likely that the difference of spelling has its basis in a difference of pronunciation. The vowel in a word like בֵּית was, at the time when the basic text was formed, a different vowel from the vowel in צֵל, even if the Masoretes later came to classify them and mark them as the same vowel. This is not controversial; probably everyone accepts that it is so. Because the pronunciation was different, scribes were little tempted to confuse the two spellings; later, when the pronunciation had become the same, the fixation of the text prevented anything more than very occasional shifts across the dividing line.

It is in a case like this, where we have a constant, a spelling structure that corresponds consistently with a verbal type, that we can be sure of identifying something in the language of the earlier stages of the text that is different from the language of its later stages. This is something that reappears several times in this present study and is basic to its philosophy.

———————

Not that there are no exceptions; there are some, and of several kinds. Some of them are rather like the long spellings of *e* that are well known from Qumran: Dt 25⁷ מֵאֵין 'he refused'; Dt 33¹² כְּתֵיפָיו 'his shoulders', apparently an error of printing in BHS, since the manuscript does not have it, but at least a sign of how such spellings could arise; Jos 9¹¹ זְקֵינֵינוּ 'our elders', certainly an abnormal spelling by our standards but recognized and catalogued by the Masora (which couples and contrasts it with Ex 10⁹, which lacks the extra yod); Mi 1⁸ אֵילְכָה 'I will go' (the added yod induced, perhaps, by the immediately preceding אֵילִילָה?); Jb 6²⁷ רֵיעֲכֶם 'your friend' (could this be a mere mistake, where רֵעֵיכֶם 'your friends' was intended, but the yod put in the wrong place and the form then diagnosed and vocalized as singular?); certainly 2C 5² יַקְהֵיל, where the Chronicles text has followed its common policy of using a longer spelling than Kings to the point where it produces an anomalous spelling in place of 1K 8¹ יַקְהֵל; or did Chronicles have a straight imperfect here rather than a jussive, and if so perhaps Kings had the same, spelt short?

Such are a few examples, and doubtless there are more; some possible cases will be mentioned below. But, even when put at its highest, the number of such spellings is very small indeed, so small that they hardly enter into our calculations for the proportions of one spelling or another. They are highly sporadic and very occasional anomalies. Most scholars will judge them, doubtless rightly, to be very late last-minute intrusions of something like the Dead Sea Scroll style of writing. They are not sufficient in number to alter the recognition that we have just reached, the recognition of a zone of virtually non-varying spellings. On the other hand they are significant as indications that, by the time these spellings were written, the spelling with yod had already become a spelling of the vowel *e*, and was definitely not the sign of a diphthong.

For this is a central question in this type of word. Where yod is written, as in בֵּיתִי 'my house', is this because it was still *bayti* with the diphthong (which separated it from the type of צֵל 'shadow' which had no yod), or was it because it was a long vowel, *bētī*, which was different in this respect from the short vowel, as it then was, in *ṣil* 'shadow' (later to develop into *ṣel*)? The question is a rather difficult one.[1] It affects a number of questions in the history of the text, and some further evidence bearing upon it will be presented shortly.

---

[1] Cf. D.N. Freedman in *Textus* 2, 1962, pp. 95f., where he seems to be uncertain as between the two possibilities.

The importance of these considerations is illustrated when we go on to consider another group of forms. There are a number of feminine nouns of the pattern of בְּרֵכָה 'pool', טְרֵפָה 'carrion', שְׁפֵלָה 'low hills', שְׂרֵפָה 'burning'. These are not infrequent words, and familiar. In all the cases cited, the second vowel is written without yod, and it would be assumed that this is the normal pattern. But in the word for 'darkness' Ps 139[12] has the form with yod, חֲשֵׁיכָה: perhaps another sign of the very occasional late spelling? And it is somewhat more serious with Ashera, the name of a female deity or of a cult object like a tree, for there, out of a total of 40 cases, we have in the singular 2K 17[16] אֲשֵׁירָה and in the plural Mi 5[13] אֲשֵׁירֶיךָ and Dt 7[5] וַאֲשֵׁירֵהֶם. This last is doubly peculiar, for it puts in the anomalous yod in the middle syllable and leaves out the yod, normally present, that precedes the suffix: it may perhaps be judged a case where a yod was added to a form previously without yod, and it was simply put in the wrong place in the word. But, even so, there remains a significant outcrop of yods in this particular word. I have no particular suggestion to offer.

In the case of p^eleṭa 'remnant', on the other hand, I do have. This word appears at first sight to belong to the same pattern. But its spelling patterns are markedly different. There seem to be 28 cases. The spelling with yod is massively favoured: there are only three cases out of 28 without the yod, Ex 10[5] Ezk 14[22] 1C 4[43]. Two in Genesis are with yod, which is thus the majority spelling in the Torah. Moreover, the plural noun p^eleṭim has a spelling with yod at Nu 21[29] Is 66[19], two out of the total of five of this form.

The contrast in spelling pattern, as against words like בְּרֵכָה and טְרֵפָה, is unmistakeable. One cannot doubt what must be the natural interpretation: פְּלֵיטָה must go back to a form of the diminutive type qutailat, and meant 'small remnant' or the like.

But this, if it is right, immediately shows that the spelling of the text preserved something that had been lost from distinctiveness in the Masoretic morphology, something that must have gone back a considerable distance in time. On the other hand, if it is right, it means again something that we must touch upon several times: that the form as written in the short-spelling book of Exodus is the philologically secondary form.

We have now to open up the question a little more by adding some further evidence. We began by contrasting two types, e derived from ay which is written with yod, and e derived from short i which is never written with yod, or only in very occasional and isolated places. There are some words, which have perhaps come from a different type of root or have developed by a different track, and which, when they have an *e* vowel, pass back and forward across the divide between spelling with yod and spelling without yod. Such words often look as if they have a background in a root with *w* rather than in one with *y*. Thus *ḥel* 'rampart' is spelt with yod at Na 3⁸ Ps 48²⁴ 122⁷ but חֵל without yod at 2S 20¹⁵ 1K 21²³ Is 26¹ Ob 20 La 2⁸; Zc 9⁴ could be a case with yod, or could be from חַיִל 'force'. By contrast with חֵל 'rampart', all the *e*-containing forms of חַיִל 'force' are spelt with yod, the normal pattern.

Again, חֵיק 'bosom' is normally spelt thus with yod (about 35 times) but is found without it in Pr 21¹⁴ בְּחֵק, Jb 19²⁷ בְּחֵקִי, and at Pr 17²³ the Masora requires מֵחֵק though Leningradensis writes מֵחֵיק against it. These are two out of the five cases in Proverbs, and the only case of this word in Job. In other similar words we have occasional unusual spellings, e.g. 2C 2¹⁶ גֵּירִים, 2S 22²⁹ נֵירִי 'my light', on which cf. p. 173.

More significant still are examples that recur more regularly and also appear in more central portions of the Bible. Consider the case of *ṣeda* 'food for journey', where the masculine noun form is צַיִד, which might look like a root with yod in it, but the verb has the form צוּד which suggests rather a root with waw.

A צֵדָה	42²⁵ 45²¹ Ex 12³⁹		Jud 7⁸ 20¹⁰
B צֵידָה	(Gn 27³ K)	Jos 1¹¹ 9¹¹	
B	1S 22¹⁰ Ps 78²⁵		

Fig. 54: *ṣeda* 'food for journey', all cases in the Bible

(Gn 27³ has Q צַיִד; Jos 1¹¹ is without yod in some texts.) The two spellings occur roughly the same number of times, and the Torah supports the spelling without yod.

A similar case is that of the measure 'ephah': this is usually spelt אֵיפָה with yod but the short spelling הָאֵפָה is found at Lv 5¹¹ 6¹³, two out of the three cases in this book; the total in the Torah is eight (incidentally, Ex 16³⁶ is also defective in some texts). Thus there are two, possibly three, exceptions, out of eight in the Torah and out of forty occurrences in all. The ratio within the Torah is particularly to be taken seriously. It is of interest, in addition, that this word is understood to be from Egyptian *aypat,[1] which might lead us to expect a consonantal yod; the LXX recognized it correctly and ren-

---

[1] Cf. J. Černy, *Coptic Etymological Dictionary* (Cambridge, 1976), p. 121.

dered with οιφι, the (Copticizing) Greek form still in use in Egypt in their time.

Again, 'ema 'terror', clearly with yod in the root (cf. the adjective אָיֹם 'terrible'), appears as אֲמָתְךָ, אֵמָתוֹ without yod in Jb 13²¹ 9³⁴, cf. אֲמָתִי Jb 33⁷ and אֵמִים Jb 20²⁵. Job has two cases without suffix, אֵימָה plene, Jb 39²⁰ 41⁶. There is also Ps 88¹⁶ אֵמֶיךָ. Apart from these there are about ten cases of this word, all spelt with yod. It looks as if affix effect allowed the yods to be omitted: but this could be so only if they were not still consonantal. We may add the tribal term 'Emim', thrice in the Torah, with yod at Gn 14⁵ and without at Dt 2¹⁰,¹¹.[1]

A word that is rather frequent, though only within one rather narrow context, is the term 'elam (or 'ulam), used for a part of Eze-kiel's temple. The form in Kings is אוּלָם, אֻלָם with u vowel; in Ezk 40 it occurs about sixteen times: thrice אֵילָם with yod, thirteen times אֵלָם without yod. The LXX dealt with this word by translit-erating it as αιλαμ. The spellings with yod, as in BHS (for there is much variation in this respect), are at Ezk 40²²,²⁴,²⁵. In any case it looks very much as if the two Hebrew writings are different spell-ings of what must have been one and the same pronunciation.

A small example: the word for 'marble' seems certainly to have yod in the root, as seen from the form שַׁיִשׁ (1C 29²); but the same word, absolute without suffix, occurs with e vowel and without yod, שֵׁשׁ Ct 5¹⁵ Est 1⁶,⁶.

Some of these words, though apparently having a yod in the root in the more proximate sense, seem to be connected more remotely with forms with u or w, and this may be the reason why their spelling varies more freely. By contrast, עַיִן 'eye' is a clear root with yod, and is written with its yod in a very large number of forms: but nevertheless Is 3⁸ gives us a solitary case of עֵנֵי 'the eyes of'.

A more broadly evidenced case concerns words of the roots אֵל and אַיִל. It is general practice to use the short spelling אֵל for 'God' and also for the homographic אֵל understood to mean 'power' in the phrase יֶשׁ־לְאֵל יָדִי; on the other hand there is a series of words of the form אַיִל (or a series of different meanings of the one word), and this generates the normal form אֵיל in the construct and before suffixes. BDB (pp. 17ff.) distinguishes at least four such words: 1. 'ram', 2. 'pillar, pilaster'; 3. 'leader, chief'; 4. 'terebinth' — and to these we may add the place-name Elim, doubtless derived from 4., and al-

---

[1] On these, plus some other cases specially relevant for the usage of Job, see my remarks in *JSS* 30, 1985, 23–27.

ways spelt אֵילִם; and with it also perhaps the other place-name Elath, Eloth.

The general practice with these words is clear, as stated above; but there are exceptions. 'Rams' are אֵלִם, without yod of the first syllable, at 2C 29²², and so also according to a wide manuscript tradition at 1C 29²¹, where however the Leningrad Codex spells אֵילִם against its own Masora, while at Ex 36¹⁹ it has אֵלִם, also against the Masora (Mm 879). These details do not have to be decided fully, but it is clear that there is *some* evidence that 'rams' were written without yod of the root syllable.

At Ps 29¹ we have the invocation:

הָבוּ לַיהוה בְּנֵי אֵלִים

and it is well known that the LXX offers a double translation of the line, taking the word אֵלִים first as 'gods' and therefore as subject; and secondly as 'rams', and therefore as the object to be offered:

ἐνέγκατε τῷ κυρίῳ, υἱοὶ θεοῦ
ἐνέγκατε τῷ κυρίῳ υἱοὺς κριῶν

The understanding as 'rams', whether literal or figurative, was not uncommon: the Syriac so translates it, and the spelling אֵלִים in some Hebrew manuscripts may reflect the same understanding. Doubtless the word was really 'God': but it was possible to understand it as 'rams' because that was a possible reading of אֵלִם, and one confirmed at least at one place in the Masoretic text. We may add that, among the cases of *'elim* meaning trees of a certain kind, Is 57⁵ בָּאֵלִים is also without the essential yod. A crossing of the boundaries between the spellings of these words was not extremely rare. This happens also with the place-name Elath, Eloth: the spelling with yod in the first syllable is found at Dt 2⁸ and several places in Kings, but 1K 9²⁶ has אֵלוֹת, omitting this yod, and 2K 16⁶ and Chronicles write אֵילוֹת.

We need not extend the evidence further. Other materials which can also be conjoined with our discussion of the vowel *sere* will be found in the sections on yod before plural suffixes, and in particular after prepositions as in אֲלֵהֶם, and in the section on Pe Yod verbs (see pp. 93–97). To the examples given on pp. 96f. we may add one or two more: מֵיתָר 'cord' is always thus with yod, but מֵשָׁרִים without yod occurs once, in some texts at least, Pr 1³, the first of five in Proverbs and one out of a total of nineteen in the Bible. The name Mephaath is מֵיפַעַת with yod at Jr 48²¹ Q 1C 6⁶⁴ but מֵפַעַת in Jos 13¹⁸.

To sum up, then, where the Masoretic vowel is *sere*, there is a fair amount of passage to and fro between writing with yod and writing of the same form without yod. On the other hand, the extent of this alternation is very slight in comparison with the very great solidity of a multitude of terms in the one spelling or the other.

But the very idea of this solidity could have been a cause of misunderstanding. One might form, let us say, the firm idea that 'between' was always בֵּין with yod, and 'son' was always בֶּן without yod — exactly the idea that most readers of Hebrew have to the present day. But suppose one then comes across a text where 'between' is actually the meaning but the word is nevertheless written as בן. If the context admitted of ambiguity, the text might then be misunderstood and thereafter transmitted incorrectly. In my own article about בֵּין 'between'[1] I called attention to two cases where this may have happened: these have been noticed, indeed, before, but not used in quite the same connection. The first is Jb 16[21]:

וְיוֹכַח לְגֶבֶר עִם־אֱלוֹהַּ   וּבֶן־אָדָם לְרֵעֵהוּ

At first sight this looks, in the latter part of the verse, like the familiar phrase 'son of man'. But good sense and syntax are provided if we understand it as 'between a man and his fellow', and that is the probable meaning. Many scholars have therefore proposed to alter the text to read וּבֵין: so already Gesenius-Buhl, p. 94b, and recently also NEB. The alteration in this mode, however, is misguided. There is reason for the alteration only if one supposes that, in order to be the word for 'between', the form must be written with yod; but what we are saying is that the practice of writing was, in this case, different from the convention to which we are accustomed, so that בן *was* in fact the writing for 'between'. But the reading tradition, misguided by that same convention, took it that בן without yod must be 'son' and vocalized the form accordingly. Some Hebrew manuscripts, however, did have the word as וּבֵין, which shows the correct understanding. In a case of this kind, it is one's very conviction that one knows the spelling conventions that causes the misunderstanding and consequent textual error.

The same is likely at Hos 13[15] בֶּן אַחִים יַפְרִיא. Whatever the general meaning of the sentence, it is very probable that 'between' is meant; and in fact many printed editions already had it as בֵּין, and still earlier the LXX had it so: ἀνὰ μέσον ἀδελφῶν. But, given the reading בֶּן of the better manuscripts, it was easy to take it as 'son', as the Targum seems to do: 'they are called sons'.

The examples suggest, then, that the defective spelling of *ben* 'between' may have existed, perhaps more extensively than we

---

[1] In *JSS* 23, 1978, 1–22, especially p. 12.

imagine, and that ignorance of its existence caused troubles in the textual tradition afterwards.[1]

This question will not be followed up further here, but cf. again below, pp. 208f.. Put simply, one's convictions about the spelling possibilities are a potential cause for distortion of the text whenever an older stage of text uses spellings that are not envisaged by these convictions. I took the matter up at this point because in the question of the vowel *sere* these convictions are likely to be very clear and very strong.

It will be convenient at this point to introduce another consideration. Given that, as we have seen, there is a high (though not an absolute) degree of fixity in the separation that Hebrew spelling makes between *sere* spelt with yod and *sere* spelt without yod, may this help us to find a historical dating for the periods represented by that distinction on the one hand, and on the other by the rise of the common vowel *sere* which came to be applied indifferently to them both?

Some suggestion may be found in the spellings of Hebrew place-names in the Septuagint.[2] Places are named as Βαιθηλ 'Bethel', Βαιθλεεμ 'Bethlehem', Αιλων 'Elon' and the like. The New Testament, however, spells these same words with η, e.g. Βηθλεεμ, Βηθσαιδα, and Josephus does the same with places mentioned in his accounts of his own time, e.g. Βηθαραμαθα, Βηθηλα, sometimes with epsilon, Βεθζαχαρια (BJ ii.59, iv.551, i.41). A similar sort of transliteration is found also in nouns that are not proper names, such as the words for parts of Ezekiel's temple: here אֵילָיו is transliterated as αιλευ, אֵלַמָּיו as αιλαμμω, repeatedly (e.g. Ezk 40^{29}). We have also referred to the transliteration of אֵיפָה 'ephah' with οιφι: since this was the regular Greek form, it does not prove that the Hebrew word was then pronounced with a diphthong *ay*, but it does leave that possibility open, and the similarity of sound would in that case make the rendering more natural and appropriate. The LXX transliteration fits in with some contemporary spellings in Greek, e.g. βαιτιανατα 'Baitianata', *Corpus Papyrorum Judaicarum* i. 2a (259 B.C.) (p. 122).

It may be thought probable that the diphthong *ay* was turning to *e* during the period of the last two hundred years from 250 BC or so, and its merger with the vowel *e* deriving from *i* took place in the

---

[1] On the above examples, see my article on בֵּין in *JSS* 23, 1978, 12.

[2] Within the LXX tradition, however, there are uncertainties. Bethlehem, for instance, is frequently Βαιθλεεμ in important manuscripts of Ruth, but seems to be Βηθλεεμ at Gn 48^7. See J.W. Wevers, *Text History of the Greek Genesis*, 1974, p. 217.

same time, the latter being marked by the rise of long spellings, with yod, in the Dead Sea Scrolls. This seems probable but we do not insist upon it and it is not essential for the rest of our argument.

A more far-reaching question concerns the relation between diphthongs and spelling practices in general. Not only in this section, but elsewhere in this book, we are finding cases where the very short spellings, such as some of those most typified in Exodus, seem also to fit with the form that is philologically secondary. For example, if we take a case from p. 141 above, if פְּלֵיטָה came from an older *pulaiṭa* or the like, does it not seem strange that the spelling with yod, פְּלֵיטָה, fits with that older linguistic form, and the shorter spelling of Exodus, פְּלֵטָה, fits with the later *p*ᵉ*leṭa*? Is it not peculiar that Exodus, which has so many short spellings that look very old, should also in a case like this have a short spelling that seems to be secondary in comparison with other spellings of the same word within the biblical text? The question is particularly obvious, of course, with the preposition plus suffix אֲלֵהֶם (see pp. 135ff.).

The answer to this must lie in a general, almost a philosophical, question of one's linguistic approach. It may be suspected that the tradition of Hebraic and Semitic studies in this respect has been overinfluenced by its own attention to the writing system. People often talk as if the *y* of the element *ay* is a consonant in a completely objective solid and tangible sense. This is no doubt because the letter yod is a written sign and is deemed to be a consonantal sign. But in fact, phonetically and acoustically, there is no absolute and objective difference between the sound of the 'vowel' *i* and that of the 'consonant' *y* (and similarly with *u* and *w*). The difference depends on language structure — to oversimplify a lot. As Abercrombie puts it, an element like the *y* in English *yet*, or the *w* in English *wet*, is 'a semivowel being a segment which defined by phonetic form is a vowel, but by phonological function is a C element [i.e. a consonant within a structure like CVC for a syllable] in a syllable pattern'.[1] Phonetically, a diphthong is a vowel: 'a vowel of continually changing quality' is Abercrombie's definition.[2] No one ever thought it otherwise, except for Hebraists with their minds dominated by the 'consonantal' character of the Hebrew alphabet. The *ay* of a form like *bayt* or *bait* 'house' (whichever way we write it in English) is as much a vowel as the *e* of a form like *bet*. The fact that the former is indicated by the presence of a yod is not because of an

---

[1] D. Abercrombie, *Elements of General Phonetics* (Edinburgh, 1967), p. 79, and see his discussion generally, e.g. on pp. 38–41, 60, 70–88.
[2] Abercrombie, p. 67.

essential phonetic difference, but because of another question, namely, what structural characteristics are held to be relevant for the use or non-use of the letters *y* or *w*. And in fact, of course, as we have been saying at some length, it is normal practice in Hebrew to write *bet* 'house of' (construct) with yod, just as we write *bayit* 'house' (absolute) with yod.[1] Thus, and this is the important point, the question whether there was a diphthong *ay* or the vowel *e* is not the same question as the question whether a yod was written or not.

This is of importance because, if it is right, it means that the passage from spelling without yod to spelling with yod can be understood as a shift in convention. It is not necessarily a phonetic change, but a change in the way in which the same phonetic reality is assessed for representation in writing. Very early portions of the Bible may well have been written in a script similar in style to the Phoenician, which is usually described as 'purely consonantal'[2]; and this would be not unlike some of the short spellings we find here and there in the Bible. The Phoenicians wrote 'house' as בת; it is usually said that they pronounced it as *bēt*, but of course a Greek form like βαίτυλος from Philo of Byblos suggests a diphthong here, and at quite a late date.[3] Whatever was historically right, we are mistaken in thinking that there is some structural reason, or some reason in principle, why they could not have written it in this way while pronouncing as *bait*: the diphthong was a vowel, which they did not represent in writing, while they wrote the consonants *b* and *t*. The same could have been done in Hebrew. The *i* component of the vowel was there but was not represented in writing. Later analysis marked this *i* component with the letter yod. This may well have happened before the vowel changed from the diphthong to the simple *e*, and independently of that shift; indeed, it is easier to understand if it took place while the *i* component was still audible. The whole thing was not at all occasioned by the monophthongization of the diphthong. Thus, although one does not doubt

---

[1] The presence of the consonantal yod in *bayit* is, after all, consequential on that (late) Hebrew development whereby a 'helping' vowel was introduced, as in *melek* 'king' and other words, which made the word into a disyllable and thus necessarily, by structural rules, *made* a consonantal yod appear here. The existence of this (necessarily written) yod then made scholars think that a 'consonantal' yod was intrinsic to the word altogether.

[2] Thus Freedman, *Textus* 2, p. 89, contemplates the 'Phoenician consonantal orthography' for the original writing of any poems written down in the age of David and Solomon.

[3] S. Segert, *Grammar of Phoenician and Punic* (Munich, 1976), p. 76, § 36.71–72.

that the form *bait* is, philologically, prior to the form *bet*, one can understand how a writing with yod could follow after, and develop out of, a writing without yod.

18. Some numerals, cardinal and ordinal

The numerals can be dealt with fairly briefly, and it is not necessary to go into all details. But they contain some features which may be surprising and also significant. Among the cardinals, only *three* and *eight* contain significant vowels of variable spelling. Numeral terms are generally of plentiful occurrence, and in many cases it is sufficient if we list the minority spellings.

The 'masculine' form of 'three', i.e. that which goes with feminine nouns, is in the absolute dominantly שָׁלֹשׁ defective. To this there are five exceptions in the Torah plus Prophets, Nu 22[32] Dt 16[16] 19[2] Ezk 41[6,22], plus the entire set in the Writings, all of which are שָׁלוֹשׁ plene without exception. Of the Torah cases, Nu 22[32] is in close juxtaposition with the identical phrase, שָׁלֹשׁ רְגָלִים, in Nu 22[28,33]; and Dt 19[2] is likewise followed by more or less the same phrase, but with שָׁלֹשׁ defective. Ezekiel has two with waw and two without. The plene spellings of the Writings include several each in Job, Proverbs, Esther and Daniel, and an ample series in Chronicles: in Chronicles the long spelling often corresponds to a short spelling in a parallel passage of Samuel and Kings.

The construct is שְׁלוֹשׁ plene only once, Ezk 40[11]. In it the Writings do not continue with the plene spelling normal in them for the absolute, for there are long runs of שְׁלֹשׁ defective in Ezra, Nehemiah and Chronicles, cf. also Esth 9[15]. This is one case, then, in which the construct state appears to favour a defective spelling.

The 'feminine' form, *š*e*loša*, has a different sort of distribution. It too is dominantly short, שְׁלֹשָׁה, but there is a series of exceptions (Mm 2959): Jos 15[14] 2S 14[27] Ezk 40[21] 48[31], plus twelve in Chronicles. In addition all cases in Esther are said to be with waw but by the text of BHS this is not correct for 9[17,18]; in any case Esther has plene dominant. Thus the position in the Writings is quite different from that which applied to *šaloš*: in it all cases in the Writings were with waw, while with *š*e*loša* considerable runs in Ezra-Nehemiah are all defective, and Chronicles itself is divided, for its twelve plene cases are much outnumbered by an even larger number of defective spellings. The construct form שְׁלֹשֶׁת seems to be thus spelt, short, in all its numerous cases in all books.

Finally we may mention 'thirty', another common form which

is steadily שְׁלֹשִׁים short, except for Esth 4[11] 1C 11[15,25] 2C 16[12]. The Esther case is the only one; the three plenes in Chronicles are only a small fraction of the total of this word there.

The number 'eight' has שְׁמוֹנָה plene in Jud 3[14] Jr 52[29] (this last is immediately followed by the short spelling of the same) and Ezk 40[31], along with all cases in Chronicles, which are about a dozen in number. Ezra and Nehemiah have four cases, but these are שְׁמֹנָה defective. In the other form, š^emona, there are again three plene spellings (2S 8[13] Ezk 40[41] Qo 11[2]) and once again all cases in Chronicles (see Masora at all these places). Ezra and Nehemiah have numerous examples, all without waw.

The distribution for the form meaning 'eighty' can be easily stated. Apart from Chronicles, there are six plene writings, שְׁמוֹנִים, Gn 5[26] Jud 3[30] 1K 6[1] 2K 19[35] Ps 90[10] Esth 1[4], out of a total of 28. Gn 5[26] is interesting, being one of a group of three (Gn 5[25,26,28]) which form the first appearance of this word in the Bible; the other two within the group are spelt short. 1K 5[29] (short) similarly alternates with 6[1] — interestingly, 6[1] is the verse that contains the key chronological statement of 480 years from Exodus to the commencement of the temple construction.[1] In Chronicles שְׁמוֹנִים plene is dominant, and there is only one case of שְׁמֹנִים short, 2C 2[17], which incidentally agrees with the phraseology as well as the spelling of 1K 5[29]; there are ten cases in Chronicles in all. Ezra, Nehemiah and the Song of Songs have the short spelling.

To sum up thus far, in these two number words we find a great preference for the short spelling in most of the Bible, with only sporadic exceptions, and on the other hand in some forms a strong preference for the long spellings, sometimes in all the Writings and often in Chronicles only. The dominance of the short שָׁלֹשׁ contrasts with the preference for long spelling in many nouns and adjectives of the same vowel pattern, e.g. כָּבוֹד 'honour', גָּדוֹל 'great'. In the construct שְׁלֹשׁ Ezra, Nehemiah and Chronicles strongly favour the short spelling. Particularly striking are the cases where Ezra and Nehemiah favour the short spelling as against Chronicles.

The ordinal numbers, however, are a greater surprise, because these are dominantly plene in spelling, and the main locus of defective spellings is — Chronicles!

Let us first take שְׁלִישִׁי 'third'. Mm 506 gives us a correct approximate picture of the situation: the short spelling שְׁלִשִׁי is found at Ex 19[11] 1S 17[13] 2S 3[3] and 'all Chronicles except seven'. In effect this

---

[1] On this see my article 'Why the World was created in 4004 BC: Archbishop Ussher and Biblical Chronology', *BJRUL* 67 (1984–5), 575–608.

means that Chronicles is the main source of the short spelling, for this book has about twelve of שְׁלִשִׁי short as against seven long.[1] The Torah has many examples, all שְׁלִישִׁי plene, except for the one case of Ex 19[11], the third of six in that book. The short spelling in Ex 19[11] is closely juxtaposed with plene spellings in the same chapter, 19[1,16], and indeed immediately follows a plene spelling only two or three words before, within the same verse. Here however there is a textual discrepancy, for BHS, correctly following its manuscript, prints the second phrase as plene, בַּיּוֹם הַשְּׁלִישִׁי, against its own Masora and a majority of other editions. Dothan prints the defective spelling but fails to note the fact in his Table of Manuscript Readings, so far as I can see. The older Kittel Biblia Hebraica printed the defective spelling and said in its note that it was so in the 'original text of Codex L', I do not know on what basis. Anyway, let us take it that Ex 19[11], in its second occurrence of our word, spells it short. Almost all cases, by the way, have the definite article. Samuel has two plene and two defective, and both the latter are וְהַשְּׁלִשִׁי with additional 'and', which might be significant. But the marked dominance of Chronicles as locus for the short spelling is the most striking fact.

The feminine forms, *šᵉlišit* etc., will be left aside for the present, and we will first of all pursue the masculine forms.

With 'fourth' the normal spelling is again רְבִיעִי with two yods, and the only exceptions (Mm 4113) are 1C 24[8] 26[11] 2C 20[26], three רְבִעִי out of about fourteen cases in Chronicles. The Torah has seven cases, all plene. 'Fourth' thus seems to have a markedly lower ratio of short spellings than 'third' has; its total number of occurrences is also lower.

'Fifth' likewise is dominantly long, חֲמִישִׁי, and the short spelling חֲמִשִׁי is found only at Ezk 20[1] Zc 7[3] (contrast plene 7[5]) 1C 12[11]. The case in Chronicles is one out of nine in the book.

'Sixth' is not relevant, but 'seventh' again produces an interesting pattern. This numeral has long runs in the Torah and in Ezra-Nehemiah-Chronicles, plus sufficient exemplification in the historical books, Jeremiah and the Minor Prophets. The dominant spelling throughout is שְׁבִיעִי plene. The exceptions are: שְׁבִעִי Ex 12[15] 16[30] Lv 25[9], plus 1C 2[15] 12[12] 24[10] 25[14] 2C 5[3]. All cases are with article. In the Torah, all cases in Genesis are plene, four in number; Ex 12[15] is the first in that book; 16[30] follows immediately after neighbouring plene writings (16[26,27,29]); Lv 25[9] is the last of a

---

[1] 1C 2[13] is plene in BHS, following the Leningrad Codex but contrary to Mm 506; Letteris, Snaith, have it defective; if this is so, the ratio is twelve to seven.

very long series in that book. Of the occurrences in Chronicles, the first four are the first four in that book, and all belong to genealogical material. 2C 5³ on the other hand is parallel to 1K 8², and uses the short spelling where Kings uses the long. In this word Chronicles is equally divided, having five short and five long. Ezra has two and Nehemiah three, all long.

By contrast 'eighth' is שְׁמִינִי plene in all sources, apparently without exception, and includes long runs in Leviticus and Chronicles (seven cases in the latter), four in Kings and so on.

'Ninth' is a much less common term than the other ordinals and occurs only eleven times in the masculine, again all with article. The dominant spelling is plene, and the three exceptions are: Jr 36⁹ Zc 7¹ 1C 24¹¹ (Mm 2670). This means one out of two in Jr 36 (36²² is plene), the one short in Zechariah as against two long in Haggai, and one short out of a total of four in Chronicles.

'Tenth' is also dominantly plene. It occurs nineteen times in all and is four times spelt short, עֲשִׂרִי: Jr 39¹ Ezk 29¹ 33²¹ 1C 24¹¹. At Ezk 29¹ the very word before is the doubly plene feminine עֲשִׂירִית. The Chronicles passage is one of four in this book. The six cases in the Torah are all plene.

The feminine forms, of the pattern šᵉlišit and the like, are largely used for fractions, 'the third part'. They will be treated together and briefly, to avoid excessive detail. It should be noted that there seem to be in this type of word an unusually large number of discrepancies between texts, made manifest by contradictions between Mandelkern and BHS. These words have four possible spellings, and all four are to be found. The most obvious point to comment on is the prominence, especially in the Torah but not only there, of spellings of the type of שְׁבִיעִת (Ex 23¹¹ Lv 23¹⁶ 25⁴,²⁰ Dt 15¹²), while for 'seventh' the non-Torah books almost always have the doubly plene שְׁבִיעִית (six cases, including Ne 10³², but שְׁבִעִית 1K 18⁴⁴ 2C 23¹). In 'tenth' the Torah has עֲשִׂרֹת Lv 5¹¹ 6¹³ Nu 5¹⁵, and so also Ezk 45¹¹; עֲשִׂרִית is found at Ex 16³⁶ Jr 32¹; the doubly plene עֲשִׂירִית at Nu 28⁵ Ezk 29¹. In 'fourth' Lv 23¹³ Nu 28⁵,⁷,¹⁴ have רְבִיעִת; Ex 29⁴⁰ Lv 19²⁴ Nu 15⁴ Ne 9³,³ have רְבִעִית; and Nu 15⁵ has רְבִיעִית. The other books, mainly Kings and Jeremiah, vary between the second and the third of these spellings. In 'fifth' we are surprised to find, out of ten cases in all, six with the doubly plene spelling חֲמִישִׁית: Gn 47²⁴ Lv 27¹⁵ 1K 14²⁵ Ezk 1² Ne 6⁵ 2C 12².

In 'eighth' and 'ninth' the only cases in the Torah are Lv 25²² שְׁמִינִת and Lv 25²² תְּשִׁיעֹת. In 'third' the Torah cases vary between שְׁלִשִׁת (Nu 28¹⁴ Dt 26¹²) and שְׁלִשִׁית (Nu 15⁶,⁷), while other books also vary, including a number of cases of the doubly long spelling.

A particularly interesting verse is 2S 18², which has two occurrences of הַשְּׁלִשִׁית followed by one of the doubly defective spelling
הַשְּׁלִשִׁת; another such doubly defective writing is וּבַשְּׁבִעִת Ex 21². In
this section I have followed the spellings of BHS throughout. It
will be noted that the pattern of spelling like עֲשִׂירְת, well represented in the Torah, has the same structure as we have observed in
the spelling of plural nouns and adjectives, such as תְּמִימִם, as seen
above, pp. 43, 45, 47.

It remains to make some general comments on the numerals.
The position of Chronicles is of particular interest. As has been
mentioned, its wide use of short spellings in some ordinals may be
connected with the presence of these numbers in genealogical texts
and other lists, something parallel to the presence of short spellings
of personal names and place-names in similar circumstances (see pp.
161–7). The implication would be that sources used by Chronicles had these short spellings and that they were just left untouched;
or, alternatively, that the later transmission of Chronicles, while it
introduced many longer spellings, was not much concerned to do
this in the genealogical sections. One could similarly account for
the short spellings like אָבֹת in the Torah, where plene spelling is
strongly dominant, as sporadic survivals from an earlier stage of
text. Striking again is the unanimity of Chronicles in spelling the
construct שְׁלֹשׁ without waw, when it is so definitely in favour of
the spelling with waw for the absolutes and also for 'thirty' and
'eighty'. This suggests a difference in pronunciation at the time,
which might be corroborated by forms like שְׁלָשְׁתָּם (e.g. Nu 12⁴)
with short *o* vowel.

A moment's consideration should be given, perhaps, to the possibility that the morphology of the numerals had not always been as
it is in the Masoretic text. The ordinals, in particular, follow a very
uniform pattern, which could suggest that the force of analogy had
succeeded in imposing this pattern on elements that were once
somewhat more different. For instance, in the case of the ordinal
'fifth' one might expect to see the form *ḥᵃmiššī* with double shin,
and this is actually found at 1K 6³¹ in some texts, e.g. Letteris, and
is cited by BDB.[1] But the main Masoretic tradition is to read as
ḥᵃmišī without dagesh. Short spellings like חמשי could be explained
as going back to such a form as *ḥᵃmiššī*, and would have the support

---

[1] Brockelmann, *Grundriss*, i, p. 491, seems to say that *ḥᵃmiššī* is the actual Hebrew
form, created by analogy and replacing the *ḥᵃmišī* that it would otherwise have been:
this is the reverse of the reality, unless one depends entirely on the (non-existent?)
dagesh at 1K 6³¹.

of the 'feminine' form חֲמִשָּׁה and the form for 'fifty'. On this basis, one might also ponder whether cases like 'third' and 'seventh' might have had different patterns at an earlier time. But the evidence does not go far enough to let us do more than hazard a thought of the possibility.

19. *Lo'* 'not'

Lo' 'not' is one of the most common words in the Bible, occurring about 5,200 times, about 515 of these in Jeremiah alone; and its spelling is overwhelmingly לֹא, defective — with, as we shall see, certain qualifications. For we have to look separately at *lo'* itself and at *lo'* in certain combinations, particularly that with the interrogative particle, *h*ᵃ-*lo'*, and similarly *b*ᵉ-*lo'*, *k*ᵉ-*lo'* and *l*ᵉ-*lo'*.

For *lo'* taken alone, the spelling is overwhelmingly short: לֹא; and the longer spelling לוֹא is said by the Masora to occur 35 times. This figure includes seven cases combined with *w*ᵉ-, וְלוֹא. The occurrences of לוֹא in these conditions seem to be:

Gn	Lv	Samuel	Kings	Is	Jr	Ezk	La	Total
1	1	2	5	1	22	2	1	35

In the books which have only a single case, the locations are: Gn 31^{35} Lv 5^1 Is 16^{14} La 1^{12}. Nothing can be easily divined from their positions within their books, for they are isolated cases within a sea of the shorter spelling. The Samuel cases are 1S 2^{24} 19^4, which also tells us little. In Kings the occurrences fall around the middle of the book, near the end of 1 Kings and the beginning of 2 Kings: 1K 18^5 20^8 22^{18} 2K 5^{17} 6^{12}. Nor does the position of the cases in Ezekiel tell us much: Ezk 16^{56} 24^{16}.

In Jeremiah something more can be told from the positions: the concentration of long spellings is clearly in the first part of the book. Eleven of them are in the first five chapters, six in the second five, and thereafter only 15^{7,11} 29^{23} 48^{27} 49^{20}. There is some textual disagreement at one or two places, such as Jr 5^{12,24}, but this will make at the most a difference of one or two to the figures either way.

One might add that, out of these 35 or so, a fairly large proportion are cases in which *lo'* is attached by maqqeph to either the preceding or the following word: so for instance 1S 2^{24} 1K 22^{18} 2K 5^{17} Jr 2^{31} 3^{12} 5^9 7^{28} 8^6 15^7; and of course some have *w*ᵉ- 'and' prefixed. These collocations might have something to do with the choice of spelling, especially in view of the decisively different distribution of *lo'* when collocated with the interrogative particle.

We see, then, that the long spelling לוֹא of *lo'* 'not' is of very small proportions in the biblical text: even in Jeremiah it is a very small fraction, and in the other books it is truly minuscule in dimensions.

When we turn to the combination h^a–*lo'*, however, we at once find a very different situation. Here we find complete books following one spelling with a consistency that we have seldom found in other words. Job and Chronicles use only הֲלֹא without exception, Judges is the same if Jud 8² is read as defective, and Psalms is the same with only one exception. On the other side, Samuel, one of the big users of the expression, has only the long spelling הֲלוֹא, and Jeremiah and the Minor Prophets are the same but with one or two exceptions only. Here then we have, at least in some books, something like a consistent spelling practice, something we have seldom found elsewhere: what is striking is that it operates thus on the combinations of *lo'*, which are not a very frequent or central expression, and that the consistent practice of one book contrasts so sharply with the consistent practice of another. The figures, broken down by books, seem to be:

	Gn	Ex	Nu	Dt	Jos	Jud	Sam	Kings	Is	Jr	Ezk	12P
הֲלֹא	5	3	6	3	1	14	0	25	6	2	8	1
הֲלוֹא	8	1	2	1	2	0	34	20	20	14	8	27

	Ps	Pr	Jb	Ru	Qo	Est	Ezr	Ne	Chr	Totals
	12	4	15	2	1	0	0	0	18	126
	1	1	0	2	0	1	1	3	0	146

Fig. 55: h^a–*lo'* 'is it not?', numbers for the different books

Minor differences in these figures should be allowed for, because of textual differences.[1] Jud 8² is plene in the Leningrad Codex and in BHS and Dothan, but since it is defective in the Aleppo Codex and in many other texts I have counted it so. If this is granted, it means that Judges joins Samuel and Chronicles in having complete uniformity in the spelling of this item. In Ezekiel, the BHS text divides seven to nine, but Ezk 17¹⁰ is plene in BHS against its own Masora, and the Masora states there are eight defective in the book. In the Minor Prophets, Zc 7⁶ is defective in some texts, and that would make a difference of one.

In several books the internal patterns deserve to be mentioned. In Genesis the first case, 4⁷, is plene, then follow the five defective;

---

[1] Cf. the treatment of the same by Andersen and Forbes, p. 187; I have been helped by the agreement of their table, apart from these small differences of text.

from 31^{15} to the end of the book all are with waw. In Exodus the one with waw is the last in the book, 33^{16}. In Numbers the two plene are the third and fourth, 14^3 22^{30}. In Deuteronomy the one plene is the second-last, 32^6. In this book we should just mention that there is one additional and peculiar case, 3^{11} הֵלֹה, which is defective in the sense of spelling without waw, but abnormal because it has he. Kings has many occurrences and a complicated pattern of distribution. Very roughly speaking, 1 Kings has frequent and abrupt variation; 2 Kings by contrast has something more like a block spelling: up to the end of ch. 13 it much prefers the plene and has a long series of it, broken by a short series of the defective in chs. 4–5; after the beginning of ch. 14 it greatly favours the defective spelling and has only two isolated examples of the plene. If we separate out the one phrase 'are they not written?', h^a-lo' hem (hemma) k^etubim, which furnishes no less than 29 of the occurrences of h^a-lo' (and which has been commented on in another connection elsewhere, see p. 114), this becomes even more clear: in 1 Kings we have much alternation, with seven defective spellings scattered in small groups among the four plene; but 2 Kings begins with a steady string of six plene, up to the end of ch. 13, while from the beginning of ch. 14 we have a solid line of eleven short, with only one single plene spelling ($2K$ 15^{21}; all this, incidentally, follows the text of BHS, and is altered somewhat with a text such as that implied by Mandelkern).

In Isaiah it is worthwhile to consider the division at the end of ch. 39. Up to this point, the book has four without waw and five with waw; after 40^1, the expression h^a-lo' is used much more freely, and the spelling with waw is much more dominant, there being only two without it, 44^8 and 57^{11}, as against fifteen with it. Jeremiah's two short spellings are at Jr 14^{22} 26^{19} (see Masora there). Ezekiel wavers: the book starts with one sole defective at 12^9, then follow a series plene, then from 18^{25} to 26^{15} a series of defective, five in number, interrupted by a solitary exception at 24^{25}; and the last three in the book are plene. In the Minor Prophets, Am 5^{20} is the second in the entire group, and the first in the book of Amos; others in Amos, and all in the rest of the series, are plene. In the Psalms the one long spelling is the last, Ps 139^{21}. In Ruth the four occurrences are located in two pairs: Rt $2^{8,9}$ both plene, $3^{1,2}$ both defective.

With b^e-lo' the distribution can be easily stated. There are six written בְּלוֹא with waw: Is $55^{1,1,2,2}$ Jr 2^{11} Qo 10^{11} (Mm 2458). This is out of a total of 31: six in the Torah, four in Isaiah, four in Jeremiah, one in Ezekiel, two in the Psalms, three in Proverbs, three in Job, two in Lamentations, two in Qohelet, and four in Chronicles.

These are in general similar proportions to the above, except that in this case Jeremiah seems to favour the short spelling more.

There is one case of k^e-lo', spelt כְּלוֹא (Ob 16), and ten of l^e-lo', of which only the first, Is 65[1], is spelt לְלוֹא. The long spellings in Isaiah and Obadiah fit in with the above, and so do defectives in Job and Chronicles; more surprising are two cases of לְלֹא defective, at Am 6[13] and Hos 2[25]. There are four instances of šello' 'that not', Ps 124[6] 129[7] Qo 2[21] 7[14], but none of these has waw.

To sum up the spelling tendencies of lo' 'not', it is true that sources around the beginning of the common era show large numbers of the plene spelling לוֹא.[1] But this is of little relevance, for the tendency to drift towards this spelling is, in the case of 'not' when taken alone, extremely slight and sporadic, even in Jeremiah where it is at its strongest. What is clear in the Masoretic text is the very drastic difference made when lo' is combined with a prefix other than w^e- 'and'. The natural interpretation of this is that it is a matter of change of stress. Perhaps lo' when alone had a sort of enclitic relationship, and was rather unstressed before the following verb or other negated word; but when prefixed by h^a- or other prefixes, it was much more emphasized, and this was, or was perceived as, a change in the character of the vowel such as to lead to a decisive or even universal preference for the plene spelling in the scribal tradition of some books. It is difficult to see that any other explanation can be equally satisfactory.

The main aspect that demands explanation lies in the unusually solid preference of some books for one spelling and of others for the opposite one. Some may think of a historical explanation for this: some books accepted revision of their spelling at a later time when the plene spelling was more general, others had already finalized their spelling before this time.[2] But this is far from persuasive. Will one really believe that the text of Samuel and the Minor Prophets — especially Samuel — was still being 'modernized' long after all such influences had been rejected by Chronicles? And, above all, why did the pressure to 'modernize' to the common late spelling לוֹא produce absolutely no cases of לוֹא alone in the Minor Prophets and only two out of two or three hundred in Samuel, and affected these books almost only, and with high consistency, in the combinations of lo' with prefixes?

---

[1] Cf. Andersen and Forbes, p. 188

[2] Andersen and Forbes, ibid., say that 'Chronicles has resisted the pressure to modernize; Samuel has succumbed completely', and conclude that 'it is reasonable to infer from this that Chronicles was written before this spelling came upon the scene'.

The fact is that the evidence does not point particularly towards historical change as a probable explanation, though it is not to be completely ruled out. Other explanations are more probable. One is that the change of stress occasioned by the prefixes attached to *lo'* was differently perceived by different groups, or assessed by some as of sufficient force to alter the character of the vowel, by others as not of sufficient such force. The other explanation is that this is a case where the force of standardization has been unusually effective. A scribal tradition could simply decide: for the purposes of this book, לא defective is the spelling — or the reverse. In many other words there might be too much variety and complication, but in this word standardization was comparatively easy. Samuel and the Twelve Prophets went one way, Judges, Psalms, Job and Chronicles went the other way. Kings wavered backward and forward but may have made some temporary efforts to standardize at certain points. The Torah showed plenty of variety, as so often (seventeen defective against twelve plene). That Chronicles, in particular, was capable of a strong standardization, and one strikingly contrary to the use of other books, is made plain also by the case of the personal name 'David' (cf. pp. 161, 165f.). We should note also the relatively high degree of uniformity in Chronicles in the spelling of the *o* vowel in other types of word, notably the plural ending *-ot*. To spell *lo'*, when with prefixes, the other way, was either the result of a different phonetic perception or that of a clear decision to standardize on a different sort of spelling for this word in particular.

20. Particle *'ot-* with pronoun suffixes attached

This matter will be treated briefly and in a simplified way, for a thorough investigation would be complicated and would take up much space. Firstly, readers will ask, are we talking about the definite object particle *'et* when suffixes are added to it? The answer is: is: yes, but not exactly. For, although by traditional grammar there is the object particle *'et* which, with suffixes, forms *'oti, 'otam* etc., and also the particle *'et* 'with' which forms *'itti, 'ittam* etc., things do not work out so clearly in practice, and there are numerous cases of *'oto, 'otanu*, and the like, which mean 'with him, us, etc.' For our present purpose these belong together: that is, if it has the *o* vowel, it belongs to the one form *'oto, 'otanu* etc., whether it is the object particle or a form of 'with'. The Masoretic lists mix the two up just as we shall do. Forms like *'itti* and the like do not belong to this question and can be ignored.

Next, readers may be warned that it is far from easy to obtain the correct facts about the spellings of these apparently minor words. Ginsburg in his edition of Levita (p. 150 n. 19) wrote that the plene writings of אוֹתָם were 'most confusingly enumerated in the Masora', and my own experience causes me to echo his judgement with feeling. Modern concordances tend not to list these small and numerous items properly, and their separating of those that belong to the object particle from those that belong to 'with' makes the task no easier.

The chief reason why these small and troublesome words should be mentioned at all is simple: like another small word, לֹא 'not', certain books show a drastic difference in usage as against certain others, so that we come a little closer once again to a sort of spelling policy for a particular book.

Thus with the first singular suffix the Masora (Mm 1238) gives us a count of 30 cases plene, אוֹתִי, plus all cases in Joshua and Judges except two (Jos 14^7 Jud 9^{15}) which are defective. Judges, as it happens, has eight cases of אוֹתִי plene against one defective. Along with Judges we note Jeremiah, which has thirteen plene against fifteen defective, and Ezekiel, which has five plene against thirteen defective. The Torah has none plene except Dt 32^{51}.

With the second person singular we will go into no further detail at this point except to say that Ezekiel is particularly notable for his use of the long spellings (see Mm 287, 541, 2565); a remark about the Torah will follow shortly.

In the third masculine singular, 'oto, special distinction attaches again to Judges, which in BHS has about sixteen plene against three or so defective. In the corresponding feminine (Mm 1009) the plene writing אוֹתָה is the dominant spelling in three books: Joshua, Judges and Ezekiel, in which there are only three defective spellings in all (Jos 8^{24} 18^5 Ezk 21^{16}). Joshua has about nine plene, Judges has ten, Ezekiel over twenty.

The third plural 'otam is a more common expression than the others, with well above 400 cases in all, nearer to 500. The Torah has an interesting pattern:

	Gn	Ex	Lv	Nu	Dt	Total
אֹתָם	30	57	41	35	20	183
אוֹתָם	4	2	9	12	12	39

The figure 39 for the plene spellings is in agreement with the Masora, but some latitude for text variations must be allowed here and there. In Genesis it is to be noted that the four plene spellings come at the end of the book: 41^8 49^{28,29} 50^{21}, so that in the last two

chapters of the book the plene spelling dominates. Exodus is dominantly defective and no particular significance can be seen in the
position of the two long spellings (Ex 14^9 29^3). In Leviticus the
plene spellings do not begin until ch. 10, by which time thirteen
defective spellings have been used. Numbers shows a rise in the
proportion of plene spellings and Deuteronomy carries the same
even farther.

Judges shows consistency here once more, and spells all occurrences אוֹתָם (18 times). Jeremiah is a voracious user of 'otam and
prefers the plene spelling by about 34 cases to sixteen, and Ezekiel
is the same, with about fifty plene and 25 defective.

We return to the position of the Torah in general. We saw that
with the first singular 'oti it was almost totally defective; and with
the third masculine singular it was solidly defective also. In the
third plural 'otam, however, though favouring the short spelling,
and especially so in Exodus, it shows an increasing liking for the
long spelling at the end of Genesis, and again as we move from the
middle of Leviticus towards the end of the Torah. To this we add
the second singular masculine, the Torah's position to which we
postponed from just above:

In the first person 'oti, as remarked above, the Torah was entirely
defective until one case in Deuteronomy, and this was particularly
noticeable in Genesis, which uses this particle a lot (23 cases). With
the second person masculine the position is suddenly reversed:

A	אֹתְךָ	Gn 7^1		28^3 30^{26,30}			41^{41} 45^{11}		23^{33}
B	אוֹתְךָ		17^2 20^6		40^{19} 41^{39}			Ex 9^{15}	
A			27^8						
B		25^{9,22}	32^{10}						

Fig. 56: 'ot^{e}ka in Genesis and Exodus

The contrast as against the spelling with other personal suffixes
is striking, and especially the preference of Exodus for the longer
spelling. I have no special explanation to offer for this.

In general, the matter of 'ot- with suffixes is interesting for some
striking permutations within the Torah, and for the strong preference of some books, especially Jeremiah and Ezekiel, for the plene
writings; and above all for the near-universal acceptance of a consistent spelling practice by one book, Judges, a book which also comes
close to the position of consistency with לא 'not', but there being as
consistently defective as it here is consistently plene. Chronicles
also seems to have consistent defective spelling in אֹתוֹ and אֹתָם,
being thus as consistent as Judges, but also consistent with its own

spelling policy with לֹא 'not'. The Torah is far from steady in its role as a short speller: it has, in addition to those mentioned above, two out of the dozen plene spellings of אוֹתָהּ (Nu 22³³ 30⁹) and one (Dt 6²³) of the first plural אוֹתָנוּ.

21. The spelling of some personal names and place names

For the student of spelling, much the most outstanding name in the Bible is that of David. For the name 'David' is one of the rather rare phenomena in which the books disagree with one another but come near to total inner consistency within themselves. A simple table will set out the essentials:

A דָּוִד — all cases in Samuel (some 575 in number), all or practically all in Psalms (about 90 — Ps 122⁵, plene in Leningradensis, should perhaps be defective, and if so the Psalms are unanimous), all in Kings (about 90 again) except three (1K 3¹⁴ 11⁴,³⁶), and all in Isaiah and Jeremiah (9 and 15, respectively); Ezekiel has one plene out of four (Ezk 34²³); also the one or two cases in Proverbs, Ruth and Qoheleth.

B דָּוִיד — all cases in Chronicles (well over 200), Ezra, Nehemiah, and the Minor Prophets with some doubt about Hos 3⁵; also Ct 4⁴.

This degree of consistency, coupled with the complete and drastic contrast between the two groups of books, is surely unparalleled in the entire field of biblical spelling.

Less unusual are the names which, though they might have varied, have one single spelling throughout, or one overwhelmingly frequent spelling with only very few exceptions. The very common מֹשֶׁה 'Moses', as has already been mentioned (p. 35 above), is never written with waw, though that would have seemed quite possible. Aaron, similarly, is always אַהֲרֹן in all books and in large numbers, although the ending -on could well be susceptible of variation and does vary in Arnon, Dibon, Hetzron, Sihon (see below). The same is true of Joseph, always written with waw: there is indeed one case of a spelling with added he, יְהוֹסֵף Ps 81⁶, but in respect of the presence or absence of waw, which is our central interest here, there is no variation; contrast the variety of spellings within the verb יסף itself (above, pp. 89f.). Moreover, this spelling is constant, not only in all cases of the patriarch Joseph, but also in all cases of the various other individuals who bear the same name.

Joshua is another of the same kind. Spelt יְהוֹשֻׁעַ over hundreds of cases, he is isolatedly written יְהוֹשׁוּעַ at Dt 3²¹ (the second of nine in that book) and at Jud 2⁷ᵇ, the third of a run of four within the space of three verses.

Jacob, similarly, is normally spelt without waw, יַעֲקֹב, and this is so over almost all of the 350 or so examples. It is a surprise, therefore, to find him written as יַעֲקוֹב in Lv 26⁴², the only case in that book, and the other four in Jeremiah, thus:

A יַעֲקֹב Jr 2⁴ 5²⁰ 10¹⁶,²⁵ 30⁷,¹⁰,¹⁰   31⁷,¹¹   46²⁷ ²⁸
B יַעֲקוֹב   30¹⁸   33²⁶   ²⁷ 51¹⁹

Fig. 57: the name 'Jacob', all cases in Jeremiah

Note that variation is confined to the latter part of the book; there is rapid alternation at 46²⁷.

Plenty of other names could be added that have the same spelling always: Lot is always plene, Noah and Nob always defective; Sodom is always סְדֹם; Edom is always long, אֱדוֹם, though some texts have a short spelling at Ezk 25¹⁴ᵃ; 'Amorite', אֱמֹרִי, with 86 cases, is invariably defective. Hebron and Heshbon are always only plene, though found in a variety of places. We should have added the name 'Saul', שָׁאוּל, always with waw over 400 or so instances, although qal passive participles, which have the same morphological form, vary quite often into the shorter spelling, e.g. Dt 32³⁴ כָּמֻס and חָתֻם.

These examples might lead one to suppose that the standardization of spelling had gone farther in personal and place names than in other words of potentially variable spelling. Unfortunately, however, we also have many cases of names in which a very high degree of variation is to be found: the case of Absalom was already displayed (p. 23 above).

A prominent case is the name Benjamin. It heavily prefers the shorter spelling, and there are only seventeen plene writings out of some 160 occurrences (Mm 262). Apart from Genesis, these plene writings are scattered in ones and twos through a variety of books, but in Genesis they are more concentrated and display a marked alternating pattern:

A בִּנְיָמִן   ²⁴   ³⁶   ¹⁵   ³⁴ 44¹²   ¹⁴,¹⁴ 46¹⁹,²¹
B בִּנְיָמִין Gn 35¹⁸ 42⁴ 43¹⁴ ¹⁶,²⁹   45¹²   ²⁷

Fig. 58: the name 'Benjamin', all cases in Genesis

Other Torah books than Genesis are entirely defective, and notably so Numbers, the only other with fairly frequent examples.

Might it be relevant that the Genesis cases are names of an individual person, while those in Numbers, like the long series in Judges, really concern a tribe or a geographical expression? (The one plene case in Judges, 5[14], is a stirring personal appeal.) Anyway, the word *yamin* 'right (hand)' is one of the most solidly plene of words, when apart from the name Benjamin, having apparently no cases at all without yod even when with following suffixes. The seemingly related name Mijamin has six cases in Ezra-Nehemiah-Chronicles and is equally divided between spellings with yod and those without.

Rapid alternation is still more notable with the name of Sihon, king of the Amorites, in the Torah, where we have:

A סִיחֹן Nu 21[21,23,23,26] [28] [34] 32[22] Dt 1[4] 2[24] [30,31,32] 3[2,6] 4[46]
B סִיחוֹן [27] [29] [26]

A 29[6]
B 31[4]

Fig. 59: the name 'Sihon', all cases in the Torah

In Numbers the alternation occurs at a point where a poem, doubtless ancient, is included within the narrative. It is not clear, however, what difference this may have made, since the name is spelt both ways within that poem. The poem also includes the names Arnon, Dibon and Heshbon, all of which have the same *-on* ending as Sihon. Heshbon is written with waw here and everywhere else; Arnon is without waw, though Numbers spells it with waw elsewhere (21[13,14], also 21[26] in some editions), and Dibon is here with waw, though Numbers writes it also without.

Zebulon has two spellings. In the Torah זְבוּלֻן, with waw in the central syllable, is dominant; the first three in Genesis, however, Gn 30[20] 35[23] 46[14], have the spelling with waw in the final syllable, זְבֻלוּן, a spelling that is used in all cases in the Writings except for one, 1C 27[19]. Judges is almost equally divided (three against four) and the Song of Deborah has one of each (5[14,18]); cf. Mm 218. The structure of the spelling זְבוּלֻן, dominant in the Torah, may be comparable to that of the many plurals like תְּמִימִם.

The place-name Tyre also has lively vicissitudes in its spelling. The dominant use is צֹר, short. Ezekiel, who uses this word a lot, varies as follows:

A צֹר Ezk 26[2,3,4,7] 27[2] 29[18]
B צוֹר [15] [3,3,8,32] 28[12]

Fig. 60: the name 'Tyre', in Ezekiel

Numerous other names in the narratives show substantial variation. The name ʿoreb, of a Midianite prince or a rock so named,
occurs four times in one verse, Jud 7²⁵, and is עֹרֵב short in the first
and last, עוֹרֵב long in the second and third. Gehazi in 2 Kings varies
back and forward. The common noun ʾeškol 'bunch of grapes' is in
the singular אֶשְׁכּוֹל plene, four times, including two in Numbers,
and only once defective (Ct 1¹⁴, paradoxically); the man Eshkol
who was an associate of Abraham is always spelt defective. But the
valley with the same name is twice defective and twice plene in the
Torah, Nu 13²³ Dt 1²⁴ and Nu 13²⁴ 32⁹, respectively (Mm 92).
Horeb is normally defective but once, surprisingly, plene, חוֹרֵב, at
Ex 33⁶. Zadok, often mentioned, is written short only at 1 K 1²⁶. It
would be tedious to heap up further examples. We pass on to one or
two more general comments.

The first such general point is that among names, taken very
generally, and especially when we look at the lists of names in the
genealogies and lists of places, that is, away from the main narratives and speeches, we find the presence of defective spellings, or
even their prevalence, such as in other words would be surprising.
A good first example is the place-name Debir, found in Joshua,
Judges and Chronicles. There are plene writings at Jud 1¹¹,¹¹ 1C
6⁴³ (though there may be textual variations here, for all these are
without yod in Mandelkern's registration), and also in the personal
name of 'Debir king of Eglon' at Jos 10³ (surely this must be a
mistake for Eglon king of Debir?). But all other cases, ten in
number, all in Joshua, are written as דְּבִר or (with local suffix) דְּבִרָה.
This degree of defective spelling is highly unusual for ordinary
words of the language: consider the common בְּרִית with its nigh-
universal yod, or other place-names such as כְּרִית Kerith, לָכִישׁ Lachish.

Moreover, consider the common noun dᵉbir, familiar as the term
for the inner sanctuary of Solomon's temple. There are sixteen
cases: eleven in Kings, four in Chronicles, one in Psalms (Ps 28²).
All of these alike are דְּבִיר plene (Mandelkern registers 1K 6¹⁶ as
defective). The difference from the place-name Debir is striking,
especially when Kings, often a locus for short spellings, spells long,
while Joshua, often a long-spelling book, spells short. Has there
not been some process under which proper nouns were transmitted
in a different way from common nouns?

For we can add many cases of the same sort of thing, often names
of otherwise unknown persons or places. Harim is invariably חָרִם:
eleven cases, mainly in Ezra and Nehemiah. Hashum, found five
times in these two books, is always חָשֻׁם defective. Yattir is יַתִּר

defective at Jos 21[14] 1S 30[27] 1C 6[42], and יְתִיר with yod only at Jos 15[48]. Assyria, אַשּׁוּר, is a common word, but only 1C 5[6], in the midst of genealogical material, has the short spelling אַשֻּׁר. Consider also such surprisingly short writings as: יְהוֹיָכֻן Jr 52[31], יאָב 1K 1[19], מאָב 2S 8[12], יאָשׁ 2C 24[1].

We should add, briefly, that spelling variation in names is found not only in typically Hebrew forms but also in foreign names and outlandish forms: Ziklag is normally צִקְלַג, but we have צִיקְלַג 1C 12[21]; conversely Phinehas is usually פִּינְחָס long, but without the yod only at 1S 1[3], the first of seven cases in Samuel referring to the son of Eli. Cyrus is כֹּרֶשׁ without waw only at Ezr 1[1b,2] (plene 1[1a]). Sennacherib is סַנְחֵרֹב without yod only at 2K 19[20].

There seems, then, to be a high proportion of short spellings in many personal and place-names. As has been seen, some really common names like Moses, Aaron, Jacob, have plene spelling rarely or never; Benjamin, though varying in spelling, heavily prefers the shorter, as does Sihon in the Torah. Places like Debir fit in with this trend. And the enormous solidity of Samuel, Psalms and some other books in the short spelling of David fits in with it also.

If we suppose that the text at an earlier stage used a larger degree of defective spelling, then a hypothesis like the following might fit the evidence. As the degree of plene spelling increased, many names might be left as they had been. Names could have a conservatism about them: the name was, perhaps, the name as it had been spelt for ages, and it should stay that way. Moreover, many names were buried in genealogical and geographical lists, and if they were there they were left untouched: hence the short spellings of names in Joshua, Chronicles and the like. The spelling of many names thus remained unchanged at a time when similar words which were not proper names were changing in their spelling.

In the case of names which were really common and conspicuous, because they took a central place in narrative, there was a tendency to reach near-unanimity in the spelling: so with Moses, Aaron, Jacob, David in major blocks of books, Solomon also perhaps (for the standard spelling of this name, שְׁלֹמֹה, is also of an unusual type[1]).

Many major cases of this kind opted for the short spelling. The case of Joseph may be a special one in this respect, because of the

---

[1] Solomon could, one supposes, have been written שְׁלוֹמֹה, but it never appears so. The place Socoh so appears, שׂוֹכֹה Jos 15[35]. Names ending in –o seem to be spelt sometimes with he but mostly with waw, e.g. Jericho mainly יְרִיחוֹ but 2K 25[5] יְרֵחוֹ and 1K 16[34] יְרִיחֹה with he; similar variation with Shiloh.

association with the Pe Waw verb type, and similarly that of Saul, since the spelling with waw seems much preponderant in the passive participle (cf. above, pp. 113f.).

Many other names began to drift towards a longer spelling: so cases like Benjamin within the Genesis narrative, and sporadically elsewhere, so Sihon, and so a few cases even within the most consistently spelled names, e.g. Jacob within the latter part of Jeremiah. In Absalom (p. 23 above) the plene spelling became dominant: possibly this case might have been influenced by the element שָׁלוֹם, which as an independent word is dominantly written with waw.

The case of David is a very prominent one but fits in also quite well. The only difference was that the short spelling of this name, though immensely dominant in many books, came to be felt to be less appropriate in other circles, beyond doubt later, and the longer spelling דָּוִיד was adopted with a high and unusual consistency in some books like Chronicles and crept in sporadically in some others like Kings and Ezekiel. There is no certain way of telling whether the long spelling was already adopted in the original composition of (say) Chronicles or whether it was made as a systematic change during the later transmission. The very systematic character of it might favour the latter rather than the former. This is supported also by the facts of the Minor Prophets: their fairly consistent use of the long spelling is not likely to go back to the original composition, since the cases in Amos and possibly Hosea may be quite early.

The case of the name David, however, brings us again to our central question: what caused it to happen? Was it a scribal matter, a feeling that the form *dawid* ought to be written with yod by current conventions, just as was done with common terms like יָמִין, בְּרִית? Or was it motivated by a change in the language itself, for instance by a shift of stress which made the final syllable more prominent, or by a change of vowel length by which *dawid*, which had a short final vowel, came to have a long *ī*? In this respect it is proper to remember that the terminations *–im* and *–ot* of the plural tend to be very constantly written plene in Chronicles, and this may be connected with the same facts. In Nehemiah, on the other hand, this is less so, which may point in the other direction. Perhaps the two possibilities come together as one in this case: a shift in pronunciation caused the spelling conventions to alter.

There remains another feature that deserves to be mentioned in connection with names of high frequency and high variation in spelling such as Absalom. This is the alternation in names beginning with the element *yo-* or *yᵉho-*. By our definition of the subject this stands somewhat outside the field, since for me *yonatan* is a different form from *yᵉhonatan* and not a different spelling of the same form. Nevertheless there may be a linkage in terms of the mechanism of scribal behaviour. The name Jonathan, as we express it in English, is a good example. The son of Saul begins his biblical existence as יוֹנָתָן (1S 13²), and there are thirteen cases of this spelling in 1S 13–14, a territory that is thus strongly dominated by this particular spelling. But in the midst of this territory the other spelling, יְהוֹנָתָן, appears twice at 14⁶,⁸, right in the midst of a long run of the spelling without he. Thereafter the spelling without he continues to dominate completely until the end of ch. 14. In the next three chapters, 15–17, Jonathan is not mentioned at all. But when he reappears in the story at 18¹ he is יְהוֹנָתָן with he, and he remains so throughout a large number of cases in 1–2 Samuel, the only exception being 1S 19¹, a verse that contains both spellings together. Chronicles mentions Jonathan much less often, but when it does it uses the spelling with he except at 1C 10². There are various other Jonathans than the son of Saul, about fourteen of them, mostly mentioned once or twice only, and some have one spelling, some the other, some both. But in general it is difficult to doubt that this variation in the writings of the name Jonathan belongs to the same genus of variation as that found in the writing of a name like Absalom in the same book, except that the amount of rapid variation is less.

CHAPTER THREE
Parallels and Combinations

A further important body of evidence now falls to be investigated, namely the material offered by the parallel passages, passages in which more or less the same content is restated in two or more places, so that the same verbal material, or more or less the same, reappears under the different spelling tendencies of different books, or different parts of the same book. I have found this evidence from parallel passages to be very significant indeed, perhaps more significant for interpretation than any other single factor, and it has greatly influenced the direction in which my thinking has moved in the course of this long period of research.

Many such parallel passages exist in the Hebrew Bible, but three areas have proved to be particularly significant, and these are the ones that will be presented here. These are: (a) the poem which is found as 2 Samuel 22 and also as Psalm 18; (b) the account in Exodus of the construction of the Tabernacle, where the earlier chapters, 25–30, tell how Moses was instructed to make the tabernacle and its furnishings, while the later chapters, 35–40, tell us how this work was carried out, often in words basically almost identical; (c) some examples of passages where Chronicles reuses the wording of Samuel and Kings.

A useful instrument in this work, but one that must be used with caution, is *Parallels in the Bible*, arranged by Abba Bendavid (Jerusalem: Carta, 1972). This prints the texts in parallel columns and marks in red ink any words or even single letters that differ between one text and another. It is, however, rather a popular than a strictly scholarly work. Its text is not based, like academic editions, upon the best manuscripts, and sometimes fails to mark the differences correctly in red. But, though everything in it must be checked against a more reliable source, it remains a quick and handy instrument of work.

Since it is obviously impossible within this work to print every word of every parallel, it has been necessary to pick out the words that are more typical and to leave unmarked the many words that could potentially differ in spelling but are in fact spelt alike in both of our parallels as compared. In the first comparison, between 2 Samuel 22 and Psalm 18, however, a list calling attention to many such words is provided.

For guidance to the reader in perusing the comparisons, a partial preview of the conclusions which were reached from them may be stated here. In very general terms we find that a passage mainly follows the tendency of the book in which it is found: for example, Ps 18 follows the general tendencies of the Psalter while 2 Samuel 22 agrees with those found elsewhere in the Book of Samuel. In a substantial majority of cases, this means that Ps 18 has the longer spelling, using waws and yods where Samuel omits them. But — and this is one of the most important aspects to come to light through these comparisons — this does not happen consistently. While the Psalm generally speaking has the longer spelling, at certain points the reverse seems to be the case and 2 Samuel has a longer spelling than the Psalm. The same is found in Chronicles in relation to Samuel and Kings. In general, Chronicles is a much longer-spelling book than Samuel or Kings, and in many forms Kings is one of the chief centres of the shorter spellings; and yet, in a substantial number of cases, never dominant but never insignificant, we find that Chronicles has the more defective spelling; one case that has already been mentioned is that of ordinal numbers like שְׁלִשִׁי 'third' (cf. above, pp. 150ff.).

In the Exodus passage both texts have the general characteristics of that book, and they have a large number of spellings in common. In spite of this they have many at which they alternate, and this alternation does not show any one clear pattern, as if to say that the earlier chapters had either a shorter or a longer tendency than the later ones within the book. Rather, there is a haphazard kind of difference, at one particular word the earlier portion having a shorter spelling, at the next the reverse.

Now there may be more than one way of explaining this, but the most probable hypothesis, I would suggest, is the following: that all these parallel texts — 2 Samuel 22 and Psalm 18, the two forms of the instructions for the tabernacle and their execution, and Samuel/ Kings and Chronicles where they are closely parallel — all of these grew from an earlier text which was on the whole spelt shorter than any of the texts that we now have in the Masoretic text. Thus, for instance, at many places Chronicles will have a longer spelling than Kings, but here and there it will have a shorter spelling of that same word or one like it, and this will mean only that at this point Kings made an amplification that elsewhere, and in general, would be more typical of Chronicles, or that Chronicles at this point omitted to make an amplification that in many cases it itself would have made. This is a much simpler and more economical explanation than to suppose that, say, Chronicles worked from the present text of Kings, adding vowel letters most of the time but occasionally removing them. The hypothesis that, where parallel texts exist, they derived from an earlier form of text that was generally shorter, and that was thereafter amplified in slightly different ways, and haphazardly rather than systematically, is the simplest explanation, and gives us means to understand the essential problem, namely the fact that the existing texts seem, in numerous individual cases, to go against their own dominant tendencies.

To say this is not to say that the only operative direction was that which led from the shorter spelling towards the longer. This was, we may suspect, the dominant direction of change, but it was not the only one. It is quite likely that from time to time words which had plene spelling came, through the optional character of the system, to be spelt without vowel letters, e.g. that a word which had been written נוֹדַע came to be written נֹדַע, the waw simply having been omitted at some stage. Nevertheless the dominant direction of change was probably from the shorter towards the longer spelling; and this agrees with what has been general opinion among scholars anyway. There is, however, at least one case in which the reverse is probable: namely, the spelling of the second person suffixes *-ta* and *-ka* with he. As has been suggested above, pp. 123ff., the evidence of the Masoretic text suggests that these longer spellings were at one time more common in the tradition. And there may be other cases in which a similar development may have taken place.

Readers may judge for themselves, however, how far they think that such hypotheses are to be acceptd. We may now proceed to the presentation of the main blocks of evidence to be considered.

1. 2 Samuel 22 and Psalm 18

The chart that follows (p. 171) displays the main spelling differences between the two versions. On the left I have placed words in which the Samuel spelling is shorter than that of the Psalm, on the right words where the Psalm has the shorter spelling. Square brackets are placed around an entry when the words of the two versions are not absolutely identical, so that the difference is not merely one of spelling, but where nevertheless one of the forms can be identified as being spelt in a noticeably short or long manner. Thus at v.

38 the אֶרְדּוֹף of the Psalm is not a different *spelling* of the Samuel form, for the Samuel form is the morphologically different אֶרְדְּפָה; nevertheless the presence of waw in the Psalm form marks it as a significantly long spelling, and for this reason it is registered in our listing.

Spelling comparison between 2 Samuel 22 and Psalm 18

A. Spelling of 2 Samuel shorter			B. Spelling of Psalm 18 shorter		
verse	2S 22	Ps 18	verse	2S 22	Ps 18
1	אֹתוֹ	אוֹתוֹ			
2/3	מְצֻדָתִי	מְצוּדָתִי			
5	אֲפָפֻנִי	אֲפָפוּנִי			
	יְבַעֲתֻנִי	יְבַעֲתוּנִי			
6	סַבֻּנִי	סַבְבוּנִי			
	קִדְמֻנִי	קִדְּמוּנִי			
	מֹקְשֵׁי	מוֹקְשֵׁי			
12	סְבִיבֹתָיו	סְבִיבוֹתָיו			
			14	קוֹלוֹ	קֹלוֹ
16	אֲפִקֵי	אֲפִיקֵי			
	מֹסְדוֹת	מוֹסְדוֹת			
19	יְקַדְמֻנִי	יְקַדְּמוּנִי			
20	[וַיֹּצֵא ... אֹתִי]	[וַיּוֹצִיאֵנִי]			
			26	[גִּבּוֹר]	[גְּבַר]
			29	נֵירִי	נֵרִי
			30	בְּכָה	בְּךָ
				אָרוּץ	אָרֻץ
			34	בָּמוֹתָי	בָּמֹתָי
34	יְעַמְּדֵנִי	יְעַמִּידֵנִי			
35	זִרֹעֹתָי	זְרוֹעֹתָי			
38	[אֶרְדְּפָה]	[אֶרְדּוֹף]			
	אֹיְבַי	אוֹיְבַי			
42	מֹשִׁיעַ	מוֹשִׁיעַ			
43	[אֲדִקֵּם]	[אֲרִיקֵם]			
44	יַעַבְדֻנִי	יַעַבְדוּנִי			
			45	[לְשֵׁמַע]	לִשְׁמוֹעַ]
47	יָרֻם	יָרוּם			
	אֱלֹהֵי	אֱלוֹהֵי			
48	נֹתֵן	נוֹתֵן			
	נְקָמֹת	נְקָמוֹת			
			51	מַגְדִּיל	מַגְדִּל

In this first case, in addition, we will list a number of words which are in principle of variable spelling but which are in fact spelt identically in both versions: v.1 אֹיְבָיו; v.4 אֹיְבִי; v.6 שָׁאוּל; v.7 קוֹלִי; v.18 יַצִּילֵנִי, אֹיְבִי, שֹׂנְאַי; v.23 אָסוּר / אָסִיר (the forms different, but both plene in respect of spelling); v.28 תּוֹשִׁיעַ, תַּשְׁפִּיל; v.29 יַגִּיהַּ; v.30 שׁוּר, גְּדוּד; v.31 צְרוּפָה, חֹסִים; v.35 נִחֻתָה; v.37 תַּרְחִיב; v.38 אָשׁוּב, כַּלּוֹתָם; v.40 תַּכְרִיעַ; v.41 אֹיְבַי, תִּתָּה / נָתַתָּה (these two are different forms but are alike in having he with the termination), אַצְמִיתֵם; v.43 חוּצוֹת; v.44 רִיבֵי; v.46 יִבֹּלוּ; v.49 אֹיְבָי; v.51 יְשׁוּעוֹת, עֹשֶׂה.

Some of these deserve brief annotation. The suffixed forms of 'oyeb 'enemy', all agreed between the two as defective except for v. 38 as noted, conform to the general styles of both books: in Samuel all cases of 'oyᵉbay and 'oyᵉbaw are defective except the very first, 1S 2[1] אוֹיְבָי, while in the Psalms the defective is preferred (plene אוֹיְבַי eight times out of 28, Mm 3365; and אוֹיְבָיו plene thrice in the book out of seven). The plene קוֹלִי is the normal spelling for this form in both books, with numerous cases in the Psalter. The numerous i-containing hiphils require no remark. חוּצוֹת with two waws is a long spelling but not an unusually long one, for there are numerous cases in the Latter Prophets and Writings.

A few comments on the differences between the two forms of the poem must be added. One of the commonest differences is in the spelling of the –u termination of the plural before a suffix: in Samuel regularly without waw, in the Psalm regularly with waw. The spelling with waw is a characteristic feature of the Psalter, not universal indeed but very dominant. The spelling without waw, though interspersed with the plene, is widely evidenced in Samuel, e.g. 1S 5[1] וַיְבִאֻהוּ, 6[2] הוֹדִעֻנוּ 7[3] וְעִבְדֻהוּ 8[8] וַיַּעַזְבֻנִי. Another characteristic difference is with the –ot of the plural ending, where the Psalms favour more the spelling with waw. Note however that at v. 35, where it has already one waw more than the Samuel form, i.e. the medial waw of זְרֹעֹתָי, it does not go on to add the waw of the plural termination. At v. 34 it is Samuel that has the waw of plural –ot.

Particularly characteristic is the handling of Pe Waw verbs and derived nouns. Samuel is well known as a major locus for the spelling without waw (cf. above, pp. 87–90; and my article on Job, JSS 30, 1985, especially pp. 9, 11f., 14f., 18, 21), and particularly in the root y-š-ᶜ 'save'. In our poem Samuel has מֹשִׁיעַ short at v. 42, and in addition has two short spellings מֹשִׁעִי and תֹּשִׁעֵנִי in v. 3 in words which are lacking from the Psalm version; both texts have תּוֹשִׁיעַ plene at v. 28 (characteristically, without suffix). At v. 6 Samuel has מֹקְשֵׁי and at v. 16 מֹסְדוֹת. At v. 49 however it has the doubly plene writing וּמוֹצִיאִי, which reminds rather of the Song of

Hannah at the beginning of the book, with its several long spellings like 1S 2⁶ מוֹרִיד 2⁷ מוֹרִישׁ 2⁸ לְהוֹשִׁיב. At v. 8, with the root *y-s-d*, we have different words in the two versions but both written with waw: 2S 22⁸ מוֹסְדוֹת // Ps 18⁸ וּמוֹסְדֵי but at v. 16 they disagree in the spelling. At v. 48 Samuel has *u-morid*, where the Psalm has an altogether different wording. BHS spells plene as וּמוֹרִיד but against the Masora, which requires וּמֹרִיד, and the latter is the reading of many texts.

More comment is perhaps called for by the cases where Samuel has the longer spellings than the Psalm. V. 29 נֵירִי is an unusual plene spelling, already mentioned above, p. 142. At v. 30 Samuel has the spelling בְּכָה, an unusual one and found otherwise only at Ex 7²⁹ Ps 141⁸. Samuel and Psalms, as has already been indicated, are both centres that favour the spelling of –*ta* and –*ka* with he, and we have seen that both of them have it with נְתַתָּה and the obscure תַּתָּה at v. 41. I have suggested (above, pp. 123ff.) that the spelling with he may have been more widespread at an earlier stage of the text's development; Ps 141⁸ shows that בְּכָה can be found in the Psalter. So it would be possible that the spelling of Samuel with he was the older one here.

An apparently odd spelling is 2S 22³³ מָעוּזִּי, which has no close parallel in the Psalm. At first sight it looks like an anomalous 'late type' spelling with waw marking a short vowel in closed syllable. In fact, however, whatever the explanation (see BDB, p. 731b, for an attempt to explain the peculiarity), the form as here written is well evidenced and not uncommon, being found identically at Ps 31⁵ 43² and additionally for other suffixes, while the shorter spelling מָעֻזִּי which one might consider normal is actually less common. There is no reason therefore to suppose that the spelling here in Samuel is an abnormality: if Ps 18 had had the word, it might well have spelt it in the same way.

Finally, the fact that the Ps 18 spellings can be shorter than those of Samuel, and within the same type of words in which they are elsewhere longer, makes it impossible to take the spellings of this poem as evidence of transmission through two different dialects, or other such explanations. Note particularly how Ps 18³⁰ spells אָרֻץ with the same short spelling that Samuel uses in v. 47 יָרֶם. The difference in the spelling of plural *u*, and of internal *u* vowels as well, is one that cannot plausibly be attached to any dialect difference. With *qolo* 'his voice' both Samuel and the Psalms have both spellings elsewhere: defective 1S 24¹⁷ and 1S 12¹⁴ (latter with *b*ᵉ–, also with some textual disagreement), Ps 95⁷ with *b*ᵉ–; plene 2S 3³², Ps 46⁷ 68³⁴. Our example makes both books evenly balanced in the writing of this word. As for the participle מַגְדִּל, this writing of the hiphil is uncommon in the Psalms, but cf. Ps 26⁷ לִשְׁמֹעַ, 49¹⁷ יַעֲשֶׂר 69³² מִקֶּרֶן etc.

The two forms of the text very probably reflect different stages of spelling practice, and indeed most scholars will agree, no doubt, that the spelling of the Psalm reflects a later style than that of Samuel in most respects. But I see no reason at all to suppose that the differences are connected with northern and southern locality or with dialect.[1]

2. Details of the Tabernacle in Exodus and Leviticus

The two texts are labelled as Text I and Text II. In Text I (Ex 25–30) the instructions for the work are given, and Text II (Ex 35–40 and some parts of Leviticus) tells how this work was carried out. Often the words are only slightly altered as between the two mentions of the same element, although the *order* is not always the same. The table indicates some, indeed most, of the notable differences in spelling of the same forms. At the right-hand side it is simply marked whether Text I or Text II has the longer spelling. As always, there are some doubtful cases, some of which are annotated.

	Text I			Text II		Longer spelling is in:
Exodus						
25⁶		מָאֹר	35⁸		מָאוֹר	II
25⁷		אֵפֹד	35⁹		אֵפוֹד	II
25¹⁰		אֲרוֹן (cstr.)	37¹		הָאָרֹן	I
25¹²	third	טַבְּעֹת	37³	third	טַבָּעוֹת	II
25³¹	second	מְנוֹרָה	37¹⁷	second	מְנֹרָה	I
26⁶		יְרִיעֹת	36¹³		יְרִעֹת	I
26¹⁴	first	עֹרֹת	39³⁴	first	עוֹרֹת	II
26¹⁶		אַמּוֹת	36²¹		אַמֹּת	I
26¹⁷		יָדוֹת	36²²		יָדֹת	I
26²⁴		תֹאֲמִים	36²⁹		תוֹאֲמִם	equal
26³³		אֲרוֹן (cstr.)	40²¹		הָאָרֹן (abs.)	I
26³⁴		הָעֵדָת	40²¹		הָעֵדוּת	II
27¹⁰		עַמְדָיו	38¹⁰		עַמּוּדֵיהֶם	II
27¹¹		הָעַמְדִים	38¹¹		הָעַמּוּדִים	II
27¹⁸		וְקֹמָה	38¹⁸		וְקוֹמָה	II

---

[1] Contrast D.N. Freedman, *Textus* 2, 1962, p. 89, and, earlier, *JBL* 72, 1953, 15–17.

28¹¹	חוֹתָם		39⁶	חוֹתָם	II
	שְׁמֹת			שְׁמוֹת	II
	מִשְׁבְּצוֹת			מִשְׁבְּצֹת	I
28¹²	זִכָּרֹן		39⁷	זִכָּרוֹן	II
28²⁰	בְּמִלּוּאֹתָם		39¹³	בְּמִלֻּאֹתָם	I
28²¹	חוֹתָם		39¹⁴	חֹתָם	I
28²³	טַבְּעוֹת		39¹⁶	טַבְּעֹת	I
	הַטַּבָּעוֹת			הַטַּבָּעֹת	I
28²⁵	הַמִּשְׁבְּצוֹת		39¹⁸	הַמִּשְׁבְּצֹת	I
28²⁵	כְּתֵפוֹת		39¹⁸	כִּתְפֹת	I
28²⁶	טַבְּעוֹת		39¹⁹	טַבְּעֹת	I
28²⁷	טַבְּעוֹת		39²⁰	טַבְּעֹת	I
28²⁷	כְּתֵפוֹת		39²⁰	כִּתְפֹת	I
28²⁷	הָאֵפוֹד		39²⁰	הָאֵפֹד	I
28²⁷	הָאֵפוֹד		39²⁰	הָאֵפֹד	I
28²⁸	לִהְיוֹת		39²¹	לִהְיֹת	I
28²⁸	הָאֵפֹד first		39²¹	הָאֵפֹד	alike
28²⁸	הָאֵפוֹד second		39²¹	הָאֵפֹד	I
28²⁸	הָאֵפוֹד third		39²¹	הָאֵפֹד	I
28³³	רִמֹּנֵי		39²⁴	רִמּוֹנֵי	II
28³⁴	רִמּוֹן		39²⁶	רִמֹּן	I
28³⁴	רִמּוֹן		39²⁶	רִמֹּן	I
28³⁶	חוֹתָם		39³⁰	חוֹתָם	II
28⁴⁰	וּמִגְבָּעוֹת		39²⁸	הַמִּגְבָּעֹת	I
29³	הָאֵלִים	Lv 8²		הָאֵילִים	II
29⁹	מִגְבָּעֹת		8¹³	מִגְבָּעוֹת	II
29¹²	קַרְנֹת		8¹⁵	קַרְנוֹת	II
29¹⁸	נִיחוֹחַ		8²¹	נִיחֹחַ	I
29²⁵	נִיחוֹחַ		8²⁸	נִיחֹחַ	I
31⁴	לַעֲשׂוֹת		(35³² לַעֲשֹׂת strictly a repeat within Text I)		
31⁹	כִּיּוֹר		35¹⁶ and 39³⁹	כִּיֹּר	I

No great deal of comment is required: most of the spelling differences are of types that we have discussed elsewhere. Most of the differences concern the vowel *o*, especially in the plural ending *-ot*. The spelling of the plural ending *-ot* without waw is very common among the terms for the tabernacle and its furniture; thus, where we do not mention a word, because it agrees in spelling in both texts, the reader will do well to assume that its spelling of the termination is short. The short spelling being thus frequent, it is the spellings of *-ot* with waw which will generally be in the minority.

A few words containing *o* deserve a brief note. Notice the unusual short קָמָה 27¹⁸: if the short spelling of *o* is taken to be the older, then it would be natural to take this to be so also for this word, and that could have implications for the original vowel of this root and its spelling. Note the striking alternation of *hotam* 'seal': this word occurs six times in our pair of texts, all in the identical phrase with פְּתוּחֵי 'engravings'; and these alternate perfectly, with every one of Text I spelt opposite to the counterpart in Text II, thus:

A   חֹתָם 28^{11} 28^{36} 39^{14}
B   חוֹתָם 28^{21} 39^{6} 39^{30}

Fig. 61: *hotam* 'seal', all cases of singular in Exodus

The differences between the two parallel texts in Exodus and Leviticus require little comment. On the basis of the examples I have cited, Text I has more long spellings than Text II: 27 as against sixteen as marked. But our purpose is not primarily to determine which of the two texts is the longer-spelling. For that purpose our listings might not suffice, for we do not guarantee to have listed every single word with a different spelling among these parallels. And the reader must remember that, as against these cases of divergence, there is a vastly greater number of words in which both texts are in agreement. What emerges from this study, and is significant, is that neither of the two texts shows consistency within itself. Note particularly how both texts oscillate back and forward in the spelling of repeated items such as *hotam* 'seal', *'epod* 'ephod', *rimmon* 'pomegranate', and in the plural termination *-ot*. Among spellings that would be noticed as unusually short מְאֹר, קָמָה and זִכְּרֹן are in Text I, while יְרִעֹת, רִמֹן and כִּיֹּר are in Text II. The distribution does not demonstrate, but is compatible with the hypothesis, that these portions of text had had more short spellings than we now see in them, and that waws and yods had been added, occasionally and haphazardly, in both texts at different points and in different ways.

A complicated word is *'ammud* 'pillar'. It occurs many times in our texts and I have displayed only a few examples. It occurs in the plural construct, in the plural absolute, and with various suffixes. Within Exodus it shows substantial variation in the spelling of the *u*. The singular is dominantly עַמּוּד plene as one would expect, but the defective עַמֻּד occurs at Nu 14^{14} (with the plene in the same phrase only a few words later) Jr 52^{21}. The plural *'ammudim* is a form that shows much variation, and our Text II, Ex 38, let it vary a great deal; so, later on, did 1K 7. Here is the diagram for our texts in Exodus; all cases have the article:

A   עַמֻּדִים   Ex $27^{10,11}$ 38^{10} ^{12,17}
B   עמודים $_{11}$ $_{17,28}$

Fig. 62: ʿammudim 'pillars', plural absolute, all cases in Exodus

It is reasonable to suppose that an older text had had the spelling without waw, and that ch. 38 hesitated between keeping that older spelling and transforming it to the longer.

Something quite different happens with the construct of the same noun:

A   עַמֻּדֵי 38^{17} Nu 3^{37}
B   עמודֵי   Ex $26^{32,37}$ 27^{17} 36^{36} 4^{32}

Fig. 63: ʿammude 'the pillars of', plural construct, all cases in the Torah

Here Text I stuck to the plene spelling. The two cases in Numbers have w^e– prefixed.

We shall not attempt to give a quantitative figure that would define whether Text I or Text II inclines more towards a plene spelling. Of the examples displayed in our two columns above, Text I seems to favour the shorter spelling in the first part, but from 28^{20} it has a considerable run of occurrences that favour the longer as against Text II. From 28^{33} onwards the two texts vary from each other in both directions. From 29^1 onwards, where the parallel is in Leviticus, the Exodus text (= Text I) is shorter on the whole, the exception being in נִיחֹחַ, a word in which the dominant spelling in Exodus is plene against the great majority of the Torah: this word appears short, נִיחֹחַ, at Gn 8^{21} (with article), then with waw at Ex $29^{18,25}$ as shown, without waw in 29^{41}, plene again in the first Leviticus case, Lv 1^9, then defective in all the remaining cases in Leviticus-Numbers. Even Ezekiel has the short spelling of this word throughout, except Ezk 20^{28} with suffix. The yod is always written in any case. But quantitative figures should not be relied on, since we have not displayed every one of the many items that are relevant.

Neither of the two texts shows any sign of having been modified from the existing spelling of the other. The evidence is entirely compatible with the supposition that both Text I and Text II were derived from an earlier text that was dominantly short, and that both of them independently added a certain number of waws and yods, both of them inconsistently and haphazardly. A word like to'ᵃmim at 26^{24}//36^{29} might thus have been the fully defective תאמם, which was then amplified, in one case with the yod of the termination, in the other with the waw of the first syllable.

3. Chronicles as parallel with Samuel and Kings

The parallels of Chronicles with Samuel and Kings are an obvious quarry for material for our purpose. Few would question that Chronicles built upon the narratives of these older books, and the verbal agreements are very numerous. In very general terms, Samuel and Kings are books with important areas of short spellings, and Kings especially so for many types of words; while Chronicles would commonly be regarded as a long-spelling book. And indeed there are very large numbers of words where a short spelling in Samuel and Kings is paralleled by a longer in Chronicles. This makes all the more interesting the cases where the reverse is to be found. The number of differences is so great that only a limited selection from one or two passages can be printed.

i. The Story of the Queen of Sheba

	1K 10$^{1-12}$			2C 9$^{1-12}$
v. 1	וַתָּבֹא			וַתָּבוֹא
5	וּמַלְבֻּשֵׁיהֶם			וּמַלְבוּשֵׁיהֶם
9	לְעֹלָם	v. 8		לְעוֹלָם
19	וְיָדֹת	18		וְיָדוֹת
22	לְשָׁלֹשׁ	21		לְשָׁלוֹשׁ
22	קֹפִים וְתֻכִּיִּים	21		קוֹפִים וְתוּכִּיִּים
25	מְבִאִים	24		מְבִיאִים

In this passage I have not noticed any material instance in which Chronicles has the shorter writing of the same word. The text of Kings from which Chronicles worked was not necessarily identical with that which we now have, but there is little reason to suppose that it was much different here. If it is accepted that Chronicles is the secondary text here, as it surely would generally be accepted, then Chronicles gives us a kind of show-case in which the process of revision can be watched. Many of the differences are of kinds that have already become familiar to us. The text of Chronicles brings them together and provides a convincing view of the way in which such revision took place.

ii. The Story of Rehoboam

	1K 12$^{1-19}$	2C 10$^{1-19}$
v. 5	אֲלֵיהֶם	אֲלֵיהֶם
7, 9,10,14	אֲלֵיהֶם	אֲלֵהֶם
16	אֲלֵיהֶם	לָהֶם

5	עֵד		עוֹד	
5	וְשׁוּבוּ		וְשׁוּבוּ	
11	אוֹסִיף		אֹסִיף	
12	הַשְּׁלִישִׁי	twice	הַשְּׁלִשִׁי	twice
16	וַיָּשֻׁבוּ		וַיָּשִׁיבוּ	
21	שְׁמֹנִים	11^1	שְׁמוֹנִים	

The entries are not exactly in order, because it seemed good to place at the beginning a group of examples of *'alehem*, a term that has been discussed elsewhere. In this expression Kings has the writing with yod no less than six times: in the first of these Chronicles agrees with Kings, in the next four it has the shorter spelling אֲלֵהֶם, and in the last it has לָהֶם, which is not the same form at all but may indicate something about the transmission.

In addition to this, the Chronicles text shows three forms with shorter spelling than the Kings form, namely the cases of אֹסִיף and שְׁלִשִׁי (twice).

It is logically conceivable that Chronicles shortened the spelling of these words as against Kings. But a more natural supposition is that an older text of Kings was shorter than the present one, and that in these particular words Chronicles simply retained the spelling. In the case of *'alehem* this is confirmed by the fact that Kings has — even in its present text — a considerable number of the short spelling: cf. an example at 1K 12²⁸, with Masora that says that there are thirteen defective in the book. This is relevant for any discussion of the incidence of the same form in the Torah and especially Exodus; cf. above, pp. 135ff.. Kings later revised שלשי to the spelling with two yods which was greatly dominant throughout the Bible except for Chronicles; Chronicles introduced it also, but never made it the majority spelling. With שְׁמֹנִים 'eighty', on the other hand, in this same passage Chronicles rewrites with the long spelling that is normal for it.

It is not possible to prove, but it can be made very plausible, that Chronicles worked from a text of Samuel and Kings that had shorter spellings than the texts of these books that we now have. Here and there we have outcrops of spellings in which Chronicles is shorter than Samuel or Kings, and most such spellings can be understood in this way. It is not possible to illustrate the problem further without printing many pages of text in parallel columns, and for the present purpose these short comparisons must suffice.

Exactly the same situation is found in other parallel passages of a historical kind in other books. Isaiah in ch. 36 retells the story of the Rabshakeh which is told also in 2K 18, and we find a considerable list of longer spellings in Isaiah: he has הַסּוֹפֵר long (v. 22, but not in v.3), וַיַּגִּידוּ long (v. 22), אֲלֵיהֶם with yod (v. 4, against אֲלֵהֶם 2K 18[19]), חוֹמָה twice long (vv. 11, 12), לְהַשְׁחִיתָהּ with yod (v. 10), all against shorter spellings in Kings. But at v. 14 he has יֵשַׁע against 2K 18[29] יֵשִׁיא. Did Isaiah remove a yod from a word that already had one? Possibly, but more likely Kings added its yod after the text had been used by Isaiah, who in this case left the word untouched — not surprisingly, for Isaiah is one of the most inconsistent of the books, wandering vaguely between shorter and longer writings.

A comparison of 2K 24[18]–25 with Jr 52 will also be instructive: here one will find a number of instances where the prophet has the shorter writings as against Kings.

The suggestions made above are considerably strengthened if we take into account another body of evidence, namely, the passages in Chronicles, apart from the early genealogical material, that do *not* derive from Samuel-Kings and may depend rather on the Chronicler's own pen. 2C 30, for example, the story of Hezekiah's passover, has a large measure of plene spellings and rather few of those unusual short spellings that surprise the reader of Chronicles in other parts of the book. I simply list a few examples: כַּאֲבוֹתֵיכֶם 30[7,8] [9] שׁוֹבֵיהֶם, תָּשׁוּבוּ, [10] מַשְׁחִיקִים doubly plene, so הַמַּשְׂכִּילִים [22], so infinitives like [19] לִדְרוֹשׁ. One of my modes of study is to mark with green spellings that are noticeably long, and red similarly for those that are noticeably short, and a chapter like this of Chronicles is almost entirely shaded green on my copy of BHS. This is not to say that there is a steady and systematic use of the maximal plene spellings, even in such a passage: for example, we have 30[14,27] וַיָּקֻמוּ, a rather common Chronicles spelling, which could easily have been וַיָּקוּמוּ and is so written in nearby sources, e.g. Ezr 1[5] Ne 9[3]; similarly participles like 30[10] עֹבְרִים, [16] זֹרְקִים, which might have been plene but are not, or [10] וּמַלְעִגִים which is in the same verse as the מַשְׁחִיקִים just quoted and might have been doubly plene like it but is not. Similarly we can find the construct עֲבֹדַת 'service of' written defectively in such passages, e.g. 1C 23[28,32], even though the same is often plene in Chronicles.

So we do not suppose that the passages from the Chronicler's own writing are hostile to defective spelling and favourable to the most plene spelling that can be found. This is not so. Nevertheless these passages seem to have, so far as I have thus far seen, few of these surprisingly short spellings which in the passages parallel to Kings are not uncommon.

It may be, therefore, that we should distinguish between three strata of Chronicles in respect of spelling practices. There are the sections of genealogies and lists, in which many short spellings have survived, partly because names and the like were not so often revised, partly because these sections were more remote from general usage of language altogether. There are the sections rewritten on the basis of Samuel and Kings, in which Chronicles probably introduced many additional waws and yods, but also, we have suggested, here and there retained very short spellings which in the course of time were to become shorter than those of Samuel or Kings. In the case of הֲלוֹא 'is it not that...?' we have the choice of supposing that Chronicles by deliberate policy chose to stick to the shorter spelling הֲלֹא and revised its sources accordingly, or of supposing that it was still הֲלֹא in Samuel-Kings when these were rewritten by Chronicles, and the waws were added to the texts of these books later. Finally, there are the sections that are original writing by the Chronicles or associates, in which a steadier application of plene spelling is discernible. These ideas may well be in need of revision on the basis of further study, but may serve as a useful working hypothesis for the meanwhile. They help to explain why Chronicles is so interesting for the student of spellings and why it is so resistant to classification as a 'late book' or the like. If Chronicles has many examples of the long and 'late' spellings found also in Qoheleth or Esther, it also has many associations with spellings of the Torah in certain types, and along with many similarities it has many striking differences from works like Nehemiah which one might have taken to be 'contemporary'. Chronicles is of central importance for the entire investigation of Masoretic spelling.

One last, and rather neat, little example. Hezekiah showed to the ambassadors from Babylon everything that was 'in his treasuries', and afterwards, questioned by the prophet, he said that he had shown them all that was 'in my treasuries'. Here is the way in which the words are spelt:

| 2K 20¹³ | בְּאוֹצְרֹתָיו | Is 39² | בְּאֹצְרֹתָיו |
| 20¹⁵ | בְּאֹצְרֹתָי | 39⁴ | בְּאוֹצְרֹתָי |

Now it would be logically possible that, if we take the Isaiah text as the later one, and if it had the present form of the Kings text before it, it removed the waw from the first case in Kings and added a waw to the second: or, if Kings was the later one, that it did the same thing the other way round. But is it not easier to think that the base text for them both was without waw, not least because that is much the majority spelling in the plural, especially in Chronicles, which has many examples; and with suffix consider such as Is 2⁷ מֵאֹצְרֹתָיו Jr 10¹³ בְּאֹצְרֹתֶיהָ Jr 49⁴ לְאֹצְרֹתָיו. For use of two spellings in close juxtaposition cf. 1C 26^{20}. But it should be added that there is considerable diversity between forms of the text in the spelling of this word.

With this we leave the sample studies of parallel passages that we have been able to offer, and we remain confident that these will prove to be a zone from which much valuable information will be gained in the future.

4. Combinations of variable spellings

By the nature of our study, and through the approach that has been adopted, much of the emphasis has fallen upon individual words and the variations of their spelling. It is important that this should be complemented with a study of another type, the study of phrases which contain two or more words of variable spelling. The study of such combinations can be very significant for our subject as a whole, as will be seen.

Take first the expression 'ark of the testimony', *'ron ha-'edut*. This occurs twelve times in all, and is rightly so counted by the Masora (Mm 853). Of the four possibilities three are actually found: both words spelt defective, both words plene, and the first plene but the second defective. The combination with the first defective and the second plene is not found. Here is the pattern of the spellings of this combination:

A אֲרֹן הָעֵדֻת Ex 25^{22} 30^6 39^{35}
 (both words short)
B אֲרוֹן הָעֵדוּת 26^{33} 40^3 40^{21}
 (both words long)
C אֲרוֹן הָעֵדֻת 26^{34} 30^{26} 40^5
 (first word long)
A   Nu 4^5 7^{89}
B   Jos 4^{16}

Fig. 64: the phrase *'ron ha-'edut*, all cases in the Bible

This is a sort of wave formation which exploits each of several possibilities in rough succession. It will be noted that neither Text I nor Text II of Exodus (cf. pp. 174–175 above) has a consistent spelling: both sections use all three possibilities.

A somewhat similar pattern is found with the combination *t'mol šilšom*: this again could be written in four ways, but in fact only three of the possibilities are used, and these the same three as with 'the ark of the testimony', namely: both words short, both long, and first long but second short. In the Torah we have the following pattern:

A   תְּמֹל שִׁלְשֹׁם 31^5 21^{29} 19^4
  (both words short)
B   תְּמוֹל שִׁלְשׁוֹם Gn 31^2 Dt 4^{42} 19^6
  (both words long)
C   תְּמוֹל שִׁלְשֹׁם   Ex 4^{10} $5^{7,8,14}$ 21^{36}
  (first word long)

Fig. 65: *t^emol* plus *šilšom*, all cases in the Torah

Genesis begins with the longest spelling combination, then moves to the shortest; Exodus uses the shortest, but only once, and apart from that one case it uses the mixed spelling with the first word long and the second short. The diagram makes no difference for the presence of propositions like *min* or *k^e-*, or for the cases which have *gam* before both words (Ex 4^{10}).

After we leave the Torah, spelling A, both words short, is not again found, and the dominant spelling is B: so Jos 3^4 4^{18} 20^5 1S 10^{11} 14^{21} 19^7 2S 5^2 2K 13^5 Rt 2^{11} 1C 11^2. Only in Samuel do we have exceptions, and they spell with first word long: 1S 4^7 21^6 2S 3^{17}. Some of the Samuel cases are אֶתְמוֹל or אֶתְמוֹל but these have been included as being the same thing as *t^emol*. 1C 11^2 is parallel to 2S 5^2 and thus shows the same spelling as the latter.

Chronicles is fond of the expression 'the first and the last', both words plural and with the article; the expression occurs in this way nine times in the book. Here again we find a sort of wave formation. There are three combinations in use, and the choices made are not the same as in the other two examples just given: the *-on-* element of the adjectives may be short in both, or long in both, or the word 'first' is short but 'last' is long. Although the combination appears nine times, only once (at 2C 12^{15}) are the spellings identical with the previous time.

A *-on-* short in both   1C 29^{29} 20^{34} 26^{22}
B *-on-* short in 'first',   2C 9^{29} 12^{15} 25^{26}
     long in 'last'
C *-on-* long in both 16^{11}
A 35^{27}
B   2C 28^{26}

Fig. 66: *ha-rišonim w^e-ha-'ah^aronim*, all cases in Chronicles

One other case in Chronicles may be mentioned: at 1C 23[27], in 'the last words of David', where we have 'last' but not 'first', BHS prints הָאַחֲרֹנִים defective, but the Masora, which states 'six plene', requires הָאַחֲרוֹנִים here also.

As a last example of phrases with combinations of variable spellings, consider this very striking case. In the tragic story of Amnon's sick love for his half-sister, in 2 Samuel 13, the same phrase 'let my sister Tamar come in' occurs twice, but the variable spellings are reversed between the first and the second:

2S 13[5]   תָּבֹא נָא תָמָר אֲחוֹתִי
2S 13[6]   תָּבוֹא־נָא תָּמָר אֲחֹתִי

It is really rather hard to say that this is not a stylistic touch on someone's part.

Yet this is the crucial question in this portion of our subject: was there an element of deliberate design in these configurations of spelling? Or can they be explained through an involuntary process whereby a waw is added here, a yod subtracted there, and the result is a pattern of fancy?

Many more such combinations of spellings can be found, though the ones already set out are perhaps the most elaborate or the most striking ones known to me at present. Another comes with the expression 'menservants and maidservants' in Genesis:

Gn 12[16] 20[14]   וַעֲבָדִים וּשְׁפָחֹת   (first long, second short)[1]
Gn 24[35]   וַעֲבָדִם וּשְׁפָחֹת   (both short)
Gn 30[43]   וּשְׁפָחוֹת וַעֲבָדִים   (both long)

These are all the cases of this phrase in the Torah. The phrase, with the third spelling, both long, occurs also at 2K 5[26] Qo 2[7]. The noun 'maidservants' is found also at Gn 33[1,2,6], with article, all three alike הַשְּׁפָחוֹת plene. As remarked above (p. 45), עֲבָדִם is a rare type of spelling and a unique one in this common word.

Here is a smaller example again of the same sort of thing:

Dt 28[11]   וְהוֹתִרְךָ יהוה לְטוֹבָה
Dt 30[9]   וְהוֹתִירְךָ יהוה ... לְטֹבָה

— this one depends however on the text, for the Leningrad Codex actually has לְטוֹבָה at 30[9], but the defective spelling is required by its own Masora (Mm 1222).

---

[1] Note that at Gn 12[16] these two words are immediately followed by the further doubly short writing וַאֲתֹנֹת 'and she-asses'; cf. above, pp. 48f..

5. Other groupings of spellings

Apart from the possibility of more complex recurrent patterns, one should also note groupings of the less usual spellings which come together in two or more words in juxtaposition. To take an obvious example: 1K 2[6] ends the verse with the sentence with the command 'and you shall not let his grey hairs go down to Sheol in peace', i.e.:

וְלֹא־תוֹרֵד שֵׂיבָתוֹ בְּשָׁלֹם שְׁאֹל

Now these last two words, with which the sentence ends, both have unusually short spellings. The spelling שָׁלֹם, as already stated (above, p. 53), is a rare one, occurring only eight times; though Kings has three of these eight, it has about thirty of the more normal spelling שָׁלוֹם. Again, שְׁאוֹל 'the underworld' is dominantly plene and, apart from the cases with the locative suffix -a, there are only two without waw, this one and one at Jb 17[16]. Kings has the long spelling just a few lines on, at 2[9], again the last word in the sentence. Thus we find that two rather unusual defective spellings occur together; and, of course, another בְּשָׁלֹם has been written just before, at 2[5].

Other groupings of the same kind can be found. Gn 45[22] has first of all חֲלִפוֹת שְׂמָלֹת and then at the end חֲלִפֹת שְׂמָלֹת with both words fully defective. Ex 4[8] has twice the two short spellings of the phrase לְקֹל הָאֹת, although it spells with waw both הָרִאשׁוֹן and הָאַחֲרוֹן (contrast Ex 12[15] הָרִאשֹׁן and 12[18] בָּרִאשֹׁן both without waw, the only cases of this defective spelling).

CHAPTER FOUR
Interpretation and Implications

In the end we come back, then, to the fundamental question from which we began: can we make some sense of the extraordinary variability of the spellings of the traditional Hebrew Bible text? Is there some rationale behind it, and if so, what is it? Can the highly variable spellings be explained at all? What factors brought this variability into existence? And why did the scribal tradition not settle for a clear, simple and consistent system, which would not have been so difficult to produce?

Scholars have often despaired of any answer. The learned Bergsträsser (1918) deplored that 'grosse Willkür und Inkonsequenz', a high degree of arbitrariness and inconsistency, applied to the use of the vowel letters.[1] Apart from this despondent generalization, and a few very obvious remarks about familiar examples, some of them wrong in any case, as we have seen,[2] Bergsträsser had little to say about the matter. The slightly later grammar of Bauer and Leander (1922) also noted the lack of consistency in the provision of vowel letters, but it did also express a reason why any of them were provided at all: they were 'probably originally placed there, in order that words that were written alike, but were to be read differently, should be distinguished outwardly as well'.[3] In saying this the learned authors appealed to an important paper by the honoured Septuagint scholar A. Rahlfs, published in 1916.[4]

The article of Rahlfs has three aspects which are particularly relevant for the present study. Firstly, he related the spelling differences to the historical development of Hebrew writing as it could be known on the basis of evidence from inscriptions. Secondly, he thought that, here and there, the longer spellings had been put in in

---

[1] G. Bergsträsser, Hebräische Grammatik (Leipzig, 1918), p. 45, §7e.

[2] Cf. above, pp. 13, 25f.

[3] H. Bauer and P. Leander, *Historische Grammatik der hebräischen Sprache des Alten Testaments* (Halle, 1922), pp. 91f., §7a.

[4] A. Rahlfs, 'Zur Setzung der Lesemütter im Alten Testament', *Nachrichten* of the Göttingen Academy, phil.-histor. Klasse, 1916, pp. 315–47.

order to resolve ambiguities of interpretation that would otherwise have been present. Thirdly, however, he thought in the end that some of the variations were more purely stylistic in character: just as Gn 1 varied, on the level of the actual verbal composition, between forms like לְמִינוֹ and לְמִינֵהוּ, which were semantically identical and yet provided a certain variety to the narrative, so on the graphic level any passage might vary stylistically between, let us say, שֵׁמֹת without waw and שֵׁמוֹת with waw. The second and the third of these three aspects will be matters to which we shall return.

Later this century the American school in the tradition of Albright, in this matter represented primarily by Cross and especially by Freedman, attempted a historical approach on the basis of epigraphic evidence. They sought to establish a chronology of orthographic developments, and historical reconstruction was central to their approach. Their work suggested that the variation of spellings within the traditional Bible text came from the superimposition of later orthographical practices upon the earlier. In favourable circumstances, however, one could 'restore' the original text, because one could detect traces which, properly interpreted, went back to the very composition of the books themselves. Cross and Freedman were extremely precise about what had happened afterwards: Cross tells us that in the establishment of the Masoretic or proto-Masoretic text 'a single orthographic tradition, in part archaizing to pre- or non-Maccabaean spelling practices, was *systematically* (my italics) imposed'.[1] Similarly Freedman writes that 'Masoretic spelling was *deliberately* designed to combine the best features of the different orthographies current in the 4th–3rd centuries... We may place the origins of Masoretic spelling as a definite orthographic system in the late third or early second century... apparently with *official* support, it gained primacy... and was ultimately successful as the *official* biblical spelling'[2] (my italics).

That I consider these ideas to be largely speculations without any good foundation will be sufficiently manifest to readers of this work. Not that one is against historical reconstruction, nor that one despises historical evidence; but I have not seen any evidence at all of these 'official' interventions in matters of biblical spelling, and it seems to me that one very large and solid piece of historical evidence, namely the facts of the Masoretic text, steadily and clearly defies explanation along the lines of Cross and Freedman's work.

---

[1] F.M. Cross in *HTR* 57, 1964, 28a; also in F.M. Cross and S. Talmon, *Qumran and the History of the Biblical Text* (Harvard, 1975), p. 185.

[2] *Textus* 2, 1962, 102.

But to this we shall return: this is only a first indication of our position.

First, however, it will be convenient to discuss the idea, rather hesitatingly put forward by Rahlfs, that the longer spellings were, at least at times, put in for the sake of intelligibility and to reduce ambiguity, particularly at the stage of the text where there was no pointing. It *may* be that the term 'mothers of reading' was coined in order to express something of the same sort of idea. But the notion, which is an obvious enough common-sense solution, quickly breaks down on two obvious considerations.

Firstly, in many cases where, in the unpointed text, ambiguity might have been very serious, no effort at all was made to overcome this ambiguity through the use of vowel letters. At Nu 9²², the first part of which unpointed reads אוֹ־ימים אוֹ־חדש אוֹ־ימים, there is a distinction between *yamim* 'days' (plural, doubtless meaning 'a year', and *yomayim* 'two days' (dual); but both alike are written as ימים, although the clear and unambiguous plene spelling for the dual, יוֹמַיִם with waw, not only was available but was actually used in all the other three places of 'two days' in the Torah, including one in Numbers itself a couple of pages later on (Ex 16²⁹ 21²¹ Nu 11¹⁹).

And cases of this kind can be multiplied infinitely. Daniel at Dn 9²⁴, in the famous but cryptic phrase 'seventy weeks', wrote שָׁבֻעִים שִׁבְעִים, with both words defective, although for any reader it could be a legitimate question which of the two words came first, and although the plene spelling שָׁבוּעַ existed in the singular and was used by Daniel himself (Dn 9²⁷).

In Jeremiah, again, there are three spellings of the plural 'prophets', נְבִיאִם, נְבִאִים, נְבִיאָם (although admittedly he uses the first of these only once, Jr 23³¹). But this prophet also uses a great deal the plural of the niphal participle נִבְּאִים, and often it is either immediately beside the word 'prophets' or is in a position where it might conceivably have been mistaken for it. Any chance of confusion could have been immediately evaded if the first or the third of the spellings had been used for the noun 'prophets', for the written yod would have made the situation clear. In fact, however, in none of the cases of juxtaposition with נִבְּאִים 'prophesying' does that elementary step of clarification appear to have been taken: on the contrary, the form נְבִאִים, which in unpointed text is the most likely to cause confusion, is the one that is actually used (cf. cases like Jr 14¹⁴,¹⁵ 23¹⁶,²⁵ 27¹⁴,¹⁵). In all these places the doubly plene writing נְבִיאִים would have been totally unambiguous, but nowhere was it used.

Another case from Jeremiah is even more persuasive. Jr 32³⁷ contains in the same verse two words that in unpointed text are written identically, as והשבתים: but one of them is וַהֲשִׁבֹתִים 'and I will bring them back' (from root שׁוּב), while the other is וְהִשַׁבְתִּים 'and I will settle them' (from root ישׁב). In their consonantal form the two are identical, and they are easy to confuse because their semantic areas are not far apart. The writer could easily have used spelling devices to make clear which word was which. For instance, he could have inserted a yod in the first, as he himself had just done at Jr 27²² וַהֲשִׁיבֹתִים; and, as for the second, the insertion of a waw in the first syllable would have been a clear indication that this was from the verb ישׁב; and such forms are used for this verb by Hosea and Ezekiel, and for other verbs in the same class by Jeremiah himself.

Conversely, it is manifest that vowel letters are included in many words where no doubt or ambiguity can be considered probable. The sequence שפר would naturally suggest 'trumpet' to any reader in almost any context, and other words with the same consonants are very rare in Hebrew; nevertheless it is dominantly spelt שׁוֹפָר with waw. There is no other word that could cause confusion to those reading בְּרִית 'covenant', and yet it is practically always written with yod. The same is the case with hᵃmor 'ass': it is not likely that readers would misidentify this as the word that means 'heap' or the one that means 'wine' or the like (Dt 32¹⁴): most contexts make it clear that it is an animal for riding or for bearing a load. Nevertheless even in the Torah the plene spelling חֲמוֹר is dominant, and in the non-Torah books it is the only spelling of the singular. But when we come to a rather difficult case, like Gn 49¹⁴, where we are told that Issachar is a חמר גרם, and it could be quite puzzling what words these were, the spelling is defective anyway and gives no indication.

Another reason lies in the manifest importance of affix effect. If yods or waws were put there in order to assist identification and reduce ambiguity, why were they so very often removed again as soon as the words in question became plural or had a pronoun suffix or even a definite article? If an ass was nearly always plene in the singular, why did asses become nearly always defective in the plural? There seems to be no answer to this argument.

The same point as the above could be repeated for a whole host of Hebrew words, for example חוֹמָה 'wall' or חוֹתָם 'seal'. Of all the vowel letters that are included in Hebrew words, only very few could reasonably be interpreted as having been put there in order to provide correct identification of the words and to remove ambiguity. Of course, there may be words in which the presence of a vowel letter did in fact assist in identification and understanding, but that does not mean that this was the reason why the vowel letters were supplied. All the evidence, taken as a whole, makes it impossible as a general explanation.

Moreover, it should be obvious that, if the inclusion of vowel letters was motivated by the desire for clarity in identification of words as against others with which they might be confused, the logic of this could lead in only one direction, namely towards the maximal use of plene spelling. If reduction of ambiguity is the motive, there cannot be any good reason for defective spellings, which by their own nature increase ambiguity. Yet defective spelling is manifestly widespread in the Bible. It is particularly strongly represented in the key zone of the Torah. On the whole, the spelling of the Bible is much more defective than is realized by the modern reader and scholar, who is deceived by grammars and by more recent usage into thinking of Hebrew in terms of a more plene spelling than is actually found. And defective spelling is, as has often been noticed, particularly strong in verb forms; but it may well be that verb forms have a higher degree of ambiguity, easily to be overcome through plene spelling, than other classes of words have: consider, for example, how in unpointed script the writing נשא could be 'he carried' (נָשָׂא) or 'carrying' (the participle נֹשֵׂא), and the ambiguity could be easily removed by writing the latter with a waw, but in fact the spelling is overwhelmingly without waw, and the one case written with waw (Lv 15^{10}, see above, p. 68) has no ambiguity about it anyway. Thus, to summarize, if the purpose of the choice is to avoid ambiguity, there is no reason in favour of defective spellings. The massive use of defective spelling in the Bible must, I submit, mean that the avoidance of ambiguity between reading as one form and reading as another was not a general guiding principle in the choice between variable spellings.

In this respect the operation of post-biblical and especially of modern spelling has been of quite different character. The reader of a modern Hebrew newspaper, seeing the writing אמר, can be pretty sure that it is 'amar (past) because, if it had been 'omer (participle, present in effect), it would have been written with waw. This is because the principle has been accepted in the culture generally, that vowel letters should generally be used in as consistent a manner as possible in order to reduce ambiguity. But in biblical writing this was not so. A person seeing אמר had no decisive reason to assume that it was not 'omer (participle) or 'amor (infinitive absolute) or ^{e}mor (imperative) or 'omar (1st singular imperfect), rather than the past; indeed, he had no reason even to take it as a probability. For instance, the writing נשא, unpointed, is actually more often the participle, נֹשֵׂא, than it is the perfect qal נָשָׂא. Or, again, in later times, the reader, faced with the writing ישב, might well be entitled to reason: surely if *yašib* (hiphil of שׁוּב) had been meant, a yod would have been put in. For the reading of the biblical text this entire logic is absent or at the most is subsidiary, tentative and precarious. A form ישבו could be *yašᵉbu* or *yošibu* (both from ישב), *yašubu* or *yašibu* (both from שׁוּב), and a variety of other forms as well. The spelling could not — in unpointed text — discriminate between all of these by vowel letters but it could easily discriminate several groups of possibilities and thus reduce ambiguity. In very many cases, however, it did nothing of the sort. We may conclude, therefore: it is possible that the will to use vowel letters to reduce ambiguity had *some* part in the production of the spelling patterns we find in the Bible, but if it had some part there must have been other factors which worked against it and meant that it was only very partially effective.

We may remind ourselves that the Bible was not just any document. It was sacred scripture, to be read officially in the synagogue by readers who knew this scripture extremely well in every detail. Such people were not so likely to be perplexed by an ambiguous written form like ישבו: from long practice in recitation they knew what the form was. This was not a newly arrived letter or a marketplace document that had to be deciphered in order for the meanings, and thereby the full audible form of the text, to be worked out. The failure of the biblical text to provide spellings that would resolve ambiguities is made much more understandable when this situation is taken into account. Even when the vocalization was not marked in the form of graphic signs, the oral reading tradition operated in the same way as such a vocalization.[1]

As was already indicated above, however, these remarks are not intended to deny that the vowel letters, once they were present, may have acted to improve identification of the words and to remove ambiguity. Presumably this is why they were called 'mothers of reading'. And yet one should not exaggerate the degree of assistance that is provided through their presence. Perhaps one can say this: that the assistance provided by the presence of vowel letters is

---

[1] See my discussions of this aspect in: 'Vocalization and the Analysis of Hebrew among the Ancient Translators', *VTS* 16, 1967, 1–11; and 'Reading a Script without Vowels', in W. Haas (ed.), *Writing without Vowels* (Manchester, 1976), pp. 71–100. On the later history of Hebrew spelling see the works of W. Weinberg, especially his *The History of Hebrew Plene Spelling* (Cincinnati, 1985).

at its greatest where they are *always* written, or at least written in very high proportion: I think, particularly, of the final vowels which indicate plurals, feminines and the like, which are almost always there, or of cases like the waws of Pe Waw hiphils, which are very commonly there and especially so in the Torah.

What has been said about this question should also be nuanced in another way. What I have opposed is the idea that in particular texts, at this point or at that, vowel letters were inserted in order to reduce ambiguity at that place, and that this was a major basis for the introduction of them at all. In saying this I do not wish to obscure the semantic function of plene spelling in another sense: namely, that the semantic function of reducing ambiguity formed part of the reason for the whole general slow development of spelling from a shorter to a longer style. This may or may not have had an important place: in any case I would not wish to question it in principle. Thus I have implied above (pp. 100–103) that the dominantly defective spelling of the imperfect qal of בוא, along with the dominantly plene spelling of the corresponding hiphil, had the semantic effect of distinguishing between two sets of forms that would otherwise have been very easily confusable. But this, if so, would probably be a motive in the general movement of spelling over a wide area, and not an individual decision of scribes at each point where they saw a potentially confusing word.

Another possibility, however, which has some degree of overlap with the view we have just discussed, is the following. It would be conceivable that a scribe, on introducing a new word, might think of spelling it plene early in his use of it, in order to help as far as was possible in the identification of it, even if thereafter he were to return to a more normal and defective spelling.[1] And indeed we have seen cases where something of the kind might be plausible: in one of our first examples we saw that תּוֹלְדוֹת doubly plene was the first case of this word in Genesis, and the tendency of Genesis to have a number of longer spellings in comparison with the core of the Torah in Exodus could be taken in the same way. Psychologically, such a procedure would be intelligible. Nevertheless it is not a probable account of the thought behind the variable spellings. Firstly, there is far too much negative evidence, far too many cases where nothing of the kind was done. In fact, if anything, I would guess (for precise measurement is hardly possible for this matter)

---

[1] Andersen and Forbes, pp. 217–20, had considered a similar idea, and rightly come to the conclusion that there is nothing in it. The examples they give are useful illustration.

that we more often find the reverse, namely that a word is written defectively two or three times before the plene writing is introduced. Nimrod for instance, is a גִּבֹר twice before he becomes a גִּבּוֹר, all in Gn 10$^{8-9}$. And this is psychologically equally comprehensible. The scribe writes the word a couple of times and then he thinks that his readers might find this confusing and that a plene spelling could help, and would verify retrospectively their reading. Since this type of explanation works equally well either way, it is impossible for it to lead us to any kind of certainty. Although plene spellings on the first introduction of a word are to be found, there is nothing like sufficient correlation between first occurrences and plene spellings to support this idea.

Moreover, even where we do find evidence for plene spelling at or near the first occurrence of a word in a book, this does not necessarily entail the conclusion that this was done with the motive of providing clearer identification at that early point. It could be explained in other ways. For instance, consider the following: the older form of the text has a large number of short spellings, but by this time the scribal convention is to use more yods or waws in these words. At the beginning of a book the scribe has this in mind, and from time to time he puts it into practice, not systematically but haphazardly, but with the effect that longer spellings appear on some of the first pages. But gradually he comes to do less of this: perhaps he forgets about the newer spelling convention and finds it simpler just to copy the older text. So he just introduces less changes than before. The motive of assisting identification and avoiding ambiguity simply does not come into the matter. This account of the process explains the same phenomena without any need to postulate that motivation.

Another explanation based on scribal procedures that I considered was this: what if waws and yods were used simply as graphic fillers in order to secure evenness at the ends of lines? It is well known that in later times there were strict rules about this sort of thing, and various devices for filling in space were permitted. Since the use of waws and yods was optional, scribes might have just inserted them, in such words as admitted their insertion, so as to take up space. This supposition would of course explain the highly arbitrary character of the distribution, which many scholars have remarked upon, and it might also help to explain the rapid gyrations between spellings that we sometimes see.

The idea is worth considering and cannot be entirely ruled out: even if it was something that happened only occasionally it would be significant. But there are evident difficulties. Waws and yods in

Hebrew script are narrow letters and even the addition of one or two of them to a line would not take up much space: unless we are to think of going back to the stage of the older script, in which yod at least was a sizeable character. But it would not be impossible: it could mean that, where we find three or four words together, all spelt with an unusual defective spelling, or another three or four, all spelt with a high degree of plene spelling, this sort of motivation could have entered in. It is interesting; but personally I doubt it very much. In any case, this view represents the extreme of the graphic approach to our problem: if it is right, or even only partly right, the choice of spellings was a purely graphic, scribal problem, and had nothing to do with the older grammar of the language or things of that kind.

From the side of scribal explanations of the variation of spellings, however, much the most obvious explanation is one that is so obvious that no one thinks of it: spelling varied because the scribes liked it to vary. Variation was something that they liked. If they introduced the common word *gibbor* with two cases defective and then at once went over to one plene, it was because they liked to do it in this way; if they wrote *tol‘dot* with four different spellings in Genesis alone, it was because they liked to do this too. If they used sharply alternating patterns for *yoš‘be* in Judges 1 or for *šemot* in Numbers 1, (pp. 24, 22 above), it was because they liked to do it in this way. Their approach to spelling was not systematic or consistent but occasional, opportunistic and at times exceptional: they did something, but they did not do it all the time; either they did it occasionally, or they did it most of the time, but if they did it most of the time they also made exceptions some of the time. If they liked variation, they could also equally well prefer consistency for a time and produce a block spelling of a word over a long series of instances. And this explanation is particularly powerful at all these many points where the variations are so numerous and so closely packed that they cannot in any probability be attached to supposed differences in the language, such as older morphological differences, or differences of local pronunciation. No one will seriously tell us that every variation between יֹשְׁבֵי and יוֹשְׁבֵי in Ju 1 is evidence of a different pronunciation or a different local dialect. For the many areas of this kind, scribal liking for variety is by far the most powerful explanation. Only it can explain why biblical spelling is so resolutely varied and unsystematic as it is.

In other words, biblical spelling has a stylistic aspect about it. It is a kind of art form. It is somewhat comparable to calligraphy: the writer can vary this way or that and each flourish is a sign of the writer's own way or tendency. Rahlfs was right in this aspect of his approach: it is like the choice between לְמִינוֹ and לְמִינֵהוּ in Gn 1: they say the same thing, the semantic effect of the difference is negligible, but they say the same thing in slightly different ways. The scribes, consciously or unconsciously, enjoyed this fact and expressed themselves through it.

Consciously or unconsciously? We have here touched upon the next stage of the question. If we do not think of scribal artistry, we have to think of mere inadvertence and lack of interest. If we follow this line of thinking, the scribe just did not know or care or remember how he had previously spelt this or that word: the variations are then accidental, no principle of any kind governs them. And I certainly would not doubt that this may give a good account of many. But the incidence of rapid alternation rather tells against this as a general account of spelling practice. Rapid alternation indicates that one varies the spelling very soon after one has used it. Still more powerful is the evidence of the occasional combination and 'wave formation' patterns which appear from time to time (cf. above, pp. 182–85). Some of these could be coincidental, but can this be true of them all? Is it not easier to believe that some of them are the product of design, something that does not have *meaning* in the normal sense, but represents a sort of signature of the scribal tradition? On the other hand I do not believe that vast numbers of these formations are likely to exist, and would deeply regret it if the notice given to some of them were to elicit an industry of discovering some kind of secret code disseminating a hidden message through the interaction of plene and defective spellings: there is no such hidden message.

Against all this, on the other hand, there stands the fact that important tracts of the variable spellings fit in very well with patterns that, in terms of historical linguistics, are very likely to have existed in the Hebrew language in the pre-Masoretic period. We have seen this to be probable in a considerable series of highly important word-classes: for example, in some words of the pattern *qatol* like עָמֹק 'deep' (above, pp. 56ff.); in the *i* vowel of the hiphil; in the waw consecutive imperfect; in some cases of the vowel *sere* with or without yod; in the endings of the second person singular masculine, –*ta* and –*ka*; in the –*na* of the feminine imperfect and imperative plurals. These are the more certain areas, and the same principle may well extend over others. In many such areas it is likely that the defective spelling fits with a morphology and grammar of Hebrew which antedated the Masoretic period; correspondingly, the plene spellings agree with shifts, often analogical, in Hebrew morphology which by Masoretic times were largely taken as normal or universal. In some areas the reverse may have happened, and the longer spelling was the older, and by later times had substantially decreased: this, we have suggested, could be the case with the –*ta* and –*ka* second person terminations. In such cases the survival of the older spelling was probably not the result of any intentional striving to preserve the older stage: the fact that so very many spellings do not retain the older style is clear evidence that changes in the spelling were readily undertaken. There is no need to posit such artificial concepts as 'archaizing': I see no evidence of any striving for 'archaic' forms of writing and no probability that anyone had such an idea in his mind. Old forms remained in the text through inertia or by accident, when large numbers of others were revised.

By the same token, however, the difference between one spelling and another does not give us the means of perception of the spelling relations as they actually were in that remote time: for, as we have just argued, many words have been altered in their spelling, and where this is so we cannot tell exactly how extensive was the spread of the older spelling. The area which is much more clear, and in which we can be much more certain, is the zone of non-varying spelling, the zone in which there is no alternation between one spelling and another, or in which such variation exists only in a minuscule degree and with an exceptional status. The largest and most obvious manifestation of this is the clear separation between the type of בֵּית and the type of צֵל, already discussed above. Although these were marked by the Masoretes with the same vowel *ṣere*, it is probable that they were phonologically distinct as vowels at the time when the text took its present form, and remained so for some considerable time afterwards, so that, apart from exceptional cases, scribal initiative was not tempted to assimilate them to one another. Such a case in one respect confirms the high degree in which the Masoretic text has preserved an earlier state of the language: on the other hand it is mistaken to take this as a principle that can be universalized, for it is true in this particular area of the language precisely because this is an area to which the conditions applying to most of the language did not apply. When we identify another such sector, such as we have suggested for the group of adjectives like עָמֹק (pp. 56f. above) or even for one single word like פְּלֵיטָה (p. 141 above), we are in effect saying that we have identified another small area that belongs to the non-varying zone.

Another aspect that cuts across this discussion is the matter of lexicalized convention, that is, the view that, for a certain lexeme, a certain spelling is the appropriate one — even if the form in question should have vowels which, in another word, might have a different spelling. The principle is one seen at enormous magnification in modern languages like English with its *him* and *hymn* or French with its *cent* and *sang*, plus a multitude of others. It has not generally been thought that anything of this kind existed in biblical Hebrew; but we have seen reason to suppose that it did. We have seen personal names, like Moses, Aaron, Jacob, of which it would be very reasonable to say that it had simply been agreed by convention, in most or all circles, that a particular spelling should be followed. Apart from proper names, the same could well be said of certain very common terms, like כֹּהֵן 'priest', which never varies, or like אֱלֹהִים which varies only extremely marginally. And we have seen words of the 'participle' form *qotel*, like סֹפֵר 'scribe', זוֹנָה 'harlot', אוֹיֵב 'enemy', שׁוֹעֲרִים 'door-keepers', of which the same sort of account seems to be plausible. Naturally, the extent to which this kind of spelling is present is minuscule in comparison with English or French, but that does not alter the possibility that it may be present in limited quantities.

And this, if it is so, greatly alters the structure of argumentation about Hebrew spellings. For it means that there is no simple and direct correspondence between spelling patterns and patterns of pronunciation. If, for example, the older books of the Bible spell the name of David almost entirely without yod, and then Chronicles spells it consistently with yod, that could mean that the pronunciation had altered by the time of Chronicles, or by the time of the origin of its present form of text — perhaps in connection with some shift of stress. But it could equally well mean that there was only a change of convention: in the past, someone said, David's name was spelt without yod, but it is now our procedure to spell it with yod, no matter whether there is any change of pronunciation (which no one, probably, would have known about in any case), and no matter whether we do the same with other words or not. If Chronicles always uses לא and never spells with waw as some other books do, it *may* mean that its pronunciation has abandoned a difference that other books still preserved, but it may also be that this is merely a matter of spelling convention: that, for the purposes of this book, all cases of *lo'* are spelt alike without waw. The probability that it is a matter of convention, and not a historical or local change in pronunciation, is made much greater by the fact that some other books, like Judges and Job (from two distant points on the spectrum of time and circumstance), do exactly the same thing. If a word has a divided spelling within the Torah and a united spelling in the non-Torah books, that does not necessarily mean that the non-Torah books had a different pronunciation for it, nor that there were two different pronunciations within the Torah: it may well mean only that the non-Torah books had a different, and an agreed, convention for that word or — to put it in another and a more historical way — that the convention used by the non-Torah books had been applied throughout their text, while in the Torah it had been applied only partially.

The discussion of Hebrew spelling has been too much dominated by the pair of concepts *phonetic spelling* and *historical spelling*. One may doubt the accuracy of the former for any writing system before the modern International Phonetic Alphabet which was scientifically designed for precisely this purpose: all other scripts are sets of conventions by which the medium of speech and the medium of writing may be related. When scholars speak of spelling as 'phonetic', they generally mean only that a written letter is pronounced as a consonant and is not a vowel letter. But this may be left aside: more damage is done by the concept of 'historical spelling'. By 'historical spelling' is commonly understood the situation of a word like בֵּיתִי 'my house': at one time there had been a consonantal yod there, that consonantal yod is no longer pronounced, but a yod is still written because it had once, 'historically', been there. But 'historically' here explains nothing: to think of it as an explanation is to commit a bad historicist fallacy. For no one wrote a yod because it had been written by people centuries before. They wrote it because it was *now*, in their time, the convention to write it. The conventions are commonly supplied out of the historical past, but that is not what makes them work.

This is important because it enables us to establish the category of morphological base spellings. The spelling with yod in בֵּיתִי 'my house' is not there because it was there as a consonant at some distant past time, but because it functions as the indicator that this word belongs to a certain class, a class to which צֵל 'shadow' does not belong. This means that the spelling difference could still be maintained as important even after the two classes of words had come to have the same vowel. Moreover, since operations of this kind worked analogically and not on the basis of past history, this enables us to see how the spelling of *e* with yod could be *introduced* in revision of a spelling where there had previously been no yod; cf. above, pp. 137, 148. And this in turn makes sense of the possibility that the waw of many Pe Waw forms may have been the later, and not the earlier, spelling in this important class of verbs.

The conjunction of these various aspects means that we have no means of returning into the past through the use of a sliding scale that works in one direction. It is probable indeed that there was a major movement from the shorter towards the longer spellings: this is generally believed, and I think rightly. But it was no simple movement. Words that had earlier been written with waw might come to be written without it, because plene spelling was optional and one did not *have to* perpetuate it: in that case the shorter spelling would be the later. In few cases, probably in no case, does the spelling give us access to the original. The spelling of a book depends not on when it was written, but on how late and how frequently it was revised, and under what conventions. Chronicles, which is the clearest proof of a strong movement towards a longer spelling, also preserves many spellings that are shorter than those in Samuel/ Kings. Strikingly short spellings can be found in books that are likely to be the latest. A few illustrations of this should be given. Of the five cases of יְבָא defective (cf. above, p. 101, Fig. 37), one is in Song of Songs, one in Qoheleth and one in Daniel (the five are: Nu 6^10 Ps 78^29 Ct 8^11 Qo 12^14 Da 11^8: Mm 871). Lamentations has יְשֵׁב defective at La 3^3: the only other such is at Ps 146^4, and this out of over 50 cases, nine of them in the Torah. It has the doubly short בְּתֻלֹת, La 5^11, the only case in the Bible; it also has La 2^10 בְּתוּלֹת, which is the spelling also at Ex 22^16. Here, then, Lamentations is shorter than Exodus. Esther would generally be counted as a 'late' book: but it has at 8^16 the only case of שָׂשֹׁן 'joy' without waw in the Bible; it has 2^6 גֹּלָה 'exile' defective, along with Na 3^10 1C 5^22, three cases out of 42 in the Bible; and, if the Masora is right, it has the rare short spelling 9^24 הִפֵּל 'he cast (lots)'.

We are sceptical, then, of all attempts to correlate the spellings, and the dates of spellings (if they could be known), with the dates, early or late, when books originated. As has just been pointed out, 'late' books like Lamentations and Esther contain some short spellings that might suggest an early date, and it is quite likely that some of these books had many more such spellings at an earlier stage, most of which were replaced by longer spellings during revision. Conversely, as was argued above (pp. 36f.), an early poem like the Song of Deborah contains many long ('late'?) spellings, and such, as will be shown, are by no means rare in the central parts of the Torah and in Exodus itself. If we eschew, then, all ideas of working from the spellings to the date of the books, we may nevertheless reasonably be asked the question: can we say something about the period to which the study of the spellings gives us access, the stage of development of the text about which they, in some measure, inform us?

The answer to this might be: something like the period 400–100 BC. For the latter limit, first of all, we would put this point: spellings of a common Dead Sea Scroll type, like כּוּלָם, גֵּירִים, רוֹעִי, do appear in the Masoretic text, but only very marginally: this could well suggest that the text was already well formed before these spellings became influential. This does not prove that these spellings were not yet in existence at all, but if they were the Masoretic text paid little attention to them and only few found entrance, so that in that sense, whatever its date, it reaches back to a stage anterior to them. In addition, it is well known that the second major Isaiah Scroll is quite close to the Masoretic text, and this confirms the existence of something close to our text by (say) the first century AD. In respect of spellings, indeed, this scroll is by no means identical with the Masoretic, but its closeness in general type is impressive. For interest I set in parallel a few cases from Is 60:

	Is 60[2]	60[5]	60[6]	60[10]	60[16]
MT	כְּבוֹדוֹ	יָבֹאוּ	לְבוֹנָה	בִּרְצוֹנִי	וּגְאַלֵךְ
Scroll	כבדו	יבוא	לבנה	ברצני	וגואלך

In these few cases, the Scroll has o defective thrice in nouns where the Masoretic is plene, and the reverse in a qal participle. The example is enough to indicate the sort of movement that may well have been taking place, in one direction or the other, over the previous century or so. It is not my purpose, however, to go farther into matters of the Qumran documents.

For the starting-point as named above, 400 BC, I would think that the agreement of Nehemiah with many characteristic spellings of the Torah must be significant. The transliterations of place-names in the LXX (above, p. 146) might also be significant; so might the view, often expressed by experts in the subject, that the LXX was translated from a text that had fewer vowel letters than the Masoretic. If I had to name a portion of text that might well have been undergoing revision down to a fairly late date within our period, I would think of the Minor Prophets, which, in spite of many short spellings of 'early' appearance, have numerous features that may point in this direction: I think particularly of the long spellings of the o vowel in the final syllable of qal imperfects, e.g. Ho 9[9] יִזְכּוֹר, יִפְקוֹד. But one cannot really make these correlations with a historical point, because all books, as we have insisted, have a mixture of spellings of very different kinds. Exodus, in spite of its many notably short spellings, has some of the opposite: Ex 23[8] צַדִּיקִים doubly plene, the only case in the Torah, similarly 15[10]

אַדִּירִים (contrast the 'Exodus-type' doubly defective spelling אַדְּרִם Ezk 32[18]) and 26[4] הַקִּיצוֹנָה.

There is no correlation, then, between the spelling tendencies and the date of origin of the books. Nor have I seen, in so far as we restrict ourselves to spelling variations, any correlation with differences of dialect. Matters of vocabulary, theme and cultural content lie, of course, beyond the field of the present study. And I do not doubt that dialect variations of a substantial kind may have existed at the time when books originated. But I find no serious evidence of them in the spellings of the Masoretic text. I have seen no constant features that run across books or sources of (say) probable North Israelite origin and distinguish them clearly from Judaean sources. There simply is *no* such correlation, or at the most tiny and insignificant fragments which have no effect on the general spelling patterns of the Bible. The spelling of the northern Hosea belongs with that of the southern Micah to the same general grouping of the Book of the Twelve Prophets. The same *kinds* of spelling variations are found in all books and all sources. The attempt of Freedman to show that spellings within Job could be explained by correlation with North Israelite dialect, and could thus determine the date and provenance of the book, was a conspicuous failure.[1] So far as I can see, the spellings of the Masoretic text show no indication of anything other than one single dialect. Even where we have seen diversities, such as the probability that the second person masculine singular termination existed in two forms, −ka and −ak, −ta and −t, and similarly −na and −an in the feminine plural imperfect, there is no indication that one of these series belonged to one dialect and the other to another: the minority spellings are distributed through a variety of books and have no correlation with matters of locality which could suggest dialectal variation. The whole idea that the idea of dialect should be invoked to help explain spelling variations should be judged to have been mistaken, and discarded.

Nor do I think that it makes sense to talk of different 'orthographies' which were successively imposed upon the text. When one reads the remarks of Cross and Freedman, quoted above, p. 187, about a 'single orthographic tradition' which was 'systematically imposed' and 'deliberately designed' and given 'official support', one wonders if those who wrote such statements had ever seriously considered the realities of spelling variation within the Masoretic text. From the most elementary beginnings of my study it seemed

---

[1] See my article in *JSS* 30, 1985, 1–33.

to me obvious that these ideas could not be right. For who 'deliberately designed' the configuration of the spellings of 'ephod' in Exodus alone that we have displayed in our Fig. 1 (p. 1)? What official decision ruled that tol*e*dot should be spelt in four different ways within Genesis (Fig. 2, p. 2)? What sort of systematic imposition was it that required that the spelling of šemot 'names' should alter back and forward eight times within the book of Numbers alone? It would have been quite easy for a spelling policy to be worked out and stated, and it would have been elementary for such a policy to deal with a simple matter like the spelling of šemot. But, clearly, nothing of the sort was done. Traces that might hint at such a policy can be seen here and there, as has been said, in certain limited matters, such as the spelling of lo' 'not'; but even this is the opposite of a general spelling policy for the Bible, for one book has directly the opposite policy from another, and in many books exceptions remain in any case, while some books remain totally divided (Kings, Jeremiah, Ezekiel) in even this simple matter. And, apart from small and limited cases like that of lo' 'not', all the evidence of the variable spellings is that policy and design had nothing to do with the matter.

In fact, the natural conclusion from the wide variation of spelling throughout the Bible is the opposite: the Masoretic text has the spellings that it has because one particular manuscript, or one small group of manuscripts, was decreed to be authoritative, and the spellings that happened to be within that manuscript or those manuscripts thereby became more or less normative. Moreover, this is just the sort of decision that 'official' or religious authority might reasonably be expected to take. This particular manuscript (I will use the singular for the sake of simplicity, and also because I think the idea of a single manuscript to be historically more probable) was taken to be standard because it was associated with some revered person, or because it was kept in a certain place in the temple, or because it was supposed to have some special history behind it. In the making of such a decision the general aspect of the spelling might indeed be noticed, and one might have said that it looked somewhat better than the sort of thing that was being written in the scriptorium at Qumran. But there is no reason to believe that the establishment and enforcement of a spelling policy on a wider front had any part at all. If there was a spelling policy which had 'official support', one must conclude that that policy was carried out with the utmost incompetence.

For the obvious character of biblical spelling is its *haphazardness*. Consistency is at a discount, and variation at a premium. As we have repeatedly observed and insisted, the variations run across all books, all sources, all periods. Exceptions are not exceptional but are the normal thing. It is reasonable to suppose that when the text, which became ancestor of our own, became decisive, it was caught in the middle of a long process of change, much of it from the shorter to the longer, some of it no doubt the opposite. Much of this change took place haphazardly: as texts were copied, a waw was added here, a yod there, and in many cases not methodically; what was done in one verse was not done in the next. The probable understanding of this is that much of it was unconscious. Scribes did not think that they *had* to add a waw or yod, that it was their duty to do so, just as they did not on the other hand think that it was their duty to copy the text without any alteration whatever. Thus from יבא (say) the text drifted towards יָבוֹא; sometimes the latter was written, sometimes it was not. If the attitude to the text had not altered, through the greater insistence on the exact *Wortlaut* and wording, no doubt the entire biblical text would have moved to a more homogeneous state of spelling than that which we now have: two or three centuries might have completed such a process. But change of that kind came largely to a stop. Our text therefore lies half-way along a process of change, largely involuntary, some of it deliberate and purposeful.

Another aspect that follows from this is that terms like 'archaizing' or 'archaism' have no meaning. Nowhere in my studies of variable spelling have I seen evidence that requires or even suggests an understanding of this kind. 'Archaizing' implies some kind of deliberate choice of the older, some intentional preference that led to spelling in styles of an earlier time. I see no reason whatever to believe that this had a part in the matter. The improbability that scribes or other 'official' persons had the historical knowledge and perspective to know what was older may be mentioned in passing; but the more serious objection is that the spellings that can reasonably be regarded as 'archaic' and the like can all be accounted for as survivals. They are old spellings which, because of the haphazard character of the change in spelling, had never been altered. Here and there in this study we have suggested that certain grammatical forms different from the grammar based on the vocalized Masoretic text existed in earlier times, and that these are reflected in the spelling. But there is nothing in the distribution of these spellings to suggest that they are there because someone deliberately intended to 'archaize'. They are not concentrated in 'late' books, which might have wanted to create an impression of the past; they are sporadically scattered over a wide variety of texts, and are usually a minority in them all. 'Archaizing' is an artificial creation born of the historical approach: it may, of course, be true of some other bodies of text, but in the traditional Bible text there is no reason to think of it.

To put it in another way, there are not really a variety of 'orthographies' embedded in the Masoretic text. Strictly speaking, there is only one orthography, which is the same for the entire Bible. But it divides into two zones. The first is the zone of non-varying spellings: it is of this zone that the term 'orthography' is really meaningful. This orthography requires, for example, that the *u* termination of plural verbs is written with waw if it is really in final position and not followed by a suffix, that the *-ti* termination of first person perfect singulars is written with yod, that the *ā* vowel even when long is not written with a vowel letter except in final position — in other words, the familiar constants of Hebrew spelling. The existence of very rare and sporadic exceptions does not alter the comprehensiveness of Hebrew orthography in this sense. Historically speaking, we may add that this unity has probably been brought into being through a process of change, a last stage of which is visible in the KQ system. But this fact does not alter the comprehensiveness of the system. It is really an '*ortho*-graphy' in the sense that it would be wrong to write otherwise, although very rare exceptions do exist.

The other zone, the zone of variable spellings, is quite different. In it there is not an 'orthography', strictly understood: choices are not between right and wrong. For a particular form there are options, at least two, often three or four. The optional character of the writing is fundamental to the understanding of it. If a scribe, copying the word יבא, added a waw and made it into יבוא, this was not because he thought that it was 'wrong' to spell it without. It was precisely because the writings were optional that it was natural to make alterations, and equally it was because they were optional that they were made haphazardly and not rigidly imposed at every point.

Historically expressed, the zone of variable spellings may be only the zone in which transition to a new spelling has been left incomplete: perhaps, if the process had gone on long enough, only יבוא would have been acceptable and יבא would then have become 'wrong'. But this had not happened, and the optionality of the many variable spellings is a fundamental and inherent fact of the Masoretic text. We are aware that it works in this way now, that יבא and יבוא are different optional writings of the same form; but it is insufficiently realized that it was already so in ancient times, for example at the time when the basic selection and authorization of the ancestor of the Masoretic text was made. Many statements made about 'orthography' obscure this fact. Did the four different spellings of the one word tol‘dot in Genesis belong to different systems of orthography? Of course they did not.

'Orthographic patterns followed rigid laws', declared Cross and Freedman as a principle of their still important book.[1] This principle is entirely mistaken. It is mistaken because there are many different ways in which the medium of speech and the medium of writing may be interrelated. Change could go in opposite directions at the same time. Lexicalized preference for a particular spelling for certain words ignored the rigid laws, if there were any. Spellings that signalized the morphological base of a word were quite different in character from those that followed its phonological form alone. And optionality, so important in the Masoretic text, is the final defiance of the idea of rigid laws.

These assertions are valid not only for the Masoretic text, but also for epigraphic evidence. Epigraphy is not a simply empirical discipline that gives direct access to hard facts: on the contrary, it is a highly ideological subject, deeply dependent on the philosophical categories with which it is approached. The ideas of language which we have, the categories which we are ready to apply, the things that we hope to prove, deeply affect what we are likely to 'see' in the evidence. Highly improbable analyses of epigraphic evidence, such as the argument that קל in the Siloam inscription was qāl and not qōl, and that ים 'day' was yām and not yōm, are products of the general ideas about language and writing with which the subject was approached.[2] And, as for variety, which is so central to the Masoretic text, only a rigidly doctrinaire approach can doubt that variation of spelling, of a similar kind though much less in degree, existed in inscriptions also. Variation even within one body of text was a familiar feature of the culture.

When we see that the Hebrew Bible has really only one orthography, which included a zone of optional spelling, we can understand better how it can all be read as one whole and the numerous spelling differences trouble the reader little, so that he often remains largely unconscious of them. Apart from very sporadic and non-systemic variants, the non-varying zone remained the same

---

[1] *Early Hebrew Orthography,* pp. 59f.

[2] *Early Hebrew Orthography*, p. 50, with references to pp. 24, 53. For a recent criticism see Z. Zevit, *Matres Lectionis in Ancient Hebrew Epigraphs* (Cambridge, Mass., 1980), pp. 20f.

throughout the Bible. The variable ones differed in that they were combined in different proportions and in different tendencies in different sections of the text. But no book or section of text appears to have any solid group of spellings that differs qualitatively and in kind from spellings that are found in other portions. Seen in this way, they all formed one way of writing and there is no reason to see a conflict of orthographies in the matter. In other words, in pure principle, the whole text could in theory have been written by one man with one orthography, who just altered the mixture, changed the proportions and tendencies within the zone of variable spellings, as he moved through the books from Genesis to the Prophets and to Chronicles or Nehemiah. I do not think that it came about in this way but in principle it could have been so.

If one man, in theory, *could* have done it, there is no reason why we should think that one man *did* do it. Andersen and Forbes see in the spelling of the Hebrew Bible 'the imprint of a single mind' and the product was 'a monumental achievement'.[1] Not at all. Again the fact of the variable spellings tells against such a speculation. Did this great mind work out the four spellings of *tolᵉdot* in Genesis, and the order in which they were to come? Did it design the pattern of eight or so changes in the spelling of *šemot* within Numbers alone? In fact the totality of biblical spelling looks as if it had been arrived at by the small, slight and often involuntary choices of many small minds, rather than the masterly comprehension of one great mind. No great mind, if it had power to decide on the matter, could have worked on biblical spelling without tidying up the *Willkür und Inkonsequenz* which has troubled everybody who thought about the subject ever since.

This brings us back to the question as it is often expressed, namely, is the Masoretic text really old? This depends on what you mean by 'old'. It is certainly old in the sense that it goes back to long before the time of the Masoretes, after whom it is named, because they cared for it and provided it with vowel points, accents and Masora. The base text to which they added these was inherited by them from a time long before. It had probably changed only slowly from about the beginning of the era, and at about that time the Qumran documents show us a text that is fairly close to it in spelling. We have also suggested that the very slight influence of the sort of long spellings known from other Qumran documents may probably associate the Masoretic text with a time before these documents were written, or, more correctly, with a tradition that goes

---

[1] Andersen and Forbes, pp. 322f.

back to a time when the spelling of these documents was still unknown or not accepted. So in that sense the text is 'old'. But 'old' in
this sense is still not *very* old: it does not take us back to the time of
Jeremiah, still less to that of David.

Readers should be reminded that we are not concerned here to
discuss this question in a general way, but only in so far as we have
indications from the spellings of the text. These work in a peculiar
and slightly contradictory way. For the internal analysis of the
variable spellings, coupled with some philological information,
does suggest that certain spellings reflect grammatical patterns that
had existed in Hebrew but had been covered over by other, usually
analogical, formations in the grammar implied by the Masoretes.
This argument appears to support the antiquity of the text, at least
its relative antiquity. But the same argument carried with it the
corollary that the traditional text, as pointed and as used with the
grammar with which we read it, is not a correct replica of the text
as it was in ancient times.

For, as has been said already, it must be considered unlikely that
any book, perhaps that any passage, still retains the spelling of the
original composition, or even the spelling of a moderately ancient
time like the last century of the Judaean kingdom. Characteristic
spellings of the times of Isaiah and Jeremiah are never found in the
Masoretic text (cf. already above, p. 20). If a prophet wrote ים 'day'
or נבא 'prophet', as is quite likely, then his original spelling has been
revised out of existence. Nevertheless there are certain ancient
spellings which, through the various influences and factors that
have been traced in this study, may have been less likely to be
revised in later times, and these may well go back to a remote antiquity. The evidence of the spellings, however, because of the diversity of the influences which may have borne upon them and the
contrary directions in which revision is possible, does not enable us
to identify precisely what these oldest spellings are. Our basis for
triangulation does not permit us to go, even speculatively, beyond
about the time of Nehemiah. For it should be remembered — this
is another corollary of what has been said — that even if the spellings give us a glimpse of a pre-Masoretic grammar, and even if we
know that the base text of the Masoretic text existed already about
the first century, the grammatical difference has to be calculated
back from the Masoretic *grammar*, and not from our first knowledge of the base text itself.

An illustration from a slightly different sphere may be offered.
Gn 49, the Blessing of Jacob to the heads of the tribes, is agreed to
be a very old poem. One of its features is that it has several examples

of the third person suffix *-o*, spelt with he rather than with the usual waw, but altered to waw in the Qere: e.g. Gn 49¹¹ עִירֹה 'his ass'. It would be easy to hail these writings as additional evidence, if any were needed, of the archaic nature of the poem. But this would be a misunderstanding: for inscriptions show that the spelling with he was used right down to the exile. The spellings, being peculiar as against the normal practice of the Masoretic text, appear at first sight to show that the poem is old: but they do not show it to be old *enough*. They are evidence, not of great antiquity, but of the fact that some few suffixes escaped a revision to waw that must have overtaken the vast majority. Similarly, in Jeremiah we find several cases spelt with he which were not rewritten even within the KQ system: so Jr 2²¹ 8⁶ 15¹⁰ כִּלֹה. Such spellings are not evidence of very ancient origin, but of exceptional escape from a revision that was general but not complete.

It remains to consider the question whether the development of spellings may have affected the preservation of the text. It has been suggested, and is no new idea but has long been widely held, that older stages of the text may well have had many shorter spellings; it may, for instance, have had many more cases of אֲבֹת defective than the two cases in Exodus that we now have. But what about the more serious problem, namely that the text may have been wrongly copied, so that words came out as the 'wrong' words, as semantically different words, or were misunderstood, or were missed out? Now the present study does not tell us much that penetrates into this dark area. I would explain this as follows. Firstly, if the text went wrong in transmission, this mainly took place at a stage in time long anterior to the development of spellings that we can trace; and so our analysis of the spellings in the Masoretic text for the most part simply gives us no purchase on that sort of question. Secondly, as I have suggested, the spelling patterns of the Masoretic text support the view that it was selected because a particular manuscript (or small group) was selected, and others were ignored. Just as there was no 'official' policy about the spelling, so there was no 'official' enquiry into the varieties that might exist among the words themselves. There were, of course, variant text forms, as we know from the LXX and Qumran, but these were just not taken into consideration, and in the Hebrew text transmission they simply faded away.

Nevertheless there are some cases of textual difficulty that may well be connected with our subject. If the spelling of a word was unfamiliar to a scribe, he might mistake it for another word which its spelling might suggest. Two instances were already discussed above (pp. 145f.). Although '*iš* 'man' was spelt as אש in ancient inscriptions, the word is understood to be invariably אִישׁ plene in the Masoretic text, retaining its yod in all cases even with affixes and having over 1,650 occurrences in the singular. Now at Ezk 8² we have the phrase כְּמַרְאֵה־אֵשׁ 'like the appearance of fire', but it is not unlikely that the true text here meant 'like the appearance of a man', which would fit also with the following 'from the appearance of his loins'. The LXX has ὁμοίωμα ἀνδρός, 'the likeness of a man'. Many scholars have accepted this and it looks highly probable. If so, it does not imply that the text should be corrected to אִישׁ (as in BHS margin, etc.) but only that the vowel point be corrected to אִשׁ. The point is that the word, written as אש, and read by people who already thought, perhaps, that 'man' was always written with yod, then came to be pronounced in the oral tradition as '*eš* and taken to mean 'fire'. This could be assisted by the fact that the phrase 'like the appearance of fire' actually exists, and in a place of great importance which every Jew would know, Nu 9¹⁶ וּמַרְאֵה־אֵשׁ לַיְלָה, and also by the fact that אֵשׁ 'fire' itself follows just after in Ezekiel.

A related but somewhat different process may have taken place at the well-known place Jb 3⁸, where אֹרְרֵי־יוֹם has often been taken to be 'those who curse the sea', giving a parallel with Leviathan in the second part of the verse. If this is right, it would suggest that the text was written as ים, at a time when 'day' was also written with that same spelling. (In the present Bible text, of course, 'day' singular is always written with waw.) The writing was thus then ambiguous. The reading tradition opted for 'day' and in due course it came to be revised with the waw that was standard for that word.

It remains to say something about the practical consequences of all these considerations for various operations of scholarship in the future.

Firstly, and most obviously, all grammars should, under each class or form, give a brief indication of the spelling patterns that are to be expected. This is particularly important because paradigms and other tabulations of forms tend, for obvious pedagogic reasons, to standardize to a high degree, commonly favouring plene spelling, and thus fail to alert the student to the spellings that he will actually encounter. No elaborate indication would be required. Thus, as an illustration, for the qal participle of triliteral verbs one might find it sufficient to put in an entry like this:

Qal active participle has dominant spelling defective as in שֹׁמֵר, but plene spelling as in בּוֹגֵד is quite frequent, e.g. in Ezekiel,

Proverbs, Qoheleth, and plene spelling is also strongly favoured in certain verbs; e.g. הֹלֵךְ, יֹשֵׁב, and several other Pe
Waw verbs.

Secondly, a full-scale grammar of the spellings of the Masoretic
text is a desideratum. This present study has limits of space and time
which made it necessary to omit many types of words which have
interesting variable spellings. For each class of word information
should be given about the spellings that occur, their proportions,
the books in which they occur, and other such data. Such a work
should be a reference handbook to accompany the normal grammar.

Similarly, thirdly, thought should be given to the preparation of
a concordance of a type that would be especially suitable for the
study of spellings. None of the existing works are entirely suitable,
although I have found Mandelkern the easiest to work with. In
particular, such a concordance should register certain forms not
under lexemes but under morphological categories; for instance, all
qal imperfects with *o* vowel spelt with waw, like יִזְכּוֹר, should be
gathered under one listing. Similarly, out-of-the-way terms like
the object particle plus suffix, אוֹתָם etc., should be fully listed, since
these are among the worst objects to discover from the current
works of reference. A modern text edition should be clearly taken
as basis; or, better still, two or three forms of text should be collated
for the purposes and the variants given. If it were possible, I would
suggest: the Aleppo Codex where extant; BHS as printed; the
Leningrad Codex as it would be if it agreed with its own Masora;
and the Bomberg Bible of 1524.

The fourth type of scholarly literature that might be expected to
look at the spelling practices of books is the commentary. The commentary writer has an ideal opportunity to observe any changes in
the spelling practices of a book, and to note unusual combinations
of different spellings, rapid alternations and other patterns. Major
changes of spelling practice within a book, if observed, could be of
significance for hypotheses about its textual history. It is therefore
all the more surprising that most commentaries, even those that
have concentrated especially on the text, have said little or nothing
about the spelling practices of the book in question. For instance,
S.R. Driver's *Notes on the Hebrew Text and the Topography of the Books
of Samuel* (Oxford, 1913), which is one of the classic commentaries
concentrating on textual matters, seems simply to have said nothing about the variations in the spelling of the names Absalom and
Jonathan which we have mentioned above (pp. 23, 167) or about

the variation in the spelling of *n ᵉbi'im* , including the unusual spelling which begins to appear at 1S 19²⁴ נְבִיאָם. This is remarkable, because Driver was keenly interested in orthography and his book was, for hundreds of students, the standard introduction to the subject.

But Driver well typifies the historicist approach to the subject. Orthography was important as a means of entering into the world of *pre-Masoretic* writing, of knowing how it had been in an earlier stage, how it had been when the LXX was translated. But the actual distribution of spellings in the Masoretic form of Samuel received from him little comment, indeed practically none. Since his time, most commentaries which have given serious discussion to the text have done the same thing: they have discussed each textual variation in detail, but have not preceded this with a description of the way in which the spellings of the text lie, just as it stands today. It seems reasonable to suggest that each future commentary should include a section on the profile of spellings in the Masoretic text of the book in question, done on the basis of the commentator's own reading, and forming a prolegomenon to his discussion of textual variations coming from other sources. I have myself begun to prepare a series of such profiles of individual books, on the basis of my own studies, and one will be included as an appendix to indicate one way in which such a work might be written. The present work will, it is hoped, at least train commentators in what to look for.

APPENDIX

Specimen Profile of One Book: the Psalms

It was suggested above (p. 211) that for each biblical book a short profile of its spelling tendencies should be prepared. Such a profile would be a cross-section across the approach through different types of words: it would form a reference chart against which the scholar, while studying particular forms, would be able to see at a glance how far they conformed to, or failed to conform to, the general tendencies of that particular book. Such a profile should not seek to present every detail but rather should give an adequate general impression of the contours of spelling within the book. It should note both elements of constancy within a book and elements which seem to vary a lot; it should note rapid alternations and also any points at which a consistent block spelling appears to commence. The task of preparation of such profiles should be a manageable one, since one book forms a more compact body of data than the whole Bible as a totality. Drafts of such profiles have been prepared by the present author or are under preparation, and this one of the Psalms is only one first attempt.

The Psalms are a particularly interesting area in which to do this, because the book consists of about 150 discrete units about the separate existence of which there can be no doubt. Only the more obvious points about the spelling of these poems will be mentioned in this draft specimen.

In the Psalms, the spelling of plural –*im* without yod is very rare: cf. 37[18] תְּמִימִם, a type more familiar from the Torah; 57[5] לְבָאִם; 111[8] עֲשׂוּיִם hardly counts, since there is a yod that is part of the stem in any case. For the same reason, cases like גוֹיִם 'nations' are spelt with only one yod, as in all other books.

The –*ot* ending of plural nouns, when without suffix, is overwhelmingly plene: exceptions spelt short include 28[5] פְּעֻלֹת 37[4] גְּבוּרֹת 90[10] מִכְלְאֹת 74[6] וְכִילַפֹּת 78[70] מַחְמָאֹת 55[22] יְשׁוּעֹת 43[5] מִשְׁאֲלֹת 42[12] 110[3] נְדָבֹת. A number of others are short words already containing a waw and therefore less likely to receive another, e.g. 56[13] תּוֹדֹת 58[3] עוֹלֹת 64[7] 65[4] עֲוֺנֹת; leaving aside such words, there are rather few short spellings of –*ot* in the central portion of the book. And after

110 there are practically no cases until near the end of the book: תוֹכֵחֹת 149[7] זְיִּת 144[12] מַדְחֵפֹת 140[12]. A number of words in the superscriptions have a spelling in which the –ot is short but a vowel in the body of the word is long: so 54[1] 55[1] 67[1] 76[1] נְגִינֹת, 45[1] יְדִידֹת.

When the plural ending –ot is followed by a pronoun suffix, the long spelling, with waw, is greatly dominant in the Psalter as a whole. Here and there, however, the incidence of short spellings rises, as in 78, which has several such as 78[28] מִשְׁכְּנֹתָיו, so also 78[63,64]. Some other cases that are short are of nouns like עֹונֹתֵינוּ (90[8]), מִצְוֹתֶיךָ (119[6] etc.) which contain a waw of their stem already. Leaving these aside, we find that there seems to be a slow increase in the number of short spellings towards the end of the book and this increases in the last few poems. Examples include: 108[12] בְּצִבְאֹתֵינוּ (against the parallel 60[12] which is plene), 109[14] אֲבֹתָינוּ, 111[4] לְנִפְלְאֹתָיו, 126[6] אֲלֻמֹּתָיו, 144[14] בִּרְחֹבֹתֵינוּ (doubly short), 145[6] נֹורְאֹתֶיךָ, 145[12] גְּבוּרֹתָיו 150[2], 146[4] עֶשְׁתֹּנֹתָיו. Since it is reasonable to think that many poems of the latter part of the book are also latish in date of origin, we seem to find, perhaps surprisingly, that the longer spellings are often in the first part of the book, the shorter in the latter part.

Among verb forms the participle deserves particular comment. The dominant spelling of the triliteral type *qotel* is short: thus 15[2] עֹזֵר 54[6] פֹּעַל and many others. Although in *yošeb* the plene spelling is frequent in the Bible as a whole, in the Psalms the shorter יֹשֵׁב is dominant, and similarly in the plural construct, where nine cases are defective, and only 84[5] 107[34] are plene. There is a preference, however, for the long יֹודֵעַ, and also for the long construct plural יֹורְדֵי. In Double 'Ayin roots long spellings are more evident: 5[6] צֹורְרֵי 7[5] הֹולְלִים, although short spellings also appear, e.g. 23[5] 31[12] שֹׁרְרָי 54[7] צֹרְרָי. Also a number of participles from triliteral roots are written with waw when with a plural ending or other suffix, e.g. 2[2] שֹׁוטְנַי 109[29] נֹוזְלִים 78[16] שֹׁולְמֵי 7[5] רֹוזְנִים (contrast 109[20]).

In Lamed He participles the dominant spelling is short. Plene writings occur sporadically, often with plural forms, absolute or construct: 2[12] 5[12] חֹוסֵי 17[7] חֹוסִים 118[22] הַבֹּונִים. Some singulars appear later, e.g. 34[23] פֹּודֶה 35[5] דֹּוחֶה 37[32] צֹופֶה 73[27] זֹונֶה.

In very general terms, the number of long spellings is higher in the earlier part of the Psalter. After Ps 45 or so it drops off markedly, but there is a revival towards the very end of the book, in 142–50. Here and there one finds a Psalm with an unusually high number of long spellings: for example, Ps 37 has six plene but three defective in the triliteral singular. At the end, Ps 145 has five long spellings but none short in the triliteral singular, but spells without waw in the plurals and suffixed forms. There are signs that point to a lexicalized preference: the common עשׂה is never plene, while חוֹסֵי, חוֹסִים 'trust' begins thrice plene (2^{12} 5^{12} 17^{7}) and then thrice defective (18^{31} 31^{20} 34^{23}) out of a total of six in Psalms. בּוֹטֵחַ with the same meaning is thrice plene (Ps 27^{3} 32^{10} 86^{2}) out of seven in the book, and the two of them that have the article are plene.

We saw that 145 has a high number of long spellings. 146 by contrast — another psalm with many participles — uses only the short spelling. 147 has no less than three plene spellings in Lamed He ($147^{2,4,11}$) but prefers short in the regular triliteral verb. To sum up, then, there is no simple correlation between spelling of the participles and position within the Psalter, but many long spellings are in the earlier part — where many of the poems, incidentally, may well be among the earliest.

Among imperfects with vowel o, and similar infinitives, there are a few spellings with waw, mainly at the beginning of the book: thus 7^{13} יִלְטוֹשׁ, and likewise $10^{9,15}$ $17^{12,12}$ 18^{38} 32^{9}, but this then drops away, and there are very few after 45: I have noted none from 45 till 87^{6}. After Ps 100 a few reappear, twice with the verb יִשְׁכּוֹן Ps102^{29} 104^{13}. Near the end of the book we have 141^{10} אֶעֱבוֹר and similarly 148^{6}. The total number of such spellings in Psalms is low.

One common word that might be considered along with participles is אוֹיֵב 'enemy', a common term in the Psalms, especially in the earlier part of the book, where the concept is more prominent. If we count all forms of this word, with or without suffix, there are slightly more spelt with the waw of the first syllable. Psalms that use both spellings include: 18, 25, 41, 68, 143. Another word of special interest that has been discussed above is שׂנא: see pp. 78f., 107.

The distribution of spellings of the second masculine singular suffixes –ta and –ka has already been discussed above (pp. 114–27) but should form part of any such profile published separately. Prominent among the Psalms using this spelling are 8, 10, 60, 89 and 139; 60 and 139 have three cases each. All these poems also have the spelling without he. The long spellings in 89 come close together towards the end of the poem, those in 139 again close together, all at the beginning. The –ta ending on verbs is far more common, and the –ka ending appears only at the end of the Psalter (139 and after).

One aspect in which the Psalms are particularly consistent is the presentation of the plural u at the end of a verb when followed by an object suffix, a form which is quite frequent in the poems. The spelling is massively in favour of the plene writing for this, and exceptions are few and sporadic: 23[4] יְסוֹבְבָה, 55[11] יְהוֹדְךָ, 45[18] יְנַחֲמְנִי, 61[8] יִנְצְרֻהוּ. 88[17] צִמְּתוּתֻנִי, 139[20] יֹאמְרֻךָ, 145[18] יִקְרָאֻהוּ and some others. This short spelling is nowhere common but, in so far as one can speak of any area favouring it, it is the area of Ps 45–64.

The above however has omitted the one Psalm that is widely divergent: 119, which has at least five short out of sixteen relevant spellings: 119[41] יַעַזְרֻנִי, [175] יְעַשְׂקֻנִי, [122] עֻדְנִי, [61] הֲלִיצֻנִי, [51] וַיְבַאֻנִי. This may be coupled with the fact noted above (pp. 132f.) that Ps 119 has a unique concentration of spellings of what are, by the Masoretic text, plural nouns with suffix but without the intervening yod which is normal. As was suggested, some of these may be singulars which came to be read as plural, and the plural reading was applied also to the verbs, but the *u* ending was not marked on the verbs by addition of a waw.

The hiphil spelt without yod in the second syllable is uncommon in the Psalms, and especially in the latter part of the book. Cases have been mentioned above, p. 174, and one may add 90[12] וְנָבִא (if this is hiphil of בּוֹא); 105[43] וַיּוֹצִא; 142[8] יַכְתִּרוּ. There are others which are suffixed and can be accounted for on that ground, such as: 27[5] יְסָתִּרֵנִי; 105[24] וַיַּעַצְמֵהוּ; 140[11] יַפְלֵם.

Passive participles written short include: 88[9] כָּלֻא; 51[8] סָתֻם; 97[11] זָרֻעַ; 112[7] בָּטֻחַ; 131[2,2] גָּמֻל; 139[20] נָשֻׂא (text?).

Here and there we have unusual short forms of *i*-containing words, such as 143[9] כִּסְּתִי 128[3] כְּשְׁתֻלֵי. There are a number of places where vowel letters are used for vowels in which they would normally not be written, e.g. 49[6] יְסוּבֵּנִי; 81[2] עוּזֵּנוּ; 84[6] עוֹז (root ‘–z–z); 107[27] יָחוֹגּוּ.

SELECT BIBLIOGRAPHY

This does not attempt to give a full listing of works relevant for the subject, but includes only those actually mentioned in the text, plus a few others which come particularly close to the same themes and should be brought to the notice of readers.

Abercrombie, D.	*Elements of General Phonetics* (Edinburgh: Edinburgh University Press, 1967)
Andersen, F.I., and Forbes, A. Dean,	*Spelling in the Hebrew Bible* (Rome: Biblical Institute Press, 1986)
Barr, James,	'Vocalization and the Analysis of Hebrew among the Ancient Translators', *VTS* 16, 1967, 1–11
do.	'Reading a script without vowels', in Haas, W., ed., *Writing without Letters* (Manchester: Manchester University Press, 1976), pp. 71–100
do.	'Some notes on *ben* "between" in Classical Hebrew', *JSS* 23, 1978, 1–22
do.	'*Migraš* in the Old Testament', *JSS* 29, 1984, 15–31
do.	'Why the World was created in 4004 BC: Archbishop Ussher and Biblical Chronology', *BJRUL* 67, 1984–85, 575–608
do.	'Hebrew Orthography and the Book of Job', *JSS* 30, 1985, 1–33
Bauer, H., and Leander, P.,	*Historische Grammatik der hebräischen Sprache* (Halle: Niemeyer, 1922)
Bendavid, Abba,	*Parallels in the Bible* (Jerusalem: Carta, 1972)
Bergsträsser, G.,	*Hebräische Grammatik* (Leipzig, 1918)
Černý, J.,	*Coptic Etymological Dictionary* (Cambridge: Cambridge University Press, 1976)
Cohen, M.,	'Ha-kᵉtib šel ha-nosaḥ ha-šomroni', *Beth-Miqra* no. 64 (1976), 54–70
do.	'Ha-kᵉtib ̌sel ha-nosaḥ ha-̌somroni, ziqato li-kᵉtib nosaḥ ha-masora u-mᵉqomo bᵉ-tolᵉdot ha-kᵉtib', *Beth-Miqra* no. 66 (1976), 361–391
do.	*Orthographic Systems in Ancient Massorah Codices* (dissertation, Hebrew University, Jerusalem, 1973)
Cross, F.M., and Freedman, D.N.	*Early Hebrew Orthography* (New Haven: American Oriental Society, 1952)
do.	'A Royal Song of Thanksgiving. II Samuel 22 = Psalm 18', *JBL* 72, 1953, 15–34

Cross, F.M., and Talmon, Sh., *Qumran and the History of the Biblical Text* (Cambridge, Mass.: Harvard University Press, 1975)

Driver, S.R., *Notes on the Hebrew Text and the Topography of the Books of Samuel* (2nd edition, Oxford: Clarendon Press, 1913)

Freedman, D.N., 'Orthographic Peculiarities in the Book of Job', *Eretz-Israel* 9, 1969, 35–44

do. 'The Masoretic Text and the Qumran Scrolls: a Study in Orthography', *Textus* 2, 1962, 87–102

Jenni, E., and Westermann, C., *Theologisches Handwörterbuch zum Alten Testament* (2 vols., Munich: Kaiser, 1971 and 1976)

Kahle, P., *The Cairo Geniza* (2nd edition, Oxford: Blackwell, 1959)

Kutscher, E.Y., *A History of the Hebrew Language* (Jerusalem: Magnes Press, 1982)

Lambdin, T.O., *Introduction to Biblical Hebrew* (London: Darton, Longman and Todd, 1973)

Levita, E., *Massoreth ha-Massoreth*, edited and translated by C.D. Ginsburg (reprint New York: Ktav, 1968)

Murtonen, A., 'The Fixation in Writing of Various Parts of the Pentateuch', *VT* 3, 1953, 46–53

do. 'On the Interpretation of the *Matres Lectionis* in Biblical Hebrew', *Abr-Nahrain* 14, 1973–74, 66–121

Rahlfs, A., 'Zur Setzung der Lesemütter im Alten Testament', *Nachrichten* of the Königliche Gesellschaft der Wissenschaften in Göttingen, Phil.-hist. Klasse, 1916, pp. 315–47

Segert, S., *A Grammar of Phoenician and Punic* (Munich: Beck, 1976)

Weil, G.E., *Massorah Gedolah* I (Rome: Pontifical Biblical Institute, 1971)

Weinberg, W., *The History of Hebrew Plene Spelling* (Cincinnati: Hebrew Union College Press, 1985)

Wevers, J.W., *Text History of the Greek Genesis* (Göttingen: Vandenhoeck and Ruprecht, 1974)

Zevit, Z., *Matres Lectionis in Ancient Hebrew Epigraphs* (Cambridge, Mass.: American Schools of Oriental Research, 1980)

Index of Biblical References

This index contains the numerical references to biblical passages given in the main text of this work. It does not include the data given within the figures and other tabulated materials, such as the plot on pp. 125–7 and the comparisons of 2 Samuel 22 and Psalm 18, of Texts I and II in Exodus, or of the specimen profile of the Psalms (pp. 168–76, 212–15), though it does include material from other areas which is mentioned in these sections.

Genesis

1^{14}	42, 48	12^{16}	48f., 184	27^{37}	118
1^{15}	42, 48	13^{10}	118	28^{16}	96
1^{16}	42, 48	14^{5}	143	30^{20}	163
1^{21}	43	15^{6}	83	30^{39}	129
1^{30}	42, 81	15^{13}	112	30^{43}	48, 184
2^{4}	1	16^{2}	29	31^{1}	13, 54
2^{7}	8	18^{25}	27	31^{14}	128
2^{10}	70	19^{16}	87	31^{15}	156
2^{11}	76, 81	19^{22}	118	31^{35}	154
2^{13}	76, 81	20^{14}	48, 184	31^{37}	86
2^{16}	112	20^{16}	86	31^{42}	86
2^{19}	8	21^{11}	61	32^{16}	49, 97
3^{9}	115, 118	21^{23}	118	33^{1}	48, 184
3^{12}	115	21^{25}	61, 86	33^{2}	48, 184
3^{17}	29	22^{17}	96, 125	33^{6}	48, 184
4^{7}	155	24^{13}	50	34^{31}	76
4^{23}	130	24^{14}	86	35^{23}	163
5^{25}	150	24^{17}	26	36^{6}	48
5^{26}	150	24^{18}	87	36^{7}	134
5^{28}	150	24^{19}	109	36^{24}	45
7^{2}	55	24^{35}	45, 48, 184	36^{43}	88
7^{8}	42, 55, 81	24^{44}	86	37^{4}	53
8^{7}	112	24^{46}	87	37^{8}	112
8^{19}	42, 81	24^{59}	97	37^{24}	42, 60
8^{21}	177	25^{12}	1	37^{25}	73
9^{12}	51, 59	25^{13}	53	38^{15}	76
9^{24}	96	25^{18}	118	39^{6}	65, 81
10^{8}	42	25^{30}	57	41	51, 75, 129
10^{8-9}	193	26^{3}	48, 125	41^{4}	96, 129
10^{9}	42	26^{4}	48	41^{7}	96
10^{18}	48	26^{18}	22	41^{8}	159
10^{19}	118	26^{32}	61	41^{20}	129
10^{30}	118	27^{3}	142	41^{21}	96
12^{2}	125	27^{7}	125	41^{24}	51
		27^{22}	29	41^{54}	48
		27^{30}	112	42	136

Index of Hebrew Words

1. Proper Nouns

Personal names and place names, the spelling of which is discussed in the text, are listed according to their common English spelling.

2. Other Hebrew Words

Verbs are listed by root consonants only. Other words are listed according to a common conventional spelling. The index lists all words discussed for their spelling in the main text of this work, but not words incidentally mentioned, nor words cited only in the plot on pp. 125–7, in the comparisons of parallel texts, or in the specimen profile of the Psalms.

Index of Names and Subjects

(The names of biblical books are listed only where comments on their general tendencies are made)

ι